French Animation History

French Animation History

Richard Neupert

WILEY-BLACKWELL

A John Wiley & Sons, Ltd., Publication

This edition first published 2014
© 2014 Richard Neupert

Registered Office
John Wiley & Sons Ltd, The Atrium, Southern Gate, Chichester, West Sussex, PO19 8SQ, UK

Editorial Offices
350 Main Street, Malden, MA 02148-5020, USA
9600 Garsington Road, Oxford, OX4 2DQ, UK
The Atrium, Southern Gate, Chichester, West Sussex, PO19 8SQ, UK

For details of our global editorial offices, for customer services, and for information about how to apply for permission to reuse the copyright material in this book please see our website at www.wiley.com/wiley-blackwell.

Library of Congress Cataloging-in-Publication Data
Neupert, Richard John.
  French animation history / Richard Neupert.
      p. cm.
  Includes bibliographical references and index.
  ISBN 978-1-4443-3836-2 (hardcover : alk. paper); 978-1-118-79876-8 (Paperback)
1. Animated films–France–
History and criticism.   I. Title.
  NC1766.F8N48 2011
  791.43'340944–dc22

A catalogue record for this book is available from the British Library

Cover image: Karaba the Sorceress, from *Kirikou et la sorciŌre/Kirikou and the Sorceress*, produced by Les Armateurs, directed by Michel Ocelot, 1998 Cover design by Simon Levy Design Associates

Set in 10.5/13pt by Thomson Digital, Noida, India
Printed in Singapore by Ho Printing Singapore Pte Ltd

1   2014

In memory of my parents
John and Caroline Neupert

Contents

Contents

Figures

Plates

Acknowledgments

This book is shaped by an enduring curiosity about French cinema. It has already been 30 years since I first studied cinema in Paris, and I have remained fascinated with French film production and its history. I owe a great deal to many influential French professors, some now good friends, from those days on, including Peter Schofer, Rick Altman, Jacques Aumont, Michel Marie, and Marc Vernet. Christian Metz even sat down with me long ago to share tips on titles and sources from his box of note cards for some of my earliest studies of cartoons. Marc Vernet continues to provide unparalleled insight and assistance, complete with his trademark wit and humor. Closer to home, David Bordwell, Kelley Conway, Eric Smoodin, Jim Peterson, and Matthew Bernstein remain constant sources of valuable information and encouragement. Here at the University of Georgia, a host of wonderful friends and colleagues have supported and contributed to this project, including Franklin College of Arts and Sciences Deans Garnett Stokes and Hugh Ruppersburg, my Department Head David Saltz, and Betty Jean Craige, Director of the Willson Center for Humanities and Arts. Crucial research and travel support came from the University of Georgia Foundation and the generous Charles H. Wheatley Professorship. I also owe a great debt, both professionally and personally, to President Michael Adams and Provost Arnett Mace.

Thankfully, my Film Studies colleagues Antje Ascheid, Chris Sieving, and Mike Hussey, as well as Jonathan Krell, Nina Hellerstein, Doris Kadish, Jean-Pierre Piriou, and Francis Assaf in French, have been very helpful fielding queries, suggesting translations, and patiently listening to me describe a latest find. Allison Lenhardt provided important feedback on early drafts of most chapters, Josh Marsh was always willing to help with images, and Kristin Nielsen and the staff from the UGA libraries repeatedly delivered pleasant and prompt assistance. And, I offer heartfelt thanks to all the bright, earnest students in my History of Animation and French Film courses. The creative and patient experts at Wiley-Blackwell, and especially Jayne Fargnoli and Margot Morse, have been a joy to work with.

Finally, I thank my wife Catherine Jones and daughter Sophie Neupert. Cathy is not only the perfect French scholar, and my first and best reader, she is the greatest of inspirations. Sophie brings a bright, unique joy to every single day. No one could find a better pair of travel companions for this or any other journey.

Screenshots from *Kirikou and the Sorceress* and *Triplets of Belleville* are reproduced courtesy of Les Armateurs.

Kirikou et la sorcière, De Michel Ocelot, © 1998 Les Armateurs/Odec Kid Cartoons/France 3 Cinéma/Monipoly/Trans Europe Film/Exposure/RTBF/Studio O

Les Triplettes de Belleville, De Sylvain Chomet, © 2002 Les Armateurs/Production Champion/Vivi Film/France 3 Cinéma/Sylvain Chomet/RGP France

1

Introduction
The Rise of Animation in France

If cinema marvelously expresses an age dominated by science, it is because cinema is "scientifically founded on movement." In effect, cinema relies upon a series of mechanisms designed to produce an illusion of anima-tion. (Guido 2007: 28)

Images remained fixed for 32,000 years. Drawings could only move once the camera was invented and put to work reproducing them 24 times a second, filming and projecting them. That is the real cinematic revolution! Animation is a completely virtual art which logically leads into the synthetic image and the modern world. The modern revolution was born with Emile Reynaud and his projected animation in 1892. Live action cinema with actors is merely a pale copy of reality. It is moving photography. . . . But the moving photograph will never be as magical as the moving drawing! (René Laloux, in Blin 2004: 148)

From the very beginning there was great potential for animation in France. Importantly, the French had built up strong traditions in the visual and graphic arts, scientific inquiry, and theatrical spectacles during the late 1800s and early 1900s. Artists from around the world came to Paris to study the fine arts and decorative arts, leading to one of the richest eras for aesthetic experimentation across the media. A number of avant-garde artists, including Marcel Duchamp, Man Ray, and Fernand Léger, were drawn toward experimenting with the representation of time and motion and became fascinated with animated cinema's potential. It is true that France never possessed large specialized commercial animation studios during the silent or classical sound eras. Nonetheless, French animation has

French Animation History
© Richard Neupert. Published by John Wiley & Sons

always existed and its animators have managed to turn out some incredibly creative and influential animation over the years. The bulk of that work has been produced by a relatively limited number of small animation firms and individual animators, often working parallel to other modern artists, exploring their media and looking for unique aesthetic approaches to animating images. Until fairly recently, animation remained on the economic periphery of French film production. French animation has also suffered from film critics and historians who have concentrated almost exclusively on France's famed avant-garde movements and narrative auteurism. Yet the history of animation is essential for understanding French film culture, its history, and its reception. Fortunately, there has been something of a renaissance in animation production within France over the past 20 years, which has motivated new interest in the long and frequently torturous history of French cartoons.

Animation has always been a more highly visible component of American film production than in France, and Hollywood cartoons have also received much more attention from film studies over the years. American animation began with a wide range of styles, techniques, and subjects during the silent era, much like in France. But American animation quickly became standardized as cartoons shifted from ink on paper to clear cels over painted backdrops. In Hollywood, animation fell into step with many conventions of live action filmmaking. By the 1930s, some major studios, including Warner Bros. and MGM, established their own animation wings while others, such as RKO and Paramount, entered into production and distribution deals with specialized animation companies like Disney and Fleischer. Hollywood's cartoon industry was built around division of labor, recurring characters and cartoon series, plus fixed durations of 6 to 8 minutes. American cartoons also received guaranteed distribution and thus predictable income. Most animation was commercially viable and highly capitalized. While there was creative differentiation from studio to studio, the output remained relatively similar, as even the series titles such as Merry Melodies and Looney Tunes (Warners), Silly Symphonies (Disney), and Happy Harmonies (MGM), suggest. Further, since the cartoons were produced under the institutionalized conditions of classical Hollywood cinema, they were also subject to regulation by the Motion Picture Producers and Distributors Association, which included censorship at the hands of the Production Code Administration. Cartoons were a very stable, successful, family friendly component of the American film industry.

By contrast, French animators worked more independently, like their colleagues in the plastic arts, or they formed small firms to create short animated motion picture commercials to be shown before the regular shows in theaters. These advertising contracts could ideally provide regular income and help bankroll more personal sorts of animated films on the side. Yet, as we shall see, animation remained a fragile cottage industry in France, an artisanal practice produced by individual auteurs or very small teams of animators. Although France was home to the world's first large movie studios, Pathé and Gaumont, animation was never a large part of their output. By the 1920s and 1930s, Pathé and Gaumont were primarily distributing independent and foreign films, including American cartoons. They did not have any sort of in-house animation unit during the years of classical cinema. Unlike Disney's animators or directors such as Chuck Jones and Tex Avery at Warner Bros., French animators never had access to long-term contracts, crews of assistants and in-betweeners, professional music and sound effects departments, or staff camera operators to compile and photograph their work. In France, animation teams were small and necessarily self-sufficient, working within an art cinema mode of production. The result is a fascinating cluster of films by individual stylists struggling to survive on the margins of a national film industry that was not really built to support their productions. Despite those conditions and challenges, the contributions of French animation have managed to be strong and varied over the past 120 years. Moreover, even before the first movies by Louis Lumière in 1895, France proved instrumental to the rise of animation and the representation of movement.

Motion picture animation fully exploits the potential of the cinematic apparatus, from camera to lab to projector. Thus, it seems valuable to situate cartoons at the very heart of cinematic technology and practice, rather than treating them as some marginal side-show or second-tier subset of national cinema. *French Animation History* investigates the rise and development of French animation, chronicles the norms and conventions of particular animators and their small, niche studios, and tests how story structures, graphic style, and sound strategies have shifted across time. Importantly, French animation exploits a wide range of techniques, some of which, from the earliest modes of animated pictures to the most contemporary computer generated and motion capture technology, even defy narrow definitions of animated cinema. While there is some reference here to television and other media, this study remains focused on cinema, helping situate animation as a vibrant, essential facet of film studies. France has also been a major player in exploring and exploiting new technologies. With the advances in computer generated imaging and digital compositing, the distinction "live action/not live" becomes less functional every day with each new development, further shifting various forms of animation to the core of film production today (Denslow 1997: 2). But even from the very earliest forms of motion devices, animation was a fundamental component for the successful recording and projection of moving images.

The Beginnings of Animation

Explanations of the origins of animation typically do not differ much from summaries of the origins of cinema itself. Survey histories often begin by mentioning cave paintings, magic lantern shows, and nineteenth-century motion devices. For many, when *Ice Age*'s (Wedge, Saldanha, 2002) wooly mammoth Manfred wanders into a cave only to discover primitive sketches of men killing his ancestors, it is a poignant self-referential acknowledgment of modern animation's place in the history of humanity's deep-seated desire to represent movement. Paul Wells agrees that animation, in one form or another, has almost always been with us and cites Lucretius as describing a mechanism for projecting hand-drawn images onto a screen as early as 70 BC (Wells 1998: 11). Much later, optics and magic lantern shows during the seventeenth and eighteenth centuries were often initiated by scientists but adapted for public presentations of various sorts of lectures and entertainment spectacles. Some historians even argue that once the magic lantern was mass produced in the 1800s, it became "the first medium to contest the printed word as a primary mode of information and instruction" (Gunning 2000: xxvii). Certainly, by the nineteenth century, when the illusion of motion became quite common thanks to a wide variety of toys, scientific devices, and serial photography experiments, there were many amusements and businesses devoted to replicating movement, rather than just presenting still images in a sequence.

Paris, along with London, Berlin, and Brussels, was among the cities boasting networks of important scientists specializing in experiments involving the capturing of fixed images and replication of motion. One of the earliest instruments was the spinning thaumatrope, which might have a drawing of an empty bird cage on one side, and a painted bird on the other.

When the device is spun around fast enough, the viewer's perception joins the two images and a relatively convincing image of a bird in a cage results. This apparatus was initially made available commercially thanks to Dr. John A. Paris in England in the 1820s. Peter Mark Roget and Belgium's Joseph Plateau were also researching "persistence of vision" during this era, continuing a long line of scientific inquiry into measuring how briefly image impressions may remain on the human eye and still be legible. Plateau's phenakistoscope, patented in 1833, allowed more stable illusions via two discs: one static disc had a slit for looking at the second spinning disc, which featured a series of up to 20 images or "phases of action" arranged around its surface. The phenakistoscope, like many early optical toy attractions, is based on circularity and repetition, and its functions are ultimately limited by the small number of images on a disk (Dulac and Gaudreault 2006: 230).

One scholar of early motion devices, David Robinson, states confidently that Joseph Plateau was the first true animator: "Plateau had devised the earliest form of moving picture" (Robinson 1991: 8). French animator Emile Cohl acknowledges Plateau's significance: "Without animation we perhaps never would have had that incomparable invention, Lumière's cinématographe. . . . Most of us owned a phenakistoscope . . . the cinema is right there" (Cohl 2007: 301). A confederation of Belgian scholars concurs: "The cinema was born in Belgium. The animated film was as well since its inventors are Joseph Plateau with his phenakistoscope and the painter Madou who drew the images onto the cut wheels that made the device work" (Sotiaux 1982: 8). As many historians will warn, declaring a "first" anything is often a risky venture. Further, even defining what might qualify as the earliest instance of animation, much less cinema, is still hotly debated. Some might productively argue that spinning discs such as the phenakistoscope function as their own "screen" and thereby qualify as animated cinema, before the fact. It proves more functional, however, to designate such early modes as "animated pictures," as in the case of a flip book, thaumatrope, and phenakistoscope, and "animated photographs" for looping devices exploiting serial photography, while reserving "animated cinema" for devices that exploit projection and/or a screen as part of their illusion of movement (the terms "animated pictures" and "animated photographs" are also employed by Dulac and Gaudreault 2006: 227–244). For our purposes, it seems valuable to investigate briefly several significant figures operating before the launch of Edison and Lumière's recorded live action films of the 1890s, since part of Robinson's important point is that cinema's first cartoons develop from techniques already pioneered and exploited in optical illusions, photographic processes, and projected spectacles that had become so important internationally during the 1800s.

The zoetrope, also known as "the Wheel of Life," was much like the phenakistoscope, though it functioned thanks to a series of small images on a band of paper, rather than a spinning disc. While not specific to France, zoetropes were manufactured there and became quite popular. During the 1860s and 1870s, one could buy assorted sets of images, arranged in bands, much like comic strips, for zoetropes. Among the available subjects are such illustrative titles as "The Rising Moon," "The Indian Juggler," and "Fly! Leave my nose alone." "The French Revolution" involves heads rolling off bodies, while others exploit abstract visuals. Further, image discs for the bottom of the zoetrope could also be purchased, such as the visually stunning but unsettling "Man Eater," in which a small black figure seems to be flung by centrifugal force into a happy tiger's mouth (for more titles and illustrations, see Robinson 1991: figs. 31–46). Hence a zoetrope could actually have two separate animated cycles going every time it was spun, with the primary series of images on the inside drum and a rotating design or sequence at the bottom. The strip on the inside of the drum provided a horizontal circularity that allowed a minimally narrative "linearization of the action performed by the subjects depicted" (Dulac and Gaudrault 2006: 235), while the bottom disc recalled the radial arrangement of the phena-kistoscope. The repetition of a limited number of images in this and other optical toys is in many ways typical of recent computer animation programs such as Flash, exploited so relentlessly by Internet web-page ads in partic-ular. We should see a direct connection between the images that represent a monkey continually running back and forth across the top of an Internet site and the often spellbinding nineteenth-century motion devices of girls eternally jumping rope, horses leaping, or couples waltzing in circles.

Importantly, during the 1860s and 1870s, a variety of devices were developed to allow for the projection of zoetrope bands and other photo-graphic images. The major French figure during this era of early animation devices was Emile Reynaud (1844–1918). In his teens, Reynaud had been an apprentice in mechanical engineering for precision machinery, where he learned to work on optical and scientific instruments. He pursued industrial design but also studied photography with Adam Salomon and learned magic lantern skills from a famous Catholic scientist and educator of the era, Abbé Moigno, also known as "the apostle of projection" (Mannoni 2000: 365). A popular scientist, subscribing to *La Nature*, the influential journal devoted to scientific applications for the arts and industry, Reynaud became frustrated with the poor image and color quality in the zoetrope and other optical devices, so he designed a superior alternative, the praxinoscope, which was patented in 1877. A series of 12 drawn images, color lithographs, on a flexible strip of paper was placed within a cylinder. In the center, a rotating "cage" of mirrors reflected the surrounding images as they passed by. The entire device looks a bit like a toy merry-go-round. Viewers looked directly at the sequence of stable images momentarily reflected on a mirror's face, rather than through slits. A candle in the middle could provide extra light for crisp resolution. During 1878, Reynaud marketed his praxino-scopes, along with packets of replaceable strips of images which typically involved subjects such as jugglers, animal tricks, or cavorting children. One series was even called "Baby's Lunch," predating Lumière's famous film by nearly two decades. In the more elaborate "theater" versions sold in folding wooden boxes, a small rectangular peep hole provided the viewer a perfect vantage point onto the reflected series of images framed by drawn sets, creating a child's replica of a small theatrical stage.

By 1879 Reynaud was producing a variation, the praxinoscope-théâtre, which printed isolated, colorful characters on the strips. An additional mirror allowed the viewer to project a background into the scene, so, for instance, a juggler could be seen in an interior room setting or outdoors in a garden. This was an early form of composite animation and delivered a new sense of depth to the presentations. Reynaud claimed eventually to have sold 100,000 praxinoscopes, which appeared in various models over the years, including one that was driven by an electric motor.

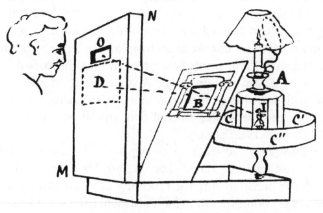

Figure 1.1   Praxinoscope patent, Emile Reynaud, 1878.

During the early 1880s Reynaud also experimented with projecting the drums of spinning images. When he presented a new projecting model of the praxinoscope to the Société Française de Photographie in 1880, for instance, he explained that the ideal goal would be for someone to invent a way to project photographic images for a better illusion of movement than drawn figures could generate (Mannoni 2000: 374). Reynaud's early prototype projector used 12 glass slides strapped together into a flexible belt of images for projection. This device also involved combining the moving figures from the glass slides with painted static backgrounds. They were both reflected onto the same mirror during projection for the composite image. But clearly Reynaud saw the continued limitations of his short series of hand-drawn images printed on slides. In 1888, Reynaud patented an important variation on the praxinoscope that allowed the projection of a large, clear, longer string of pictures.

This device, renamed the "théâtre optique," or optical theater, showed a series of images that were initially painted on glass plates connected by a flexible band that unwound from one reel and rewound onto another. These slides could briefly lie flat in front of the light source for sharp projection onto a mirror before being reflected onto the final screen. Reynaud next painted on a flexible roll of gelatine bordered by cardboard or cloth. This strip wound its way through a series of rollers before passing by the mirrored surface for projection. One of the inspirations for the overall design was apparently the mechanics of the nineteenth-century bicycle with its large front wheel, long chain, and smaller rear wheel, driven by pedals and a crank (Myrent 1989: 193). The initial patent application carefully outlined the components for the apparatus, including gears, rollers, and take-up reels, but he also left vague the definitions of the "flexible band," and allowed that the machine would work whether the "successive poses" were opaque or transparent, and he even acknowledged that the designs could be printed mechanically onto the malleable strip. A catalogue for a 1982 exhibition on "100 Years of French Animation" credits Reynaud with launching a new medium: "With characters drawn and colored on a large perforated strip of film, animation existed before the cinema!" (Maillot 1982: n.p.).

Importantly, Reynaud's optical theater allowed "unlimited durations allowing for real animated scenes" (Lonjon 2007: 201). The patent explained that this device decisively surpassed such repetitive, circular devices as the zoetrope and praxinoscope (Reynaud and Sadoul 1945: 55). A linear "show" was now possible rather than the spinning discs and strips with their brief loops that had preceded the optical theater. As Nicolas Dulac and André Gaudreault point out, "Reynaud's apparatus thus went beyond mere gyration, beyond the mere thrill of seeing the strip repeat itself . . . narrative had taken over as the primary structuring principle." Reynaud offered "a new paradigm within which narration would play a decisive role" (Dulac and Gaudreault 2006: 239). Individual titles lasted from 8 to 15 minutes and consisted of 300 to 700 images, so the duration of Reynaud's subjects far exceeds the subsequent 50-second Lumière films, anticipating instead the length of eventual one- and two-reel short films. Pauses were built into the presentations, and they still seem to have had a rather slow projection time, averaging one second per image. However, Reynaud also designed the drawings to allow for some repetitions. For instance, when Harlequin first sneaks over the wall in *Pauvre Pierrot* (*Poor Pierrot*, 1892), he acts rather hesitant. Reynaud would stop advancing the band of animation, reverse it to show the character climb back up the wall, then crank it forward again as Harlequin finally decided to drop into the garden for good (Auzel 1998: 68). When a character danced with delight, Reynaud could also draw the frames in such a way that they could be shown forward, then backward, then forward again, but it looked like three sequential dance steps. Significantly, such back and forth maneuvers were possible because Reynaud was actually projecting two images. A magic lantern projected the static painted slide of the background set which was constant, while only characters and occasional objects were drawn on the moving strip. Thus, a composite image resulted that prefigures later cel animation, where the objects changing from frame to frame were drawn on clear sheets set on top of their fixed, painted setting. So, even if a character were reversing his actions, or briefly disappearing altogether, there was always a constant projected setting visible. It would be several decades before any other animator would separate the figure and ground for animated motion pictures.

Emile Reynaud's invention back-projected the images onto a screen, which reportedly dimmed and possibly distorted the initial image somewhat for the audience watching the translucent screen from the other side. Initially, he relied upon a gas lamp powered by igniting oxygen and hydrogen for a bright light, but when bright electric lamps became available Reynaud switched over to that safer, cooler option. Beyond the moving images, an important part of the show was also the "man behind the screen" presenting his spectacle. Emile Reynaud's name figured prominently on the advertising posters for the Musée Grévin wax museum. *La Nature* even featured a famous illustration of Reynaud at the controls, operating the optical theater, and one historian points out that Reynaud looks superb in the midst of the apparatus, with his hands turning the controls: "He resembles Captain Nemo at the helm of the *Nautilus* – 20,000 leagues under his dreams" (Tchernia 1998: 5). France's *Figaro* featured a story in 1892 declaring that Reynaud's ingenious machine "creates characters whose expressions and gestures are so accurate as to give a complete illusion of life" (cited in Cayla 2007: 15).

Reynaud signed an exclusive contract with the Musée Grévin in Paris to present his shows, which he called "lighted pantomimes." Other Grévin acts performed in between each of his presentations. His earliest program included *Poor Pierrot*, which premiered on October 28, 1892 as one of three different films he presented that evening. *Poor Pierrot*, based on the well-known pantomime, features the trickster Harlequin hiding in a moonlit garden, tormenting Pierrot who has arrived to serenade Columbine, the woman of both their dreams. The mime action takes place in distinct scenes, with Harlequin showing up first to flirt with Columbine, then hiding when Pierrot arrives. Harlequin succeeds eventually in frightening Pierrot out of the yard, leaving the field free for Harlequin to woo Columbine. *Poor Pierrot* successfully synthesizes conventions from live theatrical performance with those of the comic strip. Its narrative space is shallow, with a playing space that reflects a stage setting, though the painted door in the back garden wall "opens" several times to create an increased sense of depth, reinforced by the brightly rendered moonlight pouring forth through the opening into the garden. *Poor Pierrot* contained roughly 500 drawings and initially ran for 10 minutes, and its premiere was accompanied by a piano piece written specifically for the narrative by Gaston Paulin. There were even specific songs sung in time with the characters' gestures, as well as tiny silver tabs that triggered sound effects as they passed by (Lonjon 2007: 125–128; see also Leslie 2002: 4). Georges Sadoul writes, "Reynaud's first 'pantomime lumineuse' is also the first masterpiece of the animated cartoon" (Sadoul 1972: 278) (see Plate 1).

Clown et ses chiens (*The Clown and his Dogs*), the second show on the original program, was made up of 300 images of a clown presenting various dog tricks, and ran for roughly 8 minutes. It was intensely colored and accompanied by a fast-paced waltz. Reynaud often began his presentations with *Le Bon Bock* (*A Good Beer*), a 15-minute comical playlet featuring antics among four characters at a village inn, including a waitress, thirsty hiker, a kitchen boy who repeatedly drinks the hiker's beers, and another traveler passing through. Importantly, the Grévin's manager had invited a magician he knew, Georges Méliès (1861–1938), to Reynaud's premiere. Méliès, who at this point was projecting magic lantern slides as part of his own theatrical spectacles, met with Reynaud right after the show. When Reynaud explained his labor-intensive process, the magician apparently inquired about whether some mechanical process for reproducing the images might not be possible. Reynaud mentioned that he was aware of Thomas Edison's experiments in the US but told Méliès he personally had been trying since 1888 to come up with his own more efficient process. So far the solution had eluded him (Lonjon 2007: 129–130).

Reynaud's illuminated pantomimes quickly became a central attraction for the Musée Grévin where they were part of the wax museum's daily program, running ten to twelve times on weekend days. The Grévin contract prohibited Reynaud from presenting his spectacle anywhere else as well as from selling the apparatus itself, something Reynaud had initially planned on. However, later that year the sponsors of a large charity event in Rouen convinced Grévin's manager to lend out Reynaud and his device. During one day, December 3, 1892, Reynaud gave 12 performances of the three films to a total audience of 1,300 spectators. The next day, a Rouen newspaper praised Reynaud's "elegant entertainment": "The scenery, viewpoint, characters, and costumes were all stunning successes. Everything had accurate depth and correct coloring. This is really theater in action and the illusion was perfect. We only regret that this theater could only stay in Rouen for the one day" (Lonjon 2007: 131). Back in Paris, Reynaud continued to sell his original praxinoscopes via large department stores. But he also had to repair, update, and replace his optical theater strips regularly since the gelatine surfaces were delicate, and there were no copies, so the bands of images wore out steadily from the constant use.

Thus, Reynaud provides a good model for the strengths and weaknesses surrounding the production and exhibition of animated pictures prior to the development of motion picture film stock and its ability to reproduce countless identical copies from a negative. While Reynaud paved the way in terms of subjects, exhibition, and marketing, the long-term limitations of his one-of-a-kind bands of images were obvious. When he was not selling praxinoscopes or projecting the optical theater shows, he was kept busy designing and drawing new episodes in order to continue his profitable Grévin performances. Reynaud's teenage son André also helped paint in the characters. Yet while this sort of labor-intensive moving picture mode did attract a steady audience, it was necessarily limited to one physical venue, so the profits were fixed; without an ability to copy his work, there was no hope of multiple projections in a number of theaters simultaneously. He was an artisan soon to be overtaken by the sort of mechanical reproduction that would be made possible by the highly capitalized corporate research and development of Thomas Edison and the Lumière family.

Among Reynaud's subsequent hand-made shows was *Autour d'une cabine* (*Around a Bathing Hut*), completed in 1894 for the 1895 season at the Musée Grévin. This new subject comprised 660 images, running roughly 12 minutes. Historian Georges Sadoul called it "the richest and most complex" of Reynaud's works. In addition to the bathers and their comical actions at the beach, *Around a Bathing Hut* included sea gulls circling in the sky, which opened up the action far beyond the more theatrical settings from the earlier titles (Sadoul 1949: 15). The slight diagonal perspective onto the beach scene, with a diving board intruding into the space at an angle, provides a more dynamic setting than the straight-on *Poor Pierrot* and even anticipates the framing of later Lumière films of bathers diving off piers. *Around a Bathing Hut* began with bathers frolicking on the pier, where one pushes another into the water, followed by the arrival of a "Parisian" couple. While the man goes into his beach hut to change, the wife and her dog bump into a flirtatious older dandy. When the woman enters her own hut, this fellow stoops to peek in the keyhole. Her husband soon emerges in his swimsuit and kicks the old voyeur. The couple then takes a swim, but once they return to the beach in the foreground to change back into regular clothes they find the dandy waiting in her hut. The husband pushes the man into the sea and then the little dog chases him off out of the frame. A boat heads past and its unfurled sail reads "End of the show." Thus this presentation unfolds in a series of chronological scenes that all play out on the unified section of beach, and much like Jacques Tati's *Les Vacances de M. Hulot* (1953), the story is a loose collection of anecdotes. Once again, this was not a silent presentation. Gaston Paulin wrote two songs for *Around a Bathing Hut*, one called "At the Beach" and the other "The Sea Gulls," which were performed behind the screen beside Reynaud, by a Cuban musician, Albert Faucon (Lonjon 2007: 142).

With the arrival of Edison's kinetoscope and then Lumière's cinémato-graphe screenings, Reynaud's one-man operation, with its recurring titles, soon became a quaint and dated attraction. Yet, Reynaud had developed important and influential animation techniques that helped move animated pictures beyond the repetitive sequential poses of the zoetrope. His painted human figures often moved toward or away from the audience, employing far greater depth of field and more accurate and fluid character motion than previous motion devices. Georges Sadoul points out that Reynaud made use of the zoological findings in Eadweard Muybridge and Etienne-Jules Marey's serial photography to make his own drawn horses gallop correctly and to add complex shifts in body and gesture to other characters (Sadoul 1949: 14). His significance can also be judged by the fact that an estimated half a million people attended his projections between 1892 and 1900, when Reynaud lost his contract at Grévin and was forced to discontinue his shows (Bendazzi 1994: 5). As David Robinson argues, "Indisputably the greatest animator of the pre-cinema era, Emile Reynaud, with his Pantomimes Lumineuses of 1892, provided the ultimate link between these six decades of animation devices and the motion picture proper" (Robinson 1991: 16).

Emile Reynaud's projected drawn images certainly count as moving picture animation and his shows inspired both Thomas Edison and the Lumière brothers. The Lumières had indeed visited both the Musée Grévin and Reynaud's workshop in 1894. During the late 1890s, Reynaud even used motion picture cameras to film actions, including the popular comic act Footit and Chocolate performing a pantomime version of William Tell against a black background. Such presentations were billed as animated photo-paintings (Auzel 1998: 94–95). Reynaud did not use the cinematic images themselves, rather he cut them up and colored them or traced and redrew their actions, exploiting the camera simply to streamline his process (see Bendazzi 1994: 5–6; Myrent 1989: 199). This animation technique anticipates the rotoscope developed by Max and Dave Fleischer during the 1910s, to say nothing of motion capture technology today. Interestingly, Louis Lumière also filmed the Footit and Chocolate act in 1900. Thus Reynaud's work is closely entwined with motion studies and entertainment during this era and should not be reduced to an odd, isolated side-show in motion picture animation's history.

Unfortunately, Emile Reynaud smashed his apparatus and threw most of his remaining film strips into the Seine after Musée Grévin ended his contract. Very little remains from his many intricate works, though the French Centre National de la Cinématographie (CNC) released a restored version of a portion of *Poor Pierrot* in 2007 and partial prints of *Around a Bathing Hut* circulate. These two titles had been saved by another son, Paul Reynaud. Emile Reynaud's final project involved trying to invent a commercially viable stereoscopic motion picture camera and projector, which never found financial backing. Yet Reynaud should be credited as a founding figure of international cinema alongside Edison and Lumière.

Kristen Whissel asserts that though the latter two invented more practical and marketable devices, "Reynaud first simulated movement and projected shows upon a screen" (Whissel 2007: 303). Thus, if Louis Lumière can be said to have invented a more complete form of cinema by getting Edison's kinetoscope images "out of the box," projecting them for multiple viewers, then surely Reynaud should be credited as successfully getting animation out of the zoetrope cylinder and onto the screen for a popular, paying audience, all before reels of film wound their way through Edison's kinetograph or Lumière's cinématographe.

Among the other essential figures in the development of animation, and cinema in general, is the famous photographer and scientist Eadweard Muybridge (1830–1904), who was ultimately influenced by French advances. During the 1870s and 1880s, Muybridge was a leading figure in serial photography, designing elaborate experiments involving banks of cameras to record sequentially animal and human motion. Muybridge sought to understand animation locomotion more fully by breaking down real movement via discrete photographs. His wet plates were exposed in carefully timed sequences, sometimes with exposure times as fast as 1/500th of a second, and he employed banks of individual cameras, often using 24, triggered one second apart. He arranged the photos onto plates to compare specific poses frozen in time by his apparatus. But he also transferred them onto glass discs, sometimes tracing the original photographs, other times striking positive copies from negatives, which were then projected by the zoopraxiscope. Many of Muybridge's subjects were animals and people walking laterally past his lenses, as well as naked men and women performing everyday chores. Muybridge was an important early animator, copying onto discs photographic records of people and animals undertaking some brief practical task. However, his famous horse experiments of the 1870s were of relatively poor quality. It was only after a European lecture tour, where Muybridge met Etienne-Jules Marey, among others, that his best, most scientifically useful work began. Upon returning to the United States, he set up his lab in 1884 at the University of Pennsylvania, strongly inspired by Marey in particular.

France's Etienne-Jules Marey (1830–1904) experimented with sequential "chronographic films" and time-lapse photography during the 1880s and 1890s in order to "de-animate" or break down motion into various static records to study it better, sometimes in marvelously beautiful multiple exposures. However, Marey came to his motion studies directly from the world of medicine and science. He was never interested in being the sort of public entertainer who would come to dominate early cinema and animation. Rather, Marey was an extremely accomplished physiologist who saw the practical merits of optical devices and photography for conducting and then demonstrating his research. He began his medical career interested in precise measurement of blood flow and other mechanics in humans and animals. He invented, among other things, the polygraph and the first cardiograph before inventing chronophotographic equipment to analyze movements of everything from tiny insects to humans to elephants. Much of his research work at his elaborate laboratory station was supported by the French government, and he published widely, from exemplary articles in *La Nature* to influential and often quite beautiful books on human and animal movement, including *La Machine animal* (*The Animal Mechanism*, 1873). Many of his initial chronophotographs involved multiple exposures on one large image, which resulted in fascinating, complex photos that greatly influenced later artists, anticipating, among others, Giacomo Bala's *Dynamism of a Dog on a Leash* and Marcel Duchamp's *Nude Descending a Staircase*, both 1912. For some studies, his photographed subjects would wear thin reflective metal strips on black outfits, to further isolate body parts, and these suits resemble today's motion capture suits. The precise representations by researchers like Marey also participated in the shift toward modernist representations of lived experience and helped boldly document the rift between knowledge and the limits of human perception. New functions of visual culture were being forged at a rapid rate, especially in France where a surprisingly high number of popular science societies and a vast slate of expositions allowed for scholars, researchers, and practitioners from many nations and disciplines to interact productively and follow-up on one another's experiments and triumphs (for more on modernism and shifts in visual culture, see Crary 1992).

Marey's various chronophotographs, including the famous rifle-camera invention, were constantly upgraded for his various research tasks. The initial 1882 rifle exposed a sequence of 12 images on a rotating photographic disc. Marey had read about Muybridge's horse photos in *Nature*, but he was also impressed by Pierre-Jules-César Janssen's photographic revolver which took low quality but groundbreaking photos of the planet Venus passing between the earth and sun. Already in 1888 Marey was exposing 20 images per second on a roll of sensitized paper and later he exposed longer, 90 mm wide transparent gelatine strips for large clear negatives, before finally switching to flexible 35 mm Eastman celluloid stock in the 1890s. Interestingly, Marey, Reynaud, and Thomas Edison all displayed their recent

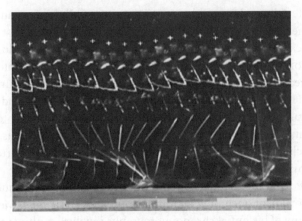

Figure 1.2   Marey's multiple exposure, produced and photographed by Etienne-Jules Marey, 1881.

inventions at the 1889 Universal Exposition in Paris, and Marey's work was greatly celebrated by physiologists, popular scientists, and photographers alike. His recurring obsessions included the study of flying birds, as well as the photographic documentation of flowing liquids and even air currents. Much of his work eventually proved crucial for early studies of air travel. For recording tiny insects scurrying past his lens, Marey reportedly managed to reach exposure times of 1/25,000th of a second (Braun 1992: 166). Marey investigated a wide range of tactics for projecting his various recorded series of photographic images, including tracing the images and even cutting up the film strips to place individual images on his crude projector. However, while Marey could reconstruct movement between his animated photographs, he was first and foremost a motion scientist. Marey wanted an apparatus to slow down some movements and speed up others: "He was not after a machine that would replicate the continuity of perceived movement. . . . The idea of reproducing movement as the unaided eye grasps it would be absurd" to Marey (Braun 1992: 174). Further, Marey was aided over the course of 14 years by Georges Demeny, a talented assistant who became frustrated by Marey's relative lack of interest in the potential for public projections or sale of their devices.

In 1892, Marey and Georges Demeny demonstrated their projecting phonoscope with a 24-frame shot of Demeny mouthing the phrases "I love you" and "Vive la France." Demeny was interested in using close-up shots of speaking subjects to help teach lip-reading to the deaf. By 1894, Marey and Demeny were filming and projecting a host of subjects. Yet the fixing and "re-animating" of images remained a research and educational venture for Marey, rather than a potentially lucrative entertainment spectacle. He had no interest in the sort of public showings that made Reynaud famous. Nonetheless, many of his chronophotography experiments also hold value as stunning visual presentations of moving pictures. As historian Marta Braun points out, Marey's work dealt head-on with the reconceptualization of time and space, influencing artists, scientists, and philosophers, including Henry Bergson: "Marey's imagery, embedded in the discourse of nineteenth-century science, comes to belong to the canon of early twentieth-century art and aesthetic modernism.... Marey's work – his subject, movement, and his method of mechanical decomposition – is at once the beginning of a new synthesis of science and labor and the focal point of the artistic dissolution of the space-time continuum" (Braun 1995: 88). This deconstruction of the visual and the ensuing exploration of rhythm between still images inspired French researchers and artists alike. According to Laurent Mannoni, "Marey's film strips are true embryonic stages of the cinema, priceless evidence of the genius of this great researcher, and just as importantly remarkable works of photographic art" (Mannoni 2000: 343). While Marey's devices may have "paved the way for the study of movement on a frame-to-frame basis" (Furniss 2007: 76), they did not yet motivate a boom in French animated pictures for popular entertainment. His animation remained closely tied to his laboratory.

By the mid-1890s, when Edison and Lumière had launched their moving picture companies, animation entered a new phase, with flexible celluloid film stock becoming the standard mode of support for the images. However, even during the rise to dominance of the 35 mm film stock, there were alternatives. Beyond the individuals and devices mentioned so far, there were scores of other techniques for representing motion, including both photographic and non-photographic means. The mutoscope, for instance, was a very popular and profitable apparatus for a short time during the 1890s. It was initially a single-viewer peep show device, something like a later rolodex, with individual cards on a drum that rotated. It was a mechanical improvement on the flip book, capable of advancing a thick stack of cards at a constant rate. The images were often recorded with a camera, transferred to the cards, then shown in mutoscopes, where the viewer turned the crank to control the sequence of printed cards. The subjects were often strongly voyeuristic and some famously erotic. A number of subjects were also hand-drawn or printed mechanically. This period of competing modes for animating images proved vital and inspiring

Figure 1.3   Marey's dragonfly, produced and photographed by Etienne-Jules Marey, 1891.

for later animators and helped prepare their audiences for diverse spectacles and increasing uses of moving, drawn images. Variations on the mutoscope would later become a useful tool for animators previewing and testing their sketches for fluid motion and accuracy.

Beyond the devices and presentational modes mentioned thus far, there was another interesting subset of motion picture animation at the turn of the century which is often overlooked today. During the 1890s, Germany's Gebruder Bing Company devised a small projection device for children that involved short lengths of flexible film stock that looped through a small projector. The images, in black and white as well as color, were printed via lithography onto a piece of Edison's 35 mm film stock. The images sat sideways on the film strip, so passed horizontally through the projector. Typical subjects included soldiers marching across the frame, acrobats and dancers performing, or children skipping rope. These attractions were brief, repetitive, and aimed at children, and sold in packs of eight. According to Robinson, "These eight films may be regarded as the origins of [the] animated cartoon in the cinema" (Robinson 1991: 18). The Bings, whose projectors are already described in Henry Hopwood's *Living Pictures*, published in 1899 (Hopwood 1970), were quickly followed by other entrepreneurs selling these expensive children's projectors, including France's Lapierre Company. These devices are another important link between the motion devices aimed at private use in the wealthy nineteenth-century home, and the earliest forms of film production and exhibition. Clearly, the animated cinema is a fascinating series of experiments, devices, and marketable products that does not begin with any single cartoon or individual. It was invented over the course of the entire nineteenth century and many of those investigations and accomplishments took place in France or were directly related to French research.

Stop-Motion Animation Attractions

In part because of the rich context of nineteenth-century France's fascination with technology, French filmmaking quickly led the world in fantasy, science fiction, and special effects techniques. Certainly, Georges Méliès established the sub-genre of the "trick film" which typically exploited stop-motion pixilation of actors and objects. However, much of his work avoided frame-by-frame construction of images, but rather exploited substitutions of objects to represent transformations. As Giannalberto Bendazzi remarks, "Screening Méliès films today is like viewing an animated film ... without animation" (Bendazzi 1994: 11). Importantly, Georges Méliès blurred the lines between live action and animation in productive ways and encouraged others to investigate methods for stopping real time and manipulating individual items between the filmed frames. On stage, before his famous trick films, Méliès regularly performed live magic acts and illusions with trap doors and lighting effects to create sudden changes as he seemingly transformed objects before the audience's eyes. He had also incorporated some lightning drawing techniques, appearing as a dessinateur express, quickly sketching portraits and caricatures of famous people, including Queen Victoria, during 1896, years before J. Stuart Blackton's lightning sketches in America (Crafton 1993a: 50). However, rather than expand on frame-to-frame animation, Méliès soon specialized in pixilation and fantastic effects. He was intent on making cinema parallel his theatrical spectacle via performance illusions rather than exploring its own full potential to animate drawings (Mitry 1967: 117).

Thanks in large part to Méliès, French cinema offered high quality special effects films, many accomplished via in-camera manipulation but also with profilmic trickery, so that the pixilation of objects, for fantasy or comic purposes, became a common strategy from the start. Stop-motion pixilated scenes helped update the sort of illusionist performances that were so popular in the late nineteenth century. Assorted objects could be filmed with a combination of regular motion, fast motion (undercranking the camera to make the process look slightly sped up), or by stopping the camera, moving something, then starting the camera anew. Pixilation has long been a favorite technique for amateur and student filmmakers as well who delight in exploiting the camera's ability to speed up clouds passing in the sky or make a friend, sitting on the floor, seem to "drive" himself down their school's corridors. Further, digital video cameras today make pixilation as easy as the push of a button, proving a continuing fascination for stop-start image technology that "moves" static objects or reduces real movement down to stroboscopic effects.

One other major participant in the cinema of attraction trick films is Segundo de Chomon (1871–1929), a Spanish immigrant who became a key filmmaker for Pathé where his work, such as *Sculpture moderne* (*Modern Sculpture*, 1908), combined the conventions and staging of the magic act with pixilation. His films were inspired by Méliès and erased barriers between realism and fantasy (Vimenet 2007: 35). Chomon was a master at spectacular special effects, including stop-motion tricks such as his character "Slippery Jim" pulling bicycle parts out of his sport coat pockets, rapidly assembling them into a real bike and then riding it on top of a train in composite shots during *Pickpock ne craint pas les entraves* (*Slippery Jim*, 1909). Chomon's work animates objects and exploits editing to substitute one object for another. In his famous *Electric Hotel* (1908), suitcases unpack themselves, brushes polish boots on their own, and the female guest's long hair braids itself. However, beyond occasional instances such as lines being scratched on subsequent frames of the film's negative to represent shocks pulsating from the hotel's electric system, Chomon's effects remain rooted in pixilation. One exception, *Chiffoniers et caricaturistes* (*Artistic Rag-Pickers*, 1908), briefly allows Chomon's performers to generate comical portraits in the lightning sketch tradition (Abel 1994: 281–282). Unfortunately, most of Segundo de Chomon's work remains lost. A recent study attributes many modes of animation to him, including silhouettes and drawing on paper, but no concrete evidence exists that can corroborate the catalogue notations and anecdotal evidence relating to this pioneering filmmaker's animated output (Tharrats 2009: 74–84).

Cinema's first attempts to adapt animated toys, scientific motion photography, and comics, among other generating contexts, reinforced the nearly magical aspect of the first animation for spectators. Much of the earliest work by animators clearly counts as what Tom Gunning (2006), André Gaudreault (Dulac and Gaudreault 2006), and others have labeled attractions, though not all may qualify as full-fledged "cinema" attractions. This famous phrase designates early cinema's dominant tendency to present overtly exhibitionistic displays to the spectator. Much like the later shocks and attractions theorized and practiced by Sergei Eisenstein, an attraction shows little evidence of character development, diegetic coherence, or narrative logic, and is specifically designed to grab the attention of the viewers and hopefully even surprise them. The first animated motion pictures gradually shift away from the "player mode of attraction," such as a zoetrope or mutoscope, to a "viewer mode of attraction," in which the spectator takes a more passive role, and this certainly would hold for Reynaud's optical theater. Narrative, as we shall see, comes more slowly to dominate animated cinema than live action films, while the various forms of animation take great advantage of cinema's ability to display its power to create illusions. The subject matter generally remained minimal, exhibitionistic gags.

During the late 1800s, France provided the most vital breeding ground in the world for scientific and aesthetic experimentation with the moving image, and it also boasted a variety of crucial venues for displaying those results. Not only was there a strong tradition of performance and a wide range of spectacles that could incorporate the latest technological advances, there was also an intricate network of professional organizations, publications, and conferences to encourage the verification and sharing of new inventions. Further, France had the added advantage of regular international conferences devoted to science and industry. It was, therefore, quite common for entrepreneurs and inventors from across Europe and the Americas to pass through Paris, and thus not only could Georges Méliès attend both the premiere projections by Emile Reynaud and Louis Lumière, but people like Thomas Edison could also meet and chat with Europe's motion image pioneers at France's international congresses and expositions. From the earliest motion toys to serial photography to Lumière's cinématographe, France helped forge the concepts and deliver the devices that would launch animation throughout world cinema.

2

Silent Animation
Emile Cohl and his Artisanal Legacy

Despite all the innovations in the early years of US cinema that eventually led to the emergence of the "cartoon," it is Fantasmagorie (1908), by Emile Cohl (1857–1938), with its surreal stick-figure animation, that should be understood as the first two-dimensional cartoon. Its bizarre narrative shows off the possibilities of the new form and signals "metamorphosis" as the core language of animated stories. (Wells 2007: 85)

France was not only the first European country to provide a spawning ground for animated cinema, it was also the site of the first organized animation studio. (Bendazzi 1994: 34)

Emile Cohl, Caricature, and the Rise of Studio Animation

Emile Cohl is an unusual figure in the cinema and his work challenges those trying to retell a smooth history of the development of animated cinema's techniques and themes. His output was as varied as it was significant. "Cohl produced a series of animated films that embrace sophisticated concepts of movement, design, humor, and format," according to Leonard Maltin (1987: 3). Donald Crafton goes further: "Cohl's films are extraordinary in their outrageousness, their outlandishness, and, frequently, their incomprehensibility" (Crafton 1990: 257). Credited with 300 films between the years 1908 and 1923, Cohl has recently received a great deal of renewed attention thanks to the 100th anniversary of his first movies. Alongside several book-length studies, including Pierre Courtet-Cohl and Bernard

French Animation History
© Richard Neupert. Published by John Wiley & Sons

Génin's *Emile Cohl: l'inventeur du dessin animé* (Emile Cohl: Inventor of Animation) (2008), the journal *1895* devoted an entire issue to Emile Cohl as an independent figure working outside the usual frames of reference: "A cartoonist, he became a photographer and illustrator but also an actor; exhibitor with an outdoor cinema, he became a filmmaker; 'effects director,' he specialized in making objects move from frame to frame, then he invented animated cinema. He was an 'indefatigable worker'" (Vignaux 2007: 17). This visual magician living on the edge of cinema was born in 1857 with the name Emile Courtet. By the time he moved into film production under his adopted pseudonym, Emile Cohl, he was already a fairly well-established figure in Parisian culture, having earned a reputation as a graphic artist and caricaturist. As Donald Crafton (1993a: 60) points out, Cohl was nearly 44 years old when Walt Disney was born and age 50 when he began animating, so he was perhaps more connected to the spirit and aesthetics of the nineteenth century than many early filmmakers. Cohl stood out in many ways from his contemporaries.

Importantly, as a young man Cohl idolized and then befriended the famous political caricaturist André Gill. The late 1800s were characterized by a fascination with new modes of representation, fueled in large part by advances in photography and scientific instruments of inquiry, including x-rays, that could document the world in new ways. Gill and Cohl mocked some of these inventions and the men of science and industry behind them. Their caricatures also explored the power of the image as they straddled the contradictory visual space between verisimilitude and distortion. Importantly, Cohl also frequented bohemian and anarchist circles, including the modernist poets, the Hydropathes, and the anti-bourgeois artistic group known as the Incoherents. The cultural climate of 1870s Paris, fueled by more permissive laws as well as the disorienting effects of absinthe, encouraged satire and literary provocation, as multiple literary and artistic societies sprang up, many with their own philosophies, journals, and cafés. Cohl's creative flair and personality made him popular among these myriad factions and his drawings appeared in 100 different publications, each with their own perspectives and favorite targets for their youthful wrath. For instance, the Hydropathes parodied French literary circles while the Incoherents aimed their spirited outrage at the prestigious artistic salons and successful artists they deplored (Courtet-Cohl and Génin 2008: 45).

The Incoherents even organized an exposition of drawings by "those who do not know how to draw" and arranged comical parades and an annual masked ball. By 1886, the Incoherents were known for "the decadent, almost maniacal pursuit of gaiety" (Crafton 1990: 47). A carnivalesque spirit ruled over their group, which adored grotesque exaggeration and incongruous combinations. One Incoherent event included Hippolyte Camille Delpy's blank canvas surrounded by a painting of a picture frame. Another member, Alphonse Allais, offered a series of monochromes of various colors with fanciful titles to justify their absence of figures. The white surface mounted on the wall was labeled *Anemic Young Girls' First Communion in the Snow*. Allais continued the gag with additional excessively silly titles to justify a wide range of monochromes, including red, blue, black, and green. Later, Cohl would revisit the idea behind Allais's series for his *Le Peintre néo-impressionniste* (*The Neo-Impressionist Painter*, 1910). In 1884, for one Incoherent salon, Cohl offered a cartoonish parody of a famous, earnest painting of a poor man fishing, *Le Pauvre pêcheur* by Puvis de Chavannes. For his version, Cohl attached a real dead herring on the end of the painted fishing line.

Pertinent French cultural contexts for Cohl and the Incoherents included "the Symbolism proper of Mallarmé, Rimbaud's poésie fantastique, and Verlaine's Decadents" (Crafton 1990: 257). During the 1880s Cohl also expanded into photography and began his own studio where he shot portraits of young artists, including Paul Verlaine. Emile Cohl clearly thrived in this era full of chaotic cultural transformations and also mastered the mechanical and chemical demands of optics, camera techniques, and film processing. Throughout his life he experimented with new cameras and processes, including multiple exposures and later "animated portraits," which were like trick calling-card photos involving three different images moving mechanically so the still photograph seemed to shift before one's eyes (Timby 2007: 109). He continued to generate all sorts of graphic media and during the 1890s his drawings became more linear and narrative. Though these comic strips remained absurd, filled with humorous, often ironic metamorphoses, they also began to resemble storyboards for short gags and fantasy films.

While Cohl's caricatures and comics typically combined humor with biting political irreverence, he also found clever ways to bring word-play into the visual realm. As François Albera explains, "What governs the delirious logic and anarchy of his gags is language" (Albera 2007: 252). Within his comics and films, politicians turn from bourgeois gentlemen into distorted clowns, a ballerina is shown to have descended from an elephant, a mother-in-law morphs into a witch, and so forth. It was typical of contemporary caricaturists to transpose "one image into its opposite in a subtle sequence of changes" (Christie 1994: 83). Cohl enjoyed presenting popular expressions literally, including scenes of hearts breaking in two or bursting into flames. In French, when people are startled they can be said to have their arms drop ("les bras m'en tombent"), so the arms regularly fall off Cohl's unfortunate characters and they often lose their heads as well. Many early films took advantage of a particularly modernist perspective allowing for humor in amputation and dismemberment, but Cohl also routinely exploited fantasy and the transformation of objects to comment upon contemporary fads, figures, and culture, connecting the popular media of the nineteenth century with the newer artistic and philosophical move-ments of his day. Cohl's compositions have been called poly-focalized and heterogeneous since many layouts included cluttered frames with several simultaneous points of interest. It is an aesthetic of bricolage combining disparate elements for a new synthesis (Kaenel 2007: 72). His busy frames defy the more commercial, efficient, and statically composed comics of his era. Beyond brutally lampooning contemporary people and events, how-ever, Cohl was also intrigued with French military history, hoping one day to make an animated version of the famous medieval Bayeux tapestry. However, eventually Emile Cohl would die poor and paranoid, with many unfinished projects and ideas.

Within the cinema, *Fantasmagorie* (1908) launched Cohl's career as an animator, and for many, this is another contender for the "first true animated cartoon." The story goes that Cohl, angered that one of this published comics (*The Thin Ceiling* from 1891) had been plagiarized and staged for a Gaumont movie, visited the studio to protest to Leon Gaumont. However, by the time Cohl left Gaumont's office he had landed an entry-level job instead of an apology. In addition to his rich past as a graphic artist, Cohl had previously written skits and plays. While working on script ideas for Gaumont, Cohl began to draw out the images for his own *Fantasmagorie*, named for a nineteenth-century apparatus that presented the illusion of ghosts conjured up by a modified magic lantern. Initially, Cohl's images were black ink on white paper, but he printed the negative, allowing stark white figures to stand out on a black background, perhaps to mimic J. Stuart Blackton's lightning sketch set-up. However, it is worth reinforcing the point that Cohl's era was not simply dominated by attempts to "make motion picture cartoons." While *Fantasmagorie* and Cohl's subsequent films certainly satisfy all definitions of animated cinema, Cohl's brand of film practice involved a mix of techniques. He manipulated a wide variety of pro-filmic elements, including drawings and cut-out paper figures but also dolls, match sticks, photographs, and other objects, even sand and clay.

The actual filming of *Fantasmagorie* was accomplished with what would become a prototype for eventual animation stands. A camera was mounted vertically above the drawing paper, which was back lit. Each image was exposed one frame at a time in the camera, and then traced over onto the next sheet before being removed, to ensure some stability between consecutive images. One account compares Cohl's painstaking solitary labor drawing and filming *Fantasmagorie* to a monk copying a medieval manuscript (Courtet-Cohl and Génin 2008: 98). Just as he had worked alone on his caricatures, comic strips, and photography, Cohl remained devoted to his status as an individual graphic artist and even at Gaumont he considered himself a "cinégraphiste" rather than an animator or filmmaker. Unlike much commercial animation later on, when individual drawings might be exposed for two or more frames to cut down on the labor, *Fantasmagorie* involves a completely new sketch for each frame. This technique allows a lively energy – every frame is different – which reinforces the frenetic action and constant transformations within this vibrant, graphic world. However, Cohl's was an extremely inefficient mode of production, so for much of his subsequent career he would have to insert some live action footage into his films to reduce both time and expense.

Watching *Fantasmagorie* remains a slightly unsettling experience for viewers even today since it moves so fast while simultaneously defying many of our expectations for how to watch a cartoon. Crafton (1990: 258) warns correctly that few in the audience can fully grasp its content in a single viewing, and Cohl's grandson seems to agree: "One almost needs to watch *Fantasmagorie* in slow motion to follow in detail all the experiences encountered by the little clown" (Courtet-Cohl and Génin 2008: 86). This short, fast cartoon, made from roughly 2,000 separate images, reveals a dizzying display of events. *Fantasmagorie* begins with Cohl's own hand painting the *fantoche* clown character in white paint on a blackboard, but then the bulk of the film unfolds without his physical presence, in the negative mode to simulate the original board. Except for one comical moment when the clown loses his head and has to be glued back together, *Fantasmagorie* presents a graphic space and time that remain independent of the artist whose job is to set free this frenetic character and, like a watchful parent in the background, patch him up when he falls. This is a major step beyond lightning sketch films that foregrounded the showman artist repeatedly standing beside his easel displaying his own talent and craft.

Furthermore, Cohl's drawings seem to be several inches tall, so the drawing surface is also much smaller than the large easels of lightning sketch animation: his figures are drawn for the camera's lens, not on large paper pads or blackboards imitating a theatrical audience's perspective. By contrast, Blackton's earlier lightning sketches in America were filmed with a frontal camera and in the same dimensions as they would have been drawn for a live vaudeville audience. Cohl's work advances substantially beyond the techniques and content of most previous work in animation and pixilation.

During the course of *Fantasmagorie*'s ever-changing action, the clown undergoes a wild array of highly dynamic escapades within a playful visual field where the borders of the frame seem less restrictive than those of a sheet of paper on an easel. *Fantasmagorie* is all about the fanciful transformation of lines and shapes into various representational images that themselves are in constant flux. For instance, a wine bottle rapidly turns into a flower and its stamen becomes the tip of an elephant's trunk (Figure 2.1). These changes are rapid and fluid. The break-neck speed and comical metamorphoses fit well within early cinema's roughhouse comic conventions, which are often built around variations on slapstick mayhem (Carroll 1991: 25). Cohl's spontaneous mode of representation moves the cinema toward a much more vital form of animation, with a character who bursts around the frame while the space dissolves and blends one setting into the next, opening up the possibilities for filmic cartoons to update and surpass the techniques of the comic strip. Nicole Brenez (2007: 24) observes that while Reynaud and Blackton contributed substantially to animation's invention, Cohl's

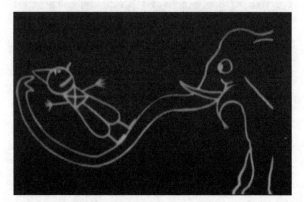

Figure 2.1   Cohl's rapidly shifting lines. *Fantasmagorie*, produced by Gaumont, directed by Emile Cohl, 1908.

Fantasmagorie amounted to a completely different sort of outcome and a redefinition of the medium.

Fantasmagorie gets underway when the stick-figure clown pulls a white bar down, forming a box with another man inside. The box shape immediately morphs into a movie theater with the clown inside a chair, which functions as both a jack-in-the box and a movie seat. The bourgeois gentleman is seated behind him. Cohl's work here is consistent with his earlier self-conscious comics and caricatural style. In that previous work, he exploited and manipulated the conventions of the two-dimensional page and comic strip windows. With *Fantasmagorie* Cohl reminds us that we are watching a rectangular screen in a cinema and he retains a frame-within-frame conceit throughout. Next, a woman with a huge hat sits down, blocking the man's view, so he plucks the giant feathers from her hat, at one point apparently even tearing a hole in the back wall to stuff them away behind the wall (and screen). He also lights a cigar which seems to ignite the woman's hair. Somehow the clown pops out of her head, spinning wildly into a new set-up as her skull becomes a hot air balloon and the man dwindles away in the corner of the frame (Figure 2.2). What makes this opening scene so challenging, in addition to the rapid change of fantastic events, is that the frame contains so many simultaneous movements. On the frame's left edge, a curtain rises and falls as several short films seem to follow one another, including soldiers marching. Meanwhile, the large woman sits, powders her face, peers through her opera glasses and wiggles her feet, oblivious of the round man behind her gesturing wildly and pulling her hat

Figure 2.2 The clown pops out of a woman's ballooning head. *Fantasmagorie*, produced by Gaumont, directed by Emile Cohl, 1908.

apart. The spectator has a rough time trying to follow all the action dispersed across Cohl's busy screen before the images flow into a whole new scene. Cohl's film frame is often as decentered as it was in his previous graphic work, while his themes also owe to his years as an Incoherent. As Hervé Joubert-Laurencin points out, "Cohl is the principal representative of an incoherent cinema. This style can be characterized as an early 'cinema of attractions' that integrates this new medium with the codes of journalistic caricature, the comic strip's vignettes, and a public provocation" (Joubert-Laurencin 2008: 113).

Throughout the remainder of the cartoon, the clown continues to appear, disappear, become entrapped, and free himself, while simple geometric shapes such as circles, lines, and boxes constantly blend into other objects. It is a film dominated by speed, transformation, and freedom of movement. The same signifiers can generate several different signifieds; no referential figure remains fixed. The playfulness of Cohl's earlier Incoherent work abounds. Here a line may be a string, a pole, then a plant stem. An elephant's eye becomes a round lamp, while the elephant's body provides the outline for a barn in the next scene. Moreover, the action reinforces the anti-bourgeois, anti-authoritarian fervor of the Incoherents. At one point the clown seems to "fish" a piece off a bourgeois gentleman (it could be his posterior), which is then swung across the frame to hit an on-coming soldier in the face. The soldier may be a visualization of a "butt-head," which is a more vulgar expression in French. Businessmen and soldiers populate this world, but are then left behind as the clown eventually rides off on a hobby-horse, seemingly to more mischief. Emile Cohl never returns at the end to regain the artist's authority or take credit for this animated marvel. There is no bracketing closure with the animator's hand. Finally, this animation is about the fanciful character, the lines, the movement – in other words, the essence of animation – rather than the artist's performance, though Cohl's playful anarchist style pervades the work.

Cohl's next film, *Le Cauchemar du fantoche* (*The Puppet's Nightmare*, 1908), continued to mimic a lightning sketch appearance and was even released in the United Kingdom under the title *Living Blackboard*. This film too is based on a series of transformations involving the sleeping *fantoche* character and objects around him. The clock becomes a ghoul, a gigantic coffee pot turns into a ladder whose white lines unravel into a rope-like spiraling line, and a butterfly pursued by the puppet transforms into a spider that captures the puppet in its web. This cartoon, like *Fantasmagorie* and the third *fantoche* puppet film, *Un Drame chez les fantoches* (*A Puppet Drama*,

1908), continues to mirror a blackboard presentation. Sébastien Denis (2007: 43) attributes Cohl's use of white lines on a black background to his application of dream theory and the limitless power of the imagination. *The Puppet's Nightmare*, like *Fantasmagorie*, proceeds at a dazzling creative pace, following dream logic without having an actual diegetic nightmare motivate the action. *A Puppet Drama* harnesses the alterity of constant visual gags in a parody of a melodramatic love triangle in which two male figures compete for the attentions of a woman, who finally gives her heart, literally, to the policeman who has protected her from both men. At the end, all four figures face the audience, smile, and curtsey before they meld into one white circle for Cohl's variation on the Gaumont symbol (Figure 2.3). These are movies about moving drawings and the magical metamorphoses and visual play possible in an animated cinema of attractions.

While working for Gaumont from 1908 until late 1910, Cohl firmly established his imaginative repertoire of themes and techniques, many of which would be reworked and combined throughout his career in his hundreds of eventual films and serials. Not all these films were fully animated. Many of them involved some creative sort of pixilation of matches or puppets or other real physical objects made to move about at strange speeds or even backwards. For instance, *Soyons donc sportifs* (*A Sportive Puppet*, 1909) exploits hinged paper figures for scenes of bicycling, swimming, and even shooting an elephant out of the sky, while *Japon de fantaisie* (*A Japanese Fantasy*, 1909) pixilates dolls and dead insects and only contains a few seconds of a drawn face. Cohl's movies were cinematic displays and experiments more than short cause-effect narratives.

Figure 2.3   Cohl's puppets bow for the camera. *Un Drame chez les fantoches/ A Puppet Drama*, produced by Gaumont, directed by Emile Cohl, 1908.

Even within his live action films, Cohl tried to include some animation, though his contractual obligations and delivery deadlines did not always allow him to spend adequate time on each project. As most animators would discover, success, or a steady contract, usually led to producers demanding a production schedule stipulating an unrealistically high output. However, early animation rarely lent itself to sped-up production schedules. "Emile Cohl found himself obliged to invent increasingly ingenious techniques to save time, including use of cut-out paper figures, marionettes, and live-action scenes" (Courtet-Cohl and Génin 2008: 99).

Les Joyeux microbes (*The Merry Microbes*, 1909) is a perfect example of the sort of hybrid film Cohl managed to generate, combining live action and animation. This format proved highly influential even if its extreme visuals and biting satire would not be repeated by many later animators. The live action story frame for *The Merry Microbes* begins with a gentleman entering a doctor's office for a check-up, proudly proclaiming he has never felt better. However, the doctor, examining the patient's blood, exclaims that he is full of dangerous microbes. The isolation of microbes was a recent trend in medicine and often ridiculed by cartoonists who regularly lampooned lofty scholars and scientists. According to Crafton, the referent for the bacteriologist was probably Dr. Doyen, "who had been a favorite butt of the caricaturists' jokes since 1899, when he had been the first to record a surgical operation on film" (Crafton 1993b: 285–289). When Cohl's dubious patient peeks into the microscope, the screen cuts to a circular mask to signal his perceptual point of view. The doctor cites five separate microbes, while the intertitles attach a personification to each: Pestilence (or the politician), Laziness (or the civil servant), Rabies (or the mother-in-law), Cholera (or the chauffeur), and Tetanus (or the drunk).

Within each short episode seemingly random lines and fragments coalesce into representational figures for some little comic strip-like gag before another set of lines begins the next view. The politician seems to go from initially drinking in a bar to becoming a statesman to being pelted with shoes and vegetables at a podium. He ducks down to protect himself but pops up as a jack-in-the box clown. Next, the lazy office worker sits at his desk, falls asleep, and once his head hits the desk he becomes covered in ink, the tool of his trade. The rabies section features an angry mother-in-law whose head rolls off, turning her into a parrot, but then she becomes an angel who morphs into a demon before disintegrating again into lines and protozoa. For cholera, swirling body parts suggest that a chauffeur has hit and dismembered pedestrians, and in the final tetanus section, a rotating

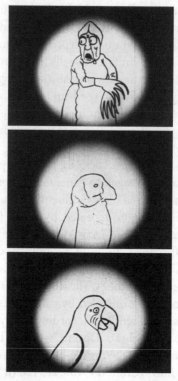

Figure 2.4   The mother-in-law microbe. *Les Joyeux microbes/The Merry Microbes*, produced by Gaumont, directed by Emile Cohl, 1909.

wheel of sketches organizes into a wino tottering along with a large bottle in his hands before he flips into the bottle, consumed by his own obsession (Figure 2.4). This animated portion of the film is all about spinning shapes and lines, and obviously draws upon motion toys and single-person viewers such as the mutoscope to present the audience with these nightmarish little visions, as seen also by the internal spectator, the patient at the microscope. Finally, the frightened patient cries "Mon dieu! How sick I am!" and breaks a painting over the doctor's head. In a fitting conclusion, Cohl has brought together many of his own graphic comic tendencies for a brief series of comic attractions that allow the frame to generate its own internal actions even if the doctor, laughing hysterically by the end at the patient's outrage, is the stand-in for a conjurer/artist.

Many of Cohl's compositions exploit circular masks or irises for the visual space of their animated sequences, similar to those employed in *The*

Merry Microbes. As Nicolas Dulac and André Gaudreault observe, optical toys and early animated picture devices were structured around rotation and brevity, while many of their spinning surfaces were round. The temporality of the device itself was typically more mechanical than narrative (Dulac and Gaudreault 2006: 228). Importantly, Cohl too retains a round visual field for many animated sequences, resulting in a much more radical temporality than that of the comical live action scenes that bracket the embedded cartoons. Such circular frames within the rectangular movie frame also reinforced the sense of exhibitionism with doubly contained images projected upon the screen. Much of the early cinema of attractions regularly placed events on display in clever ways for the viewers. As Elena Dagrada explains, such films "restructure more or less explicitly the spectator's experience as an onlooker who, outside the cinema, at fairs, or at home, was accustomed to looking through something," including mutoscopes, kinetoscopes, and peep shows (Dagrada 1990: 99). Further, when these voyeuristic devices were exploited diegetically within the film, as in a character presenting their view to the spectator, or sharing their vision, they reinforced the revolutionary nature of the visual upheaval then underway. Many of Emile Cohl's films were specifically built around perceptual depth.

One of his more clever creations, *The Neo-Impressionist Painter*, builds upon Cohl's past comic and Incoherent gags about duping the bourgeoisie. This movie again begins with a live action bracketing situation. A potential customer arrives at a painter's studio asking to see his work. The annoyed painter holds up a series of blank canvases, which were each tinted a different color in their original release prints, and explains their comically chromatic subject matter. Every new "painting" allows Cohl to bring together word-play, color, and animation as the painter explains them in sequence. Cohl inserts an animated series of events during each painting's description before cutting back to the live action framing story. For instance, the red tableau is said to be a Catholic cardinal eating lobster in tomato sauce on the shores of the Red Sea. The art collector actually looks away from the canvas, as if he were imagining what we then see in the animated sequence, a large lobster leaping out of the river and a cardinal at the table. Others include a Chinese man sailing a boat-load of corn up the Yellow River in the summer sunshine, a green devil playing billiards with green apples while drinking absinthe on the lawn, and a white tableau of a flour miller drinking milk in the snow. The most minimal joke is a totally black canvas said to be Africans making shoe polish in a tunnel at night, represented even for the viewer by simple black leader, with nothing visible in the frame at all. The entire film refers back to Alphonse Allais and the Incoherents. And Cohl's satire comes full circle with the return to live action as the bourgeois gentleman, quite excited from all the explanations, agrees to buy all the blank monochromatic canvases! Cohl manages to mock the ignorant but wealthy art collector while delivering a visualization of the verbal jokes to the movie audience.

Importantly, Cohl's tactic of cutting from live action to an animated perspective fits with early cinema techniques for emphasizing the exhibition value of various moving images. The animated painting sequences do not really offer the characters' point of view shots so much as they re-stage the action for the film viewer's maximum enjoyment (McMahan 2006: 297). The playfully satiric *The Neo-Impressionist Painter* makes full use of animation techniques as well as the coloring of the film stock itself, for a truly modern, hybrid film. Cohl created many films with these sorts of embedded animation displays. *Le Binetoscope* (*The Binetoscope*, 1910) features a live action clown who presents a series of grotesque faces that are supposedly projected from the clown's device, which has an uncanny resemblance to a computer monitor. At one point the letters of the alphabet gradually become 26 different "chattering caricatures," as if a bored schoolboy were marking up his chart of letters. A caricature is also made from numbers and another sequence animates faces by rotating in various eyes and mouth "pages" much like interactive children's "mix and match" books that provide comical options to transform people or animals. In France such books were often referred to as *livres animés* or animated books. In a final composite image, large menacing faces grimace at and then celebrate the live action clown (Figure 2.5). This short is particularly pertinent to Crafton's view of early animation: "The film is an excellent demonstration of the process of self-figuration – a characteristic of much animation as a genre after Cohl. The clown in the film may easily be seen as embodying the two aspects of Cohl's career: artist and animator" (Crafton 1990: 303–304). Throughout his career Cohl inserts characters, and often ridiculous characters at that, who somehow conjure up or create images around themselves.

In *Rien n'est impossible à l'homme* (*Nothing is Impossible for Man*, 1910) a silly drawn fellow seems to be filming the live film's action shots. From Cohl's early caricatures and comic strips through his motion pictures, internally generated images abound, whether dreamt, projected by magic lanterns, drawn on easels, or seen through microscopes. Cohl often employed such

Figure 2.5   The clown projects his binetoscope images. *Le Binettoscope/The Binetoscope*, produced by Gaumont, directed by Emile Cohl, 1910.

mixes of live and animated footage, and this format certainly influenced the American comic strip artist-turned-animator Winsor McCay. J. Stuart Blackton likely even copied his tactics (Crafton 1993a: 85). But not all Cohl's movies followed the same format at this point. His bizarre narrative *Claire de lune espagnol* (*The Moon-Struck Matador*, 1909) has an unusual amount of live action. Pedro the matador, a depressed, jilted lover moping about in a tavern, is suddenly hooked by a passing spaceship's anchor and transported to the moon. Following a series of surreal encounters with the moon, presented with only minimal animation and several clever matte shots, the unhappy matador is dropped back to earth. The matador's adventures serve as a lively parody of the cinema of Georges Méliès, complete with exploding lunar creatures and women suspended on stars in the night sky. Crafton (1993a: 74) also argues that this was the first film to combine successfully matte photography for animation and live action, proving once more Cohl's important technical inventiveness.

Le Songe du garçon de café (*The Hasher's Delirium*, 1910) is another strong example of Cohl's early style and influential story structure. In a combination of drawings and cut-outs, a waiter sleeps while angels serenade him with violins. Soon we see a collection of animated shapes, including a barrel with bottles, carafes, glasses – the stuff of the waiter's job – floating in and out of the frame and even clobbering him on the head. Much of his dream involves circular rotation combined with fanciful transformations. For instance, a bunch of grapes turn into an Eiffel Tower, then a champagne bottle, and then a beautiful woman. Most of the action takes place in a white

Figure 2.6   Waiter's fantasy. *Le Songe du garçon de café/The Hasher's Delirium,* produced by Gaumont, directed by Emile Cohl, 1910.

circle, reminiscent of the frame for *The Merry Microbes,* but the waiter, seated at frame right, watches his own dreams as if viewing a round movie screen next to him. The distorted words "alcohol" and "absinthe" appear on the screen and the waiter enters the circle, stretched into a snake-like shape, similar to the elephant's trunk in *Fantasmagorie.* Finally, angels seem to pour wine on him, but it is revealed that the live action café patrons are actually spraying him with water to awaken him. Throughout, visual humor builds upon verbal gags. Cohl manages to retain a consistent graphic style while engaging with modern art's fascination for materials, collage, and irreverent content. In these early films he synthesizes the investigation of visual and verbal humor, caricature, and cinema into a unique series of multimedia experiments that incorporate references to his own artistic journey as well as that of the young cinema and its material nature (Figure 2.6).

Emile Cohl at Pathé, Eclipse, and Eclair Studios

In 1911, Emile Cohl left Gaumont for Pathé, where he directed a number of his distinctive hybrid films incorporating live action with animated sequences as well as a conventional comedy series built around the character Jobard. Most of Cohl's narrative and exhibitionist themes were expanded at Pathé. For the live action bracketing sequences in *Le Retapeur de cervelles* (*Brains Repaired,* 1911), for instance, a frantic woman brings her delusional husband to a doctor who uses a megaphone-like device to peer into the fellow's brain. Cohl cuts away to a pixilated bug in a white oval, then a drawing of the brain dissolves into lines and patterns, including screaming faces, that recall the visuals of *The Merry Microbes*. The doctor next drills into the man's skull and extracts a long white rope from his head, said to be the string of his crazy thoughts. The screen shifts to a black frame with heavy white lines that act out a bizarre series of metamorphoses, as a broom becomes a woman and she is replaced by a champagne bottle, but there are also recurring bird-like figures and a number of characters whose heads roll off. In the end, the rope is handed to the wife, the patient is apparently cured and happy, and the film stops.

Similarly, *Le Cheveu délateur* (*The Informing Hair*, 1911) follows the same structure, with a live action bracket story, a "specialist" who conjures up an animated visual presentation full of metamorphoses, and a concluding live action epilogue. This time, however, the animation is organized around a developed, if fanciful, cause-and-effect narrative. The wealthy Mr. Martinet, suspicious of his daughter's fiancé, takes one of the man's hairs to the expert who puts it under examination. The hair somehow acts out the fellow's future, which includes absconding with the bride's money and fleeing the country. The enlightened potential father-in-law runs home with the conjurer to kick the fiancé out of his home, at which point the clever specialist proposes to the daughter and wins her hand for himself. Such films continued to include both frame-by-frame drawings and some cut-out paper objects to economize on the animated portion, while they also contained silly comic pantomimes in the tradition of Cohl's Jobard series. Cohl continued to make his moving caricatures, including *Le Musée des grotesques* (*Museum of Grotesque Portraits*, 1911), but he soon grew unhappy at Pathé and moved off briefly to Eclipse in 1912.

Cohl was clearly in high demand from studios looking to expand in novelty animated films. Two of the recently restored 1912 Eclipse films, *Les Exploits du feu follet* (*Will of the Wisp's Exploits*) and *Les Métamorphoses comiques* (*Comical Metamorphoses*), reveal that while he repeats many motifs from earlier in his career, fluid, nearly frenetic movement remains a key quality within his cinema. Neither film follows a linear storyline and both retain Cohl's bizarre trademark transformations. For *Will of the Wisp's Exploits*, a title that already suggests a nearly random series of visual gags, Cohl returns to a white puppet figure on a black background. At one point, a visual cue for music, the treble clef, becomes a physical weapon, knocking the puppet's head off. Sometimes the bottom of the frame serves as the

Figure 2.7   Cohl's ambiguous space. *Les Exploits du feu follet/Will of the Wisp's Exploits*, produced by Eclipse, directed by Emile Cohl, 1912.

ground but other times all concrete real world limits are suspended, as when the character drops out of the bottom right corner to avoid a turtle but suddenly falls back into the same frame from the top right onto the turtle. He is also attacked by a pig that seems to float in the sky (Figure 2.7). The only continuous event is the puppet's ascent to the moon and fall into the sea full of fish, another reference to Georges Méliès. This cartoon, with its mix of drawings alongside cut-out figures, remains typical of Cohl's playfulness but also proves yet again that his career does not progress in any steady fashion. Rather, he continually reworks a wide range of his own past themes and techniques.

Comical Metamorphoses returns to a film built primarily around animated caricatures. This film also lacks any bracketing situation so has no stable termination point; it functions as a series of variations on a theme and, much like a vaudeville magician's routine, it seems to end when the time is arbitrarily up. It alternates striking, staged live actions, including a man spanking a child, people in costume mugging for the camera, and a boy and girl smoking cigarettes, with short abstract animation that sometimes copies their gestures or uses some shape in the frame to motivate an animated series of transformations. For instance, when the boy insults the man and warrants a spanking, the initial sketches that follow nearly look like rotoscopes. But later a scene of the smoking children is followed up with animation of a pig being broken into pieces, while shapes from a photographic image of a picnic basket seem to motivate the animation of two stick figures fighting (Plate 2). Despite the fact that Cohl here recycles techniques and shapes from his graphic years with the Incoherents and earlier films, many of these shifts into abstract animation also anticipate future avant-garde animation, especially that of Robert Breer some 50 years later. Cohl's oeuvre constantly refers to and repeats itself in continual intertextual spirals and bursts, much like his recurring serpent figures who knot themselves up and devour their own tail before forming some familiar shape or object. Like a magic writing pad, in which images disappear but leave their mark, Cohl's animation seems to reuse shapes and situations that were just below the surface, emerging in new ways from previous films. Thus, Cohl continually cannibalizes his own products in a process that becomes a different sort of bricolage, and for Cohl that is an appropriate, anarchist artistic mode.

While Cohl's influence was already evident abroad, in 1912 he moved to Fort Lee, New Jersey to work for Eclair. His arrival there was even heralded in *A Moving Picture World*, which referred to him as "one of the best-known animated cartoonists" (Crafton 1993b: 169). One of Cohl's major American projects involved animating a cartoon series based on George McManus's popular comic strip The Newlyweds, about a family with a difficult baby named Snookums. Repeatedly, the baby, who cries loudly, disrupts the family's daily routines, often embarrassing the father by the end of each episode. Cohl's versions proved incredibly popular but also historically significant: "For the first time Eclair used a term that would be employed henceforth to describe this new genre: 'animated cartoons'"(Crafton 1990: 163). Moreover, Cohl's popular Newlyweds series motivated other comic strip artists to seek animated versions of their series, inspiring a new direction in American cartoons of the 1910s. The 14-part Eclair series was subsequently released in France, substituting the name Zozor for Snookums.

One of those installments, *How He Ruined his Family's Reputation* (*Zozor ruine la réputation de sa famille*, 1913), which is partially restored, provides a glimpse into how some of Cohl's American animation sought to bridge his own disjointed fantasy with the more linear, narrative comic strip traditions of the United States market. The story involves the Newlyweds family playing poker on a Sunday when their preacher unexpectedly shows up at the door. They hide the evidence under the couch, but while Dad tries to distract the minister, Snookums recovers the poker chips from under the couch and piles them into the minister's hat. The preacher storms out, shocked at how the family spends their holy day. One of the most striking aspects in the film is the dominance of dialogue over motion. Many of the frames are nearly covered with words, as if a

Figure 2.8   Dialogue dominates the frame in *Zozor ruine la réputation de sa famille/ How He Ruined His Family's Reputation*, produced by Eclair, directed by Emile Cohl, 1913.

static frame from a McManus comic strip, while the animated motion comes in bits and pieces between the important statements (Figure 2.8). It is as if the blank space between comic strip panels were replaced by tiny, moving cartoons. However, Cohl adds many instances of fanciful distortion that involve his trademark white lines realigning into various objects. For most dialogue scenes, the framing respects the norms of a McManus comic panel, though Cohl often overwhelms the image with words. But when possible he reverts to his own preferred visual set-up, wherein the black frame becomes a space for transformation and caricature. For instance, an image of Snookums finding the poker chips leads to a black screen with abstract shapes, then a snail smoking a pipe; then it shifts back to a profile of Snookums apparently seeing a double vision of himself seated in the preacher's hat. The preacher is even transformed briefly into a flying slug-like creature. For a scene of Snookums filling the hat with chips, the baby's two-part hinged arm rotates almost like a piston, as Cohl continues to employ several techniques within a single film. The clash of visual styles proves once again Cohl's penchant for setting competing styles side by side. By the end, the preacher's head even falls off in surprise as he sees the contents of the hat, a tactic that would certainly never appear in McManus's more realistically rendered newspaper comic.

Crafton argues that Cohl's Newlyweds was "the first modern animated cartoon series. Each installment presented a self-contained episode in the continuing adventures of the same characters, analogous to the weekly comic strip" (Crafton 1990: 166). Interestingly, however, subsequent 1910s animated series based on comic strips, such as The Katzenjammer Kids or Mutt and Jeff, retain a more unified aesthetic based on the original comic. Cohl's magical blackboard frame full of illogical transformations will not influence American animation so much as his techniques, including cut-out, articulated paper puppets. Another distinction is that Cohl zeroes in on details, pulling the comic strip characters temporarily out of their context in a way that is as striking as it is disruptive of the diegetic space. During Newlyweds Number 10, *He Poses for His Portrait* (1913), Snookums is crying loudly and his mother suggests the cat might calm him. Cohl isolates the mother in bold white lines with the other characters darkened and barely visible as a way to signify that she is the one who speaks the words scrawled across the frame. In this way, he avoids the usual dialogue balloons from the McManus comic. This cartoon too features nightmarish metamorphoses that seem to suggest the violence of Snookums' tantrum, and include the cat being stuck in a meat grinder and the father apparently swallowing baby Snookums at one point to quiet him (Figure 2.9). In Cohl's version of the series, everyone can be part of a radical and sudden fantasy moment, but it is unclear just whose subjective vision this might be. Even the fanciful genre of the American comic strip was bound by some representational rules, but Cohl regularly violated many of those norms.

Cohl and Eclair were crucial at this early stage of international animation by proving a popular comic strip could become a financially viable cartoon

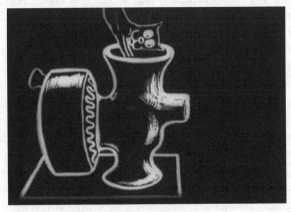

Figure 2.9   A cat is dropped into a meat grinder. *He Poses for His Portrait*, produced by Eclair, directed by Emile Cohl, 1913.

series, and many of these techniques were adopted by others. But no one else in 1910s America dared present such unusual dream imagery that meandered off from a central storyline into seemingly unmotivated mental subjective territory, much less breaking away from the typical tableau setting. Cohl's characters could bounce around in a vague, undefined cinematic space. While Winsor McCay's *Little Nemo* (1911) retained the live action bracketing from earlier Cohl movies and an animated portion of playful fantasy, by 1914 McCay's *Gertie the Dinosaur* fixed Gertie within a stable frame, a bracketing narrative to explain the animation, and functional *mise-en-scène*. Cohl's magic writing pad world of non-stop transformations failed to serve as a viable model for America's narrative brand of animated comics. A disastrous fire at Eclair Studios in March of 1914 further disrupted Cohl's influence at the time by destroying much of the evidence of his impressive American output. Cohl's luck upon returning to France in the spring of 1914 was only somewhat better. War was declared and he was put in charge of Eclair's weekly series, which placed more pressure on him to produce short material as rapidly as possible.

Connections between commercial graphic art and animated cinema continued to affect style and content at this time. The famous illustrator Benjamin Rabier (he also designed the iconic "Vache qui rit" Laughing Cow for a brand of cheese) worked with Emile Cohl on several projects, including three films based on Rabier's Flambeau the dog character. During this era Eclair was suffering from disruptions caused by World War I and released a movie Cohl had completed several years earlier, *L'Avenir dévoilé par les lignes du pied* (*The Future as Seen by the Lines in Your Foot*, 1917), in which a female fortune teller examines the soles of a man's feet to see his future. The live action bracketing story recalls many of the framing situations from Cohl's earlier films, and the woman's "vision" involves a host of now familiar metamorphoses, including a heart that bursts into flame, all organized around a man finding love and happiness. In a resolution reminiscent of *The Informing Hair*, the fortune teller ends up finagling an engagement for herself out of her presentation. Cohl also continued to rely regularly on cut-out articulated paper puppets set upon drawn backgrounds or combined with some frame-by-frame drawings. *Les Exploits de Farfadet* (*Farfadet's Exploits*, 1916), which is built around a man's troubling dreams, which are apparently caused by reactions to his medicine, employs mostly cut-out figures, though the narrative's frame recalls Winsor McCay's *Dreams of a Rarebit Fiend*. At one point in the dream the man is swallowed by a whale and escapes by yelling "I am a Boche!" The fish, disgusted by the idea of eating a German, spits the man safely out onto the beach. Repeatedly, Cohl returns to his favorite imagery and techniques as he churns out animation that remains indebted to his Incoherent past and caricatural presentation style.

However, during 1917 Cohl began a new series of shorts based on Louis Froton's popular comic strip Les Pieds Nickelés (The Leadfoot Gang), which is built around three playfully anarchistic petty thieves pursued by the hapless detective Zigouillot. While the first episode is completely lost, and the remaining volumes two, three, four, and five are only available in bits and pieces, *The Adventures of the Leadfoot Gang* display a fairly different look from Cohl's previous work. The constant sense of fantasy and transformation remains, but the visual style includes more detailed pencil drawing and the characters are inserted within rather conventionally rendered settings. Cohl successfully mixed the realistic touches and contemporary environments of Froton's comics with his own trademark sense of distortion. As Francis Lacassin explains, "This was not a simple adaptation but rather a graphic re-creation. To the [original] comic's farcical tricks Cohl added a magical dimension ... Cohl himself was plunged into a new and enriching experience" (Lacassin 2007: 213). Cohl's characters, sometimes moving as sketched cut-outs, other times bending their rubbery necks like Cohl's earlier figures, could defy gravity, temporarily lose their heads, or be smashed into fragments that reassemble on their own. The characters and settings resembled Froton's style, but the fantasy and movement sprung from Cohl. Each episode ran 7 minutes and they were released one after the other, roughly every two months (Loné 2007: 324–325). Crafton observes that the series was "innovative and improvisational. The figures move quickly without too much regard for 'naturalism'" (Crafton 1990: 163). The resulting visual style, with its jerky figure movement but subtly shaded decors, is far from the abstract fantasy worlds of most of his earlier works.

For one of his final narratives, *La Maison du fantoche* (*The Puppet House*, 1921), Cohl returned to his roots, as his *fantoche* puppet fellow, here named Fantochard, a variation on the word for homeless, wanders around an abstract, cartoony Paris looking for a room. Along the way he is offered a trunk in an attic to rent and he even attempts unsuccessfully to sleep atop the uncooperative obelisk in the Place de la Concorde. When he tries sleeping under water, the angry fish attack him repeatedly in a cycled sequence: "Nothing for rent here, filthy biped!" Lucifer will not even allow him to stay in Hell. In their book, grandson Pierre Courtet-Cohl and historian Bernard Génin find a serious change in tone within *The Puppet House* since Paris offers nowhere that Fantoche can afford to live, and he is not alone: there is not even any space under the bridges because so many poor people are camped there already (Courtet-Cohl and Génin 2008: 117). By the end the puppet draws a house on a wall and takes refuge within the sketch as he complains to the viewer about housing conditions and his treatment (Plate 3). Emile Cohl was indeed becoming much more bitter by this point in his own life. Cohl had turned 60 in 1917 and he became increasingly frustrated by the direction of commercial cinema, which seemed to have less space for him. Further, more and more attention was being directed to the successes of American animators, and especially Winsor McCay, who regularly claimed to have invented animated cartoons.

Yet Emile Cohl's cinematic contributions were truly impressive. His film work fully exploited the camera's stop-start potential to create movement emphasizing metamorphoses and transformations. He also made trick films in the tradition of Georges Méliès and Segundo de Chomon and helped expand the options for special effects. Certainly, the context of the Incoherents dominated Cohl's film career as he continued to exploit absurdly composed images in which incompatible objects and aesthetics are combined in new, comically unsettling hybrid texts. Yet Emile Cohl did not fall unexpectedly from the sky to launch animated cinema: his work is part of a larger context of art history in which the traditional beaux-arts were being reconfigured and even attacked. Conventional divisions between high and low art were eroding. A radical mix of contemporary media was suddenly possible and new strategies and materials, including collages and mechanically reproduced sounds and images, were influencing all the arts. Cohl was very much a product of his surroundings in turn-of-the-century France.

Historian Georges Sadoul asserts that thanks to Emile Cohl's variety of output, constant experimentation, and seminal influence in American animation, he was clearly the most important figure in international animation up until the mid-1910s (Sadoul 1962: 122). "One can say that Emile Cohl is the first to have explored nearly every possibility in animation: drawings, paper cut-outs, pixilated objects, and puppets" (Génin 2003: 9). Clearly, Cohl brought together a wild variety of influences from the popular graphic arts. All his work is intertextual and anticipates many surreal and cubist traits of modern art and later avant-garde animation, from Man Ray and Marcel Duchamp to Norman McLaren and Robert Breer. One student in my recent animation history class even observed on an anonymous course evaluation that s/he appreciated Emile Cohl because his style resembled Adult Swim's Superjail! Nicole Brenez concludes that Cohl's work pays homage to all his artistic friends and influences, while preserving a sense of irony throughout. Further, she argues that Cohl invented more than animation – he also launched the art film and the psychedelic cinema "under the auspices of fantasy, freedom, and joy" (Brenez 2007: 28). However, as Cohl continued into the 1920s, other animators were exploiting more efficient animation techniques and subjects were changing the norms of animated cinema. His work was already fading rapidly into the past.

Graphic Art and the Cartoon: Lortac and O'Galop

Emile Cohl's exaggerated, graphic, unrealistic animation style and his reliance on a variety of materials, including hinged cut-out figures, proved a strong influence on subsequent French animators for decades to come. That his animation could be loosely narrative or brazenly avant-garde and that it found its way into Eclair newsreels, live action comedies, and stand-alone cartoons all provided a wide range of models for animation's rich potential in French cinema. Two artisanal animators following in his wake were Lortac (Robert Collard) and O'Galop (Marius Rossillon). Lortac (1884–1973) is credited with establishing Europe's first true animation studio, while O'Galop (1867–1946) applied his graphic art background initially to public service cartoons, then to stylish adaptations of fables. At a time when many live action filmmakers were trying to figure out the best business model for small-scale production, animators were also struggling to find their niche in the French national cinema. Cohl established some ground rules, but Lortac, O'Galop, and others sought out aesthetic and economic strategies that would allow the inefficient, labor intensive genre of animation to fit within the increasingly undercapitalized and decentralized French marketplace. Recently, the French journal of early film history, *1895*, published a valuable special issue devoted to reexamining the important, but frequently overlooked careers of O'Galop and Lortac, including their cultural contexts and their output in illustrations, magic lantern art, and films (Vignaux 2009b).

As with many pioneering international animators, Lortac came to cinema via the worlds of painting and then journalistic graphic arts, including caricature and portraiture. After being seriously wounded as a soldier in 1915 when an artillery shell damaged his shoulder, Lortac found work creating puppet animation to encourage people to buy World War I bonds. These public service shorts were inserted into Eclair's newsreels during Cohl's tenure there. For Pathé, Lortac and Jean Comandon made a public health film, *La Tuberculose menace tout le monde* (*Tuberculosis Threatens Everyone*, 1917), in which people who drink and carouse excessively or eat poorly are shown to be more at risk than those living a balanced lifestyle. A cut-out paper skeleton hosts a "massacre game," as if at a country fair, where he tosses infected TB balls at people, knocking down the weak. Such educational movies provided a solid training ground for Lortac's later commercial ventures, combining humor with effective messages. Importantly, Lortac was also sent to the United States as part of a group of committed artists raising funds for the war. There he saw the animated films of Winsor McCay and a host of other American cartoons, which motivated him to launch his own studio, Publi-Ciné, when he returned to France in 1919. Despite distributing through Pathé, Lortac quickly learned how risky and unprofitable animation could be for a small independent producer and decided to diversify his products. There were few successful business models in Europe at this point, but Lortac produced a mix of short comedies, educational films, and especially commercial advertising, hence the name Publi-Ciné, a play on Publicité or advertising. Lortac also released a brief series in the spirit of the comical newspaper *Le Canard enchaîné* (*The Chained Duck*) called *Canard en ciné*, "the first cheerful animated newsreel, cooked up by Publi-Ciné." Such creative diversification, which mirrored John R. Bray's Studio in America, eventually provided a solid economic footing for Lortac's long-term stability. Publi-Ciné went on to offer a viable blueprint for fellow animators throughout Europe.

Lortac's Pucli-Ciné studio in Montrouge employed roughly 15 people, including André Rigal and Cavé, with five animation stand cameras. Crafton considers Lortac's crew "the first generation of commercial animators in France" (Crafton 1990: 206). Their techniques included the full range of alternatives, drawn and painted animation on paper and cels, cut-out figures, puppets, and occasional live action inserts. Lortac's early customers included Nicolas wine stores, Nestlé, and Citroën automobiles, for which he made *Citroën: la plus belle conquête de la femme c'est la Citroën* (*Citroën: The Most Beautiful Way to Win Over a Woman*, 1920), among many others. But Lortac's business model also allowed him to take on occasional fiction film projects, including a short series involving Toby, a policeman with an inconvenient thirst for whisky. In addition, Publi-Ciné launched several shorts involving the bumbling popular scientist Professor

Mecanist. In one episode, *L'Aspirateur du Professeur Mecanicas* (*Professor Mechanist's Vacuum*, 1921), the professor's modern vacuum ends up devouring everything in the room, anticipating a similar scene in *Yellow Submarine* (Dunning, 1968) 47 years later. In *La Sève poilifère* (*The Hair Restorer*, 1924) Mecanist devises a new hair tonic that proves all too successful at growing hair on every surface, causing comical mayhem. One historian suggests Lortac's fascination with products of the technical revolution, including robots, appliances, and products for the home, "was really expressing the mixed feelings of contemporary observers to the changing world" (Newnham 2009). Lortac was certainly participating in and cautioning against the modern transformation of France. Another short, *Les Déboires d'un piéton* (*The Challenges for a Pedestrian*, 1922), follows the trials and tribulations of a pedestrian in a town overrun with cars. But while Lortac may have lampooned modernism and its consumerism, he also profited from making commercials to market those same products, including Eyquem Spark Plugs to ensure motorists a safe trip and insecticides to increase harvests.

Lortac inserted a great deal of irony and bizarre humor into the short animated commercials at Publi-Ciné, just as he had in his fiction films. Unfortunately, Lortac's earliest commercial films also abound in racist caricature and culturally insensitive stereotypes. One of the title sequences for Publi-Ciné shows was a black usher who draws out the company name, then returns at the end to erase it. A close-up completes the show. O'Galop is credited with this sequence (Figure 2.10). Further, one commercial for

Figure 2.10   Publi-Ciné logo. Produced by Publi-Ciné, title sequence animated by O'Galop, 1920.

Pluvier plum cakes, *Faites comme le nègre* (*Do Like the Darkie*, 1920), features a caricatural black boy, with big rolling eye-balls, who invites the audience to buy this brand of sweets and send in the enclosed sweepstakes entry forms in the hopes of winning cookies or even a free car. A very different commercial for Kohler chocolate, *Le Testament de Findubec* (*The Sweet-Tooth Will*, 1920), pits two nephews against one another: the one who finds the world's tastiest treat inherits their dead uncle's money. The foolish nephew travels to Africa and China in search of exotic foods. Both regional cultures are represented via crude caricatures. The wise nephew simply buys Kohler chocolate at a local store and wins. Shopping close to home is safer than venturing into the world. Across a wide range of products, the Publi-Ciné worlds are populated by concisely typed characters springing from preexisting conventions, many of them unflattering and even cruel.

In the tradition of comic strips, short advertisements exploited such cultural shorthand and caricature to establish rapidly a milieu and concise range of themes, emotions, and outcomes. Many of these sexist and racist scenarios derived from easily recognized folklore and popular culture references. For instance, one ad by Lortac and Cavé for Nestlé yogurt features Uglyrella, a shepherdess with horrible facial blemishes who is nice to a magician disguised as a beggar. He rewards her kindness with a yogurt which will improve her health and beauty. The spots disappear as she eats one pot of yogurt, then a prince wanders past. Struck by her natural beauty he marries her and the town erects a statue in tribute to the magician and Nestlé yogurt (Figure 2.11).[1]

The overall visual style of Publi-Ciné involved carefully articulated paper cut-outs, many of which moved on the screen with surprising subtlety. For instance, the shepherdess gracefully spoons the yogurt with her articulated arm while her drawn facial expressions and eye movement remain restrained, as if she is concentrating on the yogurt's pleasant taste and healing effects simultaneously. Admittedly, as with much animation made with paper cut-outs, Lortac's characters stand and move in silhouette the bulk of the time and speak with exaggerated gestures, often freezing clumsily during shots with dialogue balloons. For instance, in one ad for a urology medicine, *La Réponse de l'au-delà* (*An Answer from the Beyond*, 1920), some contraption supposedly invented by Edison allows a suffering man to call upon the

---

[1] This film, *Comme au temps des fées* (*Once Upon a Time*, 1920), and five others, including *Faites comme le nègre*, are available on the Lobster DVD *Retour de Flamme*, Volume 3.

Figure 2.11   Lortac's Nestlé commercial *Comme au temps des fées/Like in the Days of Fairy Tales*, produced by Publi-Ciné, Directed by Lortac, 1920.

ancient Greek Dr. Aesculape for advice. The framing and setting recall Emil Cohl live action skits, but the commercial depends upon both intertitles and dialogue balloons to deliver information (Figure 2.12). While a practical, rhetorical function dominates all Lortac's work, the commercials manage to retain a sense of fantasy, with engaging figures often making eye contact with the audience to suggest a degree of irony or even satire is at work in these tiny dramas. Publi-Ciné's films were subsequently sold in the popular 9.5mm format for projection in homes and other settings beyond the commercial 35mm movie theater.

Figure 2.12   Lortac's medicine commercial *La Réponse de l'au-delà/An Answer from the Beyond*, produced by Publi-Ciné, animated by O'Galop, 1920.

But Lortac's reputation also opened other opportunities. One of his major fiction projects was funded by two Swiss producers who wanted an animated version of satirist Rodolphe Töpffer's *Histoire de M. Vieux Bois* (begun in 1921 and premiered in 1923). Töpffer's popular series was published in English as both *The Story of Mr. Wooden Head* and *The Adventures of Obadiah Oldbuck*. Töpffer (1799–1846) is credited with establishing the comic strip as a genre and during the early 1900s, the exploits of his character Mr. Wooden Head (known primarily in the US as Obadiah Oldbuck) were even staged in live theatrical presentations. Töpffer's visual style was well known, featuring finely etched caricatures, and his individual panels were as comical as they were lyrical. Given the great cultural status of Töpffer's exquisite and intelligently satirical work, the very idea of an animated adaptation raised concerns among his fans. Advance articles were generally divided at the time about whether animated cinema was appropriate for presenting Töpffer's famous tale, which includes some outrageous actions not normally associated with popular cinema, including comical suicides. But the delicacy of the line drawings, the clever irony, absurd humor, and cinematic rhythm were generally praised in the filmed version (Fondation Vevey n.d.). Lortac's 35-minute featurette was cut into three episodes for its commercial release as shorts, but its distribution seems to have been mostly limited to Switzerland during the 1920s. As Bendazzi points out, "This series by Lortac and Cavé was an example of humorous animation in a European style. It distinguished itself from the slapstick formulas of the other side of the ocean. . . . A humor based not on rhythm but on character, more like a circus act" (Bendazzi 1985: 63–64). Happily, *The Story of Mr. Wooden Head* was restored in 1971 by the Swiss Cinémathèque (see Cosandey 2009).

As late as 1940, Lortac and Publi-Ciné were still animating advertisements. During the Occupation they even made their commercials timely: a Buitoni pasta commercial argued that their vermicelli was as nutritious as (scarce) red meat, while a public service short encouraged people to recycle their prewar wool into new clothes. By the end of World War II, however, Lortac sold off his equipment to write and draw comics the rest of his life. His most lasting contributions included establishing a successful business model for this small niche in the film industry and simultaneously providing a training ground and employment for a new generation of animators and graphic artists, including fellow employees Cavé, Antoine Payen, and André Rigal, and the poster artist Raymond Savignac. Of course, he also worked briefly with that other key figure of the 1920s, O'Galop.

Marius Rossillon, a.k.a. O'Galop, was of a previous generation from Lortac. O'Galop began as an illustrator and poster artist, most famously creating the iconic figure Bibendum, the Michelin Man, back in 1898. By the 1910s he began to experiment with the cinema, reportedly animating his pen name like a lightning sketch, with the letters OGALOP cleverly turning into a drawing of a galloping horse. He also knew Emile Cohl and these two friends crossed paths regularly throughout their careers. O'Galop's work retains a flat, graphic space, much like poster art, while characters tend to move more stiffly than Lortac's cut-out figures. Their motion is quite separate from the static backgrounds and while O'Galop lacks the fanciful transitions of Cohl's work, he creates some strong, haunting images. Among the few films remaining and readily accessible are several of his public service shorts produced thanks to Dr. Jean Comandon. O'Galop also made educational health films commissioned by the Rockefeller Foundation at the end of World War I. The Rockefeller Foundation funded public awareness campaigns against alcoholism, syphilis, and tuberculosis (which killed 60,000 people each year). Fortunately, O'Galop's films on all three topics are preserved.[2] The Rockefeller project's goal was to get the word out to as large an audience as possible, so they ended up anticipating the Soviet agit-prop trains, sending "health" caravans, trucks equipped with projectors and educational films, including O'Galop and Lortac's animation, into France's small towns, distributing information and showing these cautionary movies for a period of five years. Animation, with its direct appeal to all ages and clear rhetorical delivery style, was a central component of their public health media campaign.

Among O'Galop's grimmest films is *Petites causes, grands effets* (*Great Oaks from Small Acorns Grow*, 1918), a lesson in the slippery slope toward alcoholism. A man, moving rather robotically, buys a drink each day, and quickly sinks so low he loses his family. Moreover, there is a series of images to show the effects on an alcoholic's children, who may become epileptic or even murderers (Figure 2.13). This little cartoon even ends with a guillotine, seemingly inviting the audience to decide which path they themselves will take. Throughout this and other cartoons, O'Galop's figures are outlined by dark lines which starkly delineate their cut-paper edges and reinforce their position, placed atop a drawn background. The films act as a series of poster-like scenes with some foreground movement. Characters typically pace back

---

[2] Copies may be found on Lobster Film's DVD *Retour de Flamme*, Volume 2, as well as at www.europafilmtreasures.eu.

Figure 2.13   O'Galop's murderous boy. *Petites causes, grands effets/Great Oaks from Small Acorns Grow*, produced by Jean Comandon for Rockefeller Foundation, animated by O'Galop, 1918.

and forth laterally or move in repetitive cycles. Such repeated visual stylization fits perfectly with *Le Circuit de l'alcool* (*The Alcohol Cycle*, 1918). This short film mocks the café as an extension of the distilling industry. It also reveals the cycle of exploitation at the café, as the barman pours wine into the customer's mouth and the man's money flies back to the bartender. Once the drunken patron stumbles home, O'Galop's film anticipates *Felix Woos Whoopee*, as the street lamps dance about and the world rotates, recalling some of Cohl's circular effects. Alcohol, according to this scenario, empties your pockets but fills up the insane asylums. By the end, one image of a mad man in a straitjacket refers to Cohl's mentor, André Gill, who died in an asylum. The final title announces that real athletes drink water! Crafton (1990: 334, n. 25) suspects that Emile Cohl may have worked on the backgrounds.

Similarly, *Pour résister à la tuberculose soyons forts* (*To Resist Tuberculosis, Stay Strong*, 1918) warns against assuming that pills or other antidotes can spare you from TB. A skeleton sprays germs at a thin intellectual in his garret who easily succumbs to the disease, but a round, athletic man exercising outdoors knocks out the skeleton, as the film concludes with happy, healthy families jogging, riding bikes, and rowing boats. Outdoor sports are the best defense. While the TB cartoon contains a bit of slapstick, O'Galop's educational work fails to develop the sort of satire, humor, and fluidity found in Lortac. Further, O'Galop's visual style owed much to rather dated modes of caricature. However, he also drew and directed a number of animated fiction films built around several absurd bumbling characters. He made several comedies involving Touchatout (Touchall), an inventive veterinarian, and a series of five shorts featuring Bécassotte, a rather clueless girl. After the war he also turned out a number of fables from La Fontaine, such as *La Grenouille qui veut se faire aussi grosse que le boeuf* (*The Frog Who Wished to be as Big as the Ox*, 1921) and *Le Loup et la cigogne* (*The Wolf and the Stork*, 1923). After 1924, O'Galop returned almost exclusively to print illustrations and then left Paris, taking up watercolors. As Caroline Patte laments, "It is sometimes difficult to date precisely the films of Marius O'Galop, but it is certain that with the dominance of cel animation techniques, the arrival of sound, and especially the division of labor among animation teams, he no longer found a place for his creativity in this cinematic genre" (Patte 2007: 305).

Clearly, Lortac and O'Galop followed Emile Cohl's lead, expanding upon their backgrounds in graphic arts and popular culture by entering the world of animated cinema. As Crafton observes,

> It is legitimate to think of the animators clustered around Lortac and O'Galop as a 'Cohl School,' in the sense that they tempered the American influence with his methods and his fundamental aesthetic assumptions that defined the genre. This partially explains the tenacity of the cut-out technique in France. Certainly there were shortages of celluloid caused by the war, but economic factors alone cannot account for the fact that all but one animator still relied on cut-outs as late as 1930. (Crafton 1990: 206)

Lortac and O'Galop also provided valuable examples of how tenuous the life of an animator could be, so their business models remained influential during the late silent period, when there were no equivalents to American animation producers and distributors in Europe. But their films remained in public circulation into the early sound era, thanks in large part to Pathé's marketing of home projectors and films. Sébastien Denis points out that while Cohl was not featured in the Pathé Baby catalogue of 1931, French animators, including Lortac and O'Galop, were as well represented as the Americans, though Pat Sullilvan's Felix the Cat was clearly the most popular series in France at that point (Denis 2007: 120–121). Mickey Mouse, Popeye, and Betty Boop would be topping the competition very soon as American cartoons came to dominate

French screens during the 1930s. Yet, while the small, fragile French animation studios were scratching out a viable business model, the explosion of truly avant-garde cinema during the 1920s began exploring the techniques but also functions of animation in a surprising number of extreme experiments far beyond anything practiced in other national cinemas.

But is it "Animation?" French Avant-Garde and Moving Pictures

French cinema of the 1920s included a strong array of experimental work from visual artists, especially painters and designers, as well as literary figures and poets. As Ian Christie points out, "Early animation often seems, with hindsight, like a popular version of the same concerns that pushed 'serious' artists into Modernism." Even some Cohl films are so reflexive that they parallel cubist fascination with revealing all the processes of picture making (Christie 1994: 85). A wide variety of modernists during this era also emphasized the interdisciplinary connections between the arts as well as the specificity of each medium and its forms. According to Jean Mitry, cinema brought many of these impulses together: "Attracted spontaneously to the cinema, writers, painters, and men of the theater believed that visual rhythms were the very essence and expressive purpose of the cinema" (Mitry 1997: 155). Critic and filmmaker Germaine Dulac argued that cinema was about various forms of motion and that cinematic Impressionism could reexamine the physical world from a new perspective: "We experimented with making things move through the science of optics, tried to transform figures according to the logic of a state of mind" (cited in Abel 1984: 280). Beyond the use of exotic filters and superimpositions, dizzying editing rhythms, and extreme close-ups, the avant-garde investigated the effects of slow and fast motion as well as pixilation in their efforts to explore "pure cinema" and the essence of the medium's material and potential.

Animation was an important source of inspiration to the avant-garde, which was devoted to synthesizing various aspects of popular and graphic arts into radically new forms. It is no surprise then that they occasionally returned to exploiting the moving image at its most fundamental, as had Emile Reynaud and Emile Cohl. However, the French avant-garde steered clear of the more systematic use of abstract animation then underway in Germany at the hands of Walter Ruttman, Viking Eggeling, and Lotte Reiniger. France's experimental filmmakers tended to rely on location shooting, then they enjoyed disrupting that everyday world with inserts of animated cut-out figures, title cards, and pixilation. For instance, René Clair's *Paris qui dort* (*Crazy Ray*, 1923) contains several very short animated sequences to present how the scientist's ray machine put most of the world to sleep. The demonstration resembles a blackboard, as white chalk-like lines arc across the night sky and the cut-out figure of a plane flying beyond its reach slides across the image. But the bulk of this fantasy film relies on the manipulation of camera speed making the live action world stop, start, or race about. Clair's Dada-esque *Entr'acte* (*Intermission*, 1924) continues the pattern of exploiting only a tiny bit of animation in an otherwise real world setting. Near the opening, a canon is pixilated to roll back and forth across rooftop before pointing at the camera. Later, scores of wooden matches gather in a superimposed shot with a man's hair, before igniting spontaneously. However, most of the jerky motion featured throughout *Entr'acte* is due to in-camera manipulation of speeds and post-production montage. Pixilated animation is but one brief technique among many other disorienting strategies.

Similarly, Man Ray expanded his work with camera-less photographs, known as rayograms, by setting tiny objects directly onto unexposed 35mm film strips for his 1923 work, *Retour à la raison* (*Return to Reason*). When a light source was then turned on, the shapes of the objects, including salt granules, springs, pins, and tacks, would be recorded. Projecting these initially static outlines and patterns of light creates a frenetic array of pulsating patterns across the screen, in a Dada dance of shapes, some identifiable, others not (Figure 2.14). Ray also inserts some underexposed

Figure 2.14   Man Ray's rayogram springs. *Retour à la raison/Return to Reason*, produced and directed by Man Ray, 1923.

nighttime shots of a spinning amusement park ride. This is another sort of "animation" for these modernists, since a new mechanized machine, here a gigantic spider-like contraption, could hold and spin humans about in a comical cycle. The new world was full of such devices, which seemed to mix the impulse of the early zoetrope motion machines with the robotics of contemporary mechanical engineering. Thus, rather than employing conventional animation itself, Ray was exploring cinema as a medium to foreground and create new forms of motion, from the rotation of model Kiki's naked torso to the unsettling rhythms of salt granules flickering on the screen. His ciné-poem *Emak Bakia* (1925) inserted several more rayogram sequences, but also relied on pixilated wooden shapes, dice, and leaping shirt collars, creating sequences of moving sculptures and animated "still life" studies. Plus, he added a hinged paper figure of a male leaping that recalls Marey's motion studies (Figure 2.15). Ray also helped Marcel Duchamp create a kinetic film, *Anémic cinéma* (1926), which features a number of spinning discs that mimic some of the circular word patterns and animation of Cohl and others, avoiding actual frame-to-frame techniques.

Animation for many of the avant-garde artists during this era was mostly interesting for its potential to lend motion to the inanimate, allowing objects to move on their own like kinetic sculptures, moving artworks, and robotic machines. Many of these people were also big fans of American commercial animation, including Fleischer's rather surreal Ko-Ko the clown who could pop out of his inkwell, leap off the paper, and bring

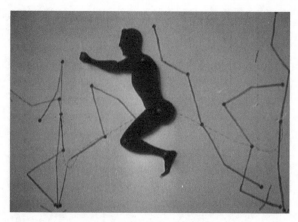

Figure 2.15   Ray's leaping man. *Emak Bakia*, produced and directed by Man Ray, 1925.

playful chaos into the live action world around him. It was the ability to create a new sort of rhythm that appealed to many of the avant-garde artists of this era, who came to see motion pictures as a way for visual artists to approximate the "pure" sensations and pacing of music. As Jean Mitry explains, "To dispense with the script ... and turn the cinema into visual music (self-expression in terms of a self-significant rhythm) was the aim of a whole generation of artists and experimenters" (Mitry 1997: 155). This "search for pure rhythm which would be for the eye what music was for the ear" found a vocal advocate in painter Léopold Survage (Mitry 1997: 112). Survage theorized a visual dynamism based on form and rhythm, and though his own film project built around color harmonies and graphic sensations was never completed, he typifies the interaction of the arts that brought painters and musicians toward the silent experimental cinema.

Fernand Léger was an established painter with his own personal cubist style when he approached the cinematic apparatus to extend his fascination with collage, graphic compositions, fragmentation, mechanically produced objects, and kinetic rhythm. Early on, Léger was drawn toward painters concentrating on geometric shapes, including Paul Cézanne and Pablo Picasso. After serving in World War I he frequented artistic circles that included Jean Epstein and René Clair. Léger had much in common with this young, rebellious generation of artists living in the aftermath of World War I. As a soldier, Léger had been gravely wounded in a mustard gas attack, and endured a long convalescence. By the 1920s, his association with other kinetic artists and filmmakers, as well as posters he created for Abel Gance's rapid-cut *La Roue* (*The Wheel*, 1923), fueled his fascination with combining media. His collaboration with American cinematographer Dudley Murphy and composer George Antheil led to *Ballet mécanique*, an aesthetic investigation of mechanical objects in time and motion. The film's opening and closing animated sequences feature Charlie Chaplin rendered in a pastiche of Léger's own visual style, though this footage was already apparently something of a found object itself, having been first created in 1920 for an unfinished project (Kermabon 2007: 291). Chaplin was a key figure to Léger and his cinema had served as an inspiration during the war. At one point, while Léger was depressed and on leave from the front, the poet Apollinaire had cheered him up with a trip to a Chaplin movie which served to prove to Léger that life still had happy surprises in store. Despite its abstraction, *Ballet mécanique* brought together many personal and artistic references (Figure 2.16). Léger's guiding concept at the time of *Ballet mécanique* was that his art could reveal the "plastic possibilities" of everyday, manufactured

Figure 2.16   Fernand Léger's Chaplin. *Ballet mécanique/The Mechanical Ballet*, produced and directed by Fernand Léger, 1924.

objects: "The fact of giving movement to one or several objects can make them plastic" (Léger 1965: 48). However, while this avant-garde film makes heavy use of rapid montage, prisms, and spinning whisks, the only real animation is limited to the framing title sequence. A schematic Chaplin, built from geometric paper cut-outs, rises into the frame and waves his hat for several seconds to salute the audience (and perhaps say "Chapeau! Hat's off to the film") before sliding back down out of view. At the close, the Chaplin fragments burst back up into the frame, in a nearly identical series of gestures before setting his hat on his head as the film cuts to black leader. While Léger and Antheil celebrate the movie as a new form of modern architecture, for us it serves as evidence of the theoretical and practical significance of animation for those exploring the cinematic medium during this era of "pure cinema" in France.

Though members of the avant-garde occasionally dabbled with animation techniques, there was no core group of experimental animators in France. Instead, brief animated sequences popped up in a various works. Pixilation in particular proved popular among some of France's most important avant-garde auteurs. After all, it fit the spirit of collage and the mixing of media that inspired so many works at this time. Jean Vigo made reference to the surreal potential of animation with several frames of doll-characters arriving on a toy train at the beginning of *A Propos de Nice* (1929). He also inserts a surprising several-second cartoon sequence into *Zéro de conduite* (*Zero for Conduct*, 1933). A doodled sketch on a desk begins to move and the figure transforms into Napoleon. This flash of childish cartooning comments upon the pompous teachers, but for us it also stands as another sort of tribute to Emile Cohl's legacy. Though it turned up in a wide array of instances, animation in France remained a rather feeble mode of production by the time of sound cinema. Nonetheless, Léger, writing about avant-garde cinema back in 1924, suggested animation might still turn out to be key to the future health of French cinema: "An epoch alive with exploration, risk, which perhaps is ended now. It continues through animation, which has limitless potential for giving scope to our imagination and humor. It has the last word" (Léger 1965: 51).

3

French Animation and the Coming of Sound

Animation is an art but also an artistic craft, a métier. *It is creation in every sense of the word. Animation's essence is to breathe life into drawings, objects, or things that do not normally move.... These elements are thrown into motion.* (Jean Image, animator, 1979: 2)

We were destined to fail because the Americans were so far ahead of us, but especially because they could sell their cartoons here so cheap. On the budgetary level, there was no way for us to compete. (André Rigal, animator, cited in Roffat 2009: 97)

During the 1930s, French animation continued many of the trends established during the previous decades of silent cinema, including a large amount of avant-garde work by national and immigrant artists. Almost all motion picture animators remained individual auteurs, struggling on the edge of the French commercial cinema and often balancing personal projects with advertising to survive. The coming of sound only complicated the economics of animation in the absence of a strong studio system. As Colin Crisp (1993: 2) points out, the decentralized, financially fragile situation of 1930s French cinema may have opened up creative potential in some areas, but these conditions closed off many other possibilities found within Hollywood's mode of production. France's cinema was built around low-budget, artisanal modes of production. The labor intensive practice of animation, which was so highly capitalized within the American studio structure during this era, never found a strong foothold within French film practice. Thus, France lacked a stable, classical period of commercial

French Animation History
© Richard Neupert. Published by John Wiley & Sons

animation. It fell upon several passionate individuals to try to forge a viable national alternative to Disney and Hollywood's major studio productions. As Jean Mitry (1980: 728) admits, France never really distinguished itself in the area of animation during the early sound cinema, beyond the work of a few exceptional individuals, including Alexandre Alexeieff and Berthold Bartosch. Although these two avant-garde artists were hardly alone, for a nation famous for its rich vitality in live action output during the tumultuous decades of the 1930s and 1940s, animation remained a weak cottage industry distinguished by unusual, even quaint, techniques more influenced by the practical and fine arts than by commercial, international norms for cel animation and its cartoon content or styles.

Ladislas Starewich's Fabled Puppets

For many historians, "breathing life" into the inanimate is at the ontological core of animation, if not of all cinema. French filmologist Edgar Morin argued that cinema "reanimates" the filmed world but also has the distinct potential to give "dynamogenic powers," motion to normally static objects. Once objects appear to move, thanks to the apparatus of animation, they become anthropomorphized with "souls," where previous to their being projected there was nothing (Morin 2005: 64–66). Further, animation has often been cited as a medium, like mythology and fables, where animals can readily become humanized for thematic purposes. Ladislas Starewich (born Wladyslaw Starewicz, also spelled Starevich) becomes a key figure for such discussions, proving the power of animation thanks to his stop-motion manipulation of insects, stuffed animals, and puppets, often in allegorical fables and children's stories. Starewich's careful pixilation of dead bugs prompts one critic to observe: "His insects' nimble gestures lead one through an array of human emotions, and to a heightened sense of sympathy" (Schneider 2000: 2). Ladislas Starewich also serves as an important figure in the transition from silent to sound animation in France, as he and his family struggled to create a viable, independent production niche within the decentralized French cinema between the wars.

A Pole educated in a Russian fine arts academy, Starewich initially learned animation techniques to illustrate insect behavior, but quickly shifted from educational films to animating dead bugs and frogs to illustrate little skits or popular folk tales. His most famous film from this era is certainly *The Cameraman's Revenge* (1912), which was a parody of pot-boiling cinematic melodramas, complete with infidelity, voyeurism, and clever reflexivity. As Crafton aptly puts it, Mr. Beetle walks in on Mrs. Beetle and Mr. Cricket "on the sofa stroking each other with their twelve legs in a way both comic and obscene" (Crafton 1993a: 239). However, during the Revolution, Starewich fled Russia, along with much of the film community. French cinema gained considerably in creative new blood from this wave of White Russian immigrants, which included actor Ivan Mosjoukine and director Alexandre Volkoff along with the newly formed Albatros Films. Starewich too moved to France where he set up a small animation studio in his home outside Paris. Once established, he also mentored other Russian expatriates, including animator Bogdan Zoubowitch. Starewich seems quickly to have stabilized his output, managing to create one or two of his fable films each year while delivering advertising and publicity work to help maintain a steady income.

The French films of Ladislas Starewich were produced in a family centered mode of production, with his daughter Irene frequently creating the costumes for his "ciné-marionettes" as well as assisting with scripts, animation, and eventually with co-directing. Wife Anna also helped construct sets and costumes, but she was never included in the credits. Irène and her younger sister Jeanne (a.k.a. Nina Star) even performed within several live action sequences. For the celebrated *La Voix du rossignol* (*Voice of the Nightingale*, 1923), Jeanne, then 10 years old, performs as a young girl who has caged a nightingale. The bird tells her stories, featuring a number of elegantly mobile insects and fairies, as the live action girl learns the nightingale must live free. Released from its cage, the bird rewards the kind girl with a beautiful singing voice. *Voice of the Nightingale* was released with Pathé color process and earned many awards, including the American Hugo Riesenfeld Award for "the most novel short subject motion picture" of 1925. The older Irène even began helping her father negotiate distribution contracts. Together, the family managed to create and market successfully their unusual brand of high quality pixilated films over the next 40 years. Whether working with real dead animals or stuffed toys, Ladislas Starewich managed to produce a fluidity in their gestures, thanks in part to his knowledge of anatomy. These smooth, purposeful, and even subtle movements of his figures gave his animation its distinction and popularity. Yet all this artistry was accomplished within quite basic facilities. From 1923 until the 1960s, an animation table roughly four meters square served as the staging area, with poles attached for mounting lighting units and a small Jupiter camera. Props such as trees might be 50 centimeters high and much of the terrain was initially shaped from molten wax (Béatrice and Martin 2003: 91). Further, he pioneered a method of working with models, whether toys or taxidermied, wherein the backs might be removed to allow the fingers of the crew to manipulate the puppets' joints and facial features easily from within. As evidence of his novel talents the French film journal *La Cinématographie française* in 1926 called Starewich the founder of a new cinematic genre (cited in Béatrice and Martin 2003: 86).

Starewich shot commercial advertisements as well, but the content for his narratives often came from reworking or re-imagining well-known tales. For *Le Rat de ville et le rat des champs* (*The City Rat and the Country Rat*, 1926), Starewich updated the La Fontaine fable adding modern touches and speed of movement. The City Rat drives a noisy car through Paris (shown via back projection), but then heads into the country where he crashes into the Country Rat's farm. The Country Rat returns to Paris with him where they join other rats in fancy evening dress, eating and drinking atop a human-sized table. The figures, which retain grotesque rat-like traits, smoothly tilt their heads, curl their lips, and roll their eyes, their gestures clearly communicating their personalities and emotions. A sort of musical revue by dancing girl rats is performed for the upper-crust revelers, complete with detailed moving backgrounds and elaborate Folies-Bergère sorts of outfits, until a real cat awakes and chases everyone away. When an alert rat screams a warning, it is signified by a drawing of a cat face bursting from its mouth. A chaotic series of desperate escapes follows as rats risk life and limb (and tails). Animator Simon Pummell comments on the grotesque action and deep anxieties present in this film: "The country rat's tail is amputated while he is disguised in women's clothing. A shot where he holds up his apparently erect tail, only to have the tip collapse and fall off, deserves a place in someone's thesis on 'The Phallic Symbol in Cinema . . .'. These are fairy tales with all the dark humor of the originals" (Pummell 1996: 123). By the end, the Country Rat walks back to his calm home, defeated, dragging a mouse trap stuck to his broken tail.

Starewich's longest and perhaps most successful film, *Le Roman de renard* (*The Tale of the Fox*), was begun during 1929 but took many years to complete. It was not initially distributed until 1937, and then it was released in a German version only before being revised in French in 1941. The reasons for the series of delays included the financial shenanigans of producer Louis Nalpas. Nalpas had arranged to use his own sound-on-disc process which quickly became obsolete. He also provided Starewich only a tiny advance of 350 francs per meter of completed film. After years of disagreements, Starewich sued Nalpas, and in 1935 they agreed to sever all contractual ties. Starewich owned the rights and had a nearly completed but silent film. Finally, in 1936, the German studio Ufa bought the rights and created a German soundtrack for its premiere. Only in 1939 did Starewich find a French producer, Roger Richebé, who acquired the German release negative plus the music and sound effects tracks, without dialogue. Thanks in part to the chaos and staggering unemployment within France's film industry during the Occupation, Richebé managed to assemble a very skillful team to re-record a more appropriate, and "French," soundtrack. Writer Jean Nohain created most of the dialogue, the music was composed by Vincent Scotto (famous for hundreds of popular songs and the sound-tracks for scores of movies including Marcel Pagnol's Fanny trilogy and Pepé le Moko), and Raymond Legrand (father of Michel Legrand) was brought in as conductor (Béatrice and Martin 2003: 176–178).

The synchronization was carefully worked out, with Irène Starewich assisting at every stage of production. Richebé could have relied heavily on voice-over narration to speed up production and cut costs, but he preferred to allow the animals to speak for themselves, despite the added difficulties. Plus, several new shots and even scenes were animated for better synchro-nization, and a whole new dream sequence was created, including an anachronistic radio broadcast, to help justify the ending. Because of the heavy Nazi and Occupation censorship, however, several lines of dialogue had to be changed (including a sarcastic reference to a "corporal of the guard" since that had been Hitler's rank). The premiere finally arrived on April 10, 1941. Reviews praised the quality of animation, the elegant voice work, and the music: "It is a tour de force of both patience and technique; hats off!" (La Cinématographie française, cited in Béatrice and Martin 2003: 189). The movie played in French theaters fairly steadily over the next two years. Despite having only eight prints in circulation, The Tale of the Fox managed to play in over 200 cinemas, attracting an estimated first-run audience of 120,000, with nearly half of that from the very successful engagements at the large César and Gaumont Palace in Paris. But, appar-ently, competition from the German propaganda feature Jud Süss (Jew Süss, Harlan, 1940) pushed it off the screens early (Béatrice and Martin 2003: 194). It was also distributed to a number of occupied and neutral European nations, from Norway to Greece. The Tale of the Fox was a rare success for French animation of this era.

Reynard, the lead fox character of the story, is a well-known figure in European folk traditions. Many poems and tales abound in the Reynard cycle, and one of the most influential was the episodic *The Tale of the Fox* composed by multiple authors in the twelfth and thirteenth centuries. There is even a highly respected International Reynard Society composed of medievalists. Thus, Starewich was working from a well-established storyline that had appeared in a wide variety of forms for hundreds of years in Western culture. The coming of sound forced Starewich to rework it with voices by a number of promising young actors, many in their first commercial roles, including Sylvia Bataille and Claude Dauphin. Moreover, Irène is credited with co-scripting and co-directing, so from that point on, she should be considered an equal creative partner in all Starewich productions. The introductory narration is presented by a rather hideous monkey who turns the book's pages to introduce the major characters who leap from the pages. This clever opening recalls that of Sacha Guitry's *Roman d'un tricheur* (*Story of a Cheat*, 1936) (Figure 3.1). Further, the animated figures move very quickly and smoothly, with fast-paced editing delivering the action in dramatic fashion. At one point, for instance, a number of characters are shown running laterally in sequential shots as they chase after the fox, and the graphic matches on each anticipate Akira Kurosawa's famous scene of panic in *Seven Samurai* (1954).

The overall plot is a series of escapades by Reynard the fox who repeatedly tricks the inhabitants of the kingdom. The land is ruled by a lion king whose lead counsel is a badger and cousin to the crafty, elusive Reynard. The fox, as in many folk tales, exploits the weaknesses and vices of those around him

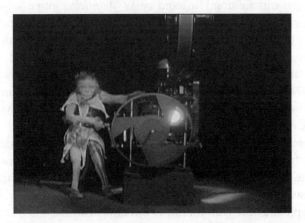

Figure 3.1 A monkey introduces *Le Roman de renard/The Tale of the Fox* (a.k.a. *Story of the Fox*), produced and directed by Ladislas and Irene Starewitch, 1946.

to get what he wants. For instance, he repeatedly outsmarts the poor local wolf, who receives quite violent treatment. Reynard, much like the later trickster in George Pal's Jasper cartoons, promises his naive neighbors that he knows where the best honey or fishing or dancing is to be found, then takes full advantage of his victims. And they are all partly to blame for what befalls them. The badger is the only animal cunning enough to get the fox to return to the castle, where he faces punishment for his crimes. But, upon an elaborate gallows set, populated by scores of animal spectators and involving intricate camera movements, the fox tempts the King with tales of riches and frightens him with rumors of a plot on his life, until Reynard gains his own freedom. Finally, the King discovers he has been publicly duped. His army unsuccessfully attacks the fox's intricately booby-trapped castle until the poor King realizes Reynard is too resourceful and the kingdom would instead benefit from making the fox a top minister in the government. Thus, the fox really is in many ways put in charge of the henhouse by the end. However, the ending displeased the fascist governments of Italy and Spain. Both regimes banned the film outright, judging the final victory of the criminal fox "immoral."

While the characters move fluidly, the backgrounds alternate between detailed three-dimensional sets and back-projected photographs and drawings, often suggesting atmosphere as well as deep space. Starewich indeed generates a complicated tale that comes to life, but unlike Disney's versions of fables, a great deal of surrealism, cruelty, and dark humor remain. As early as 1937, Walt Disney considered adapting his own version of Reynard's tale, combining it with Edmond Rostand's play *Chanticleer* into a musical, since both stories involved animal communities. Though the studio spent a great deal of pre-production time and money on the idea, they eventually decided it was too risky to use such a devious trickster as the central character. Decades later, Disney Studios used some of their 1930s designs for *Robin Hood* (1974) and its dashing anthropomorphic fox, Robin (Solomon 1995: 77–84). Disney's cartoony 2D cel characters, however, lacked the vitality and grotesque attitude of Starewich's disconcerting puppets.

Starewich's version, *The Tale of the Fox*, clearly incorporates many elements from European oral traditions and fable conventions. For instance, the lazy wolf is not just fooled by the fox: he gets frozen in the lake, is then beaten by the local men, and finally loses his tail altogether. Similarly, the fox exploits a bear's lust for honey by hammering the bear's snout into a log and then calling out to the humans who arrive to beat the immobilized, howling bear. The cute fox family even strings up a kicking bunny rabbit as they prepare to slaughter and flay it. "There is also a nice sense of irony in seeing animals dressed in furs and finery – for example, a badger in a badger fur coat – reminding us what fur coats are made from," observes Simon Pummell (1995: 61). Reynard also seduces a chicken away from her rooster husband and chicks only to devour her. Her cleanly picked bones are then laid out for all to see, including her traumatized chicks. The humor too is far from that found in American cartoons. For instance, just before the fox steals the chicken away, he comically licks her rooster husband's coxcomb in a truly lascivious manner. Even the Queen has a cruel sense of humor; she is clearly fed up with her King, invites various flirtations, and embarrasses her husband at dinner by proclaiming, "You may be a lion but you eat like a pig." And the final reflexive words in *The Tale of the Fox* are spoken by one of the fox's children: as the cub's pants fall off he turns to the camera and says, "That's all folks!"

Certainly Starewich's greatest achievement, this first-ever feature of stop-motion animation includes a host of internal narrators with stories within stories, presented as mental subjective scenes. There is also an embedded dream sequence, narrated in part by the monkey as an announcer for a fantasy battle between fox and wolf. Such a dependence upon a variety of voices makes overt reference to oral traditions while it also reinforces characterization in these bizarre stuffed animals. Edgar Morin celebrates the uncanny power of the cinema to suggest human qualities in otherwise static objects, which, "under the combined influence of rhythm, time, fluidity, camera movement, magnifications, the play of shadow and light, gain a new quality." They exhibit a "subjective presence" to the spectator: "This animation of objects takes us back, in a sense, to the universe of archaic vision, or to the gaze of a child" (Morin 2005: 66, 67). *The Tale of the Fox* makes full use of fluid movement, close-ups, subtle gestures, and motivated camera movement, but it also mimics classic realist style, including con-tinuity editing, to lend the stop-motion figures personality, emotion, and desires. They are characters who move nearly as naturally as human actors, and therein lies part of their perverse attraction. Everyone knows they are static objects, and yet we can become easily aligned with them and even feel allegiance, like the entranced children at the Punch and Judy show in *The 400 Blows* (Truffaut, 1959) (Figure 3.2).

Importantly, the fast-paced editing rhythm helps the animistic effects. *The Tale of the Fox* is composed of over 625 shots for a rapid average shot length of 5.6 seconds, with several breathless, accelerated montages. The "execution" sequence alone is said to have required over 270,000 animation

Figure 3.2   The fox beats the bear in *Le Roman de renard/The Tale of the Fox* (a.k.a. *Story of the Fox*), produced and directed by Ladislas and Irene Starewitch, 1946.

movements, involving nearly 100 figures. Unlike the earlier two-dimensional cut-out figures of Lotte Reiniger's *Adventures of Prince Achmed* (1926), Starewich's vast menagerie of stuffed animals is truly animated within a narrative space and time that demonstrates the cinema's innate ability to generate subjective presence in otherwise still objects. Moreover, while Walt Disney eventually scuttled his version of the Reynard tale, *The Tale of the Fox* did inspire and influence Wes Anderson's *The Fantastic Mr. Fox* (2009). "In [*The Tale of the Fox*], action cuts fairly abruptly between puppets of radically different scales, a technique that Anderson borrowed," according to cinematographer Tristan Oliver (Hope-Jones 2009: 76).

For all his cinematic talents, Starewich had initially worried that synchronized sound would interfere with his fantasy worlds of stuffed animals and puppets. Voices and dialogue, he assumed, would distract the audience's attention away from the delicate visual communication by the animated figures and destroy the dream-like atmosphere of his fantasy worlds. After all, what would a stuffed mouse or cat's speech "sound" like? For films such as *Le Lion devenu vieux* (*The Old Lion*, 1932), another reworked La Fontaine tale, he had added musical accompaniment and some sync sound effects, but avoided any spoken language. Starewich's trademark style mixes occasionally cute, appealing characters with a gruesome set of supporting figures. This time the main character is a once-ferocious King who now has trouble killing a fly. Here too, Starewich employs a mix of stuffed dead animals and dolls. There is an unsettling quality to the taxidermy animals, especially since they are specially designed to have moving mouths and expressive eyes. For instance, the stuffed cat who plays the accordion has grotesque, menacing jagged teeth. While the lion is a furry, sympathetic doll, most of his subjects are deliberately frightful creatures. Flashbacks reveal that when young, the King was quite daring and feared, once abducting a neighboring kingdom's princess for his bride. Sadly, the aged King is now kicked out of his own castle and dies miserably in a cave with only his memories to keep him company. It is a mournful movie with less fluid movement and rather mundane sets and action compared to *The Tale of the Fox*, but many of the same fascinating puppet characters appear, including the monkey, fox, and donkey.

Structurally, many of Starewich's short films feature characters who leave their "normal" world and descend into a dream or an underworld of deviant, frightening figures before returning back to normal life by the end. For instance, the old lion king dreamt of his dangerous past adventures and Country Rat eagerly voyaged to the threatening city before dragging himself back home where he would be secure. This pattern also holds for *Fétiche mascotte* (*The Mascot*, 1933), a tale about a child's stuffed puppy. *The Mascot* is a fairy tale combined with a working-class fantasy. A poor woman, in live action, stitches together a puppy doll, Duffy, while her sickly child's only desire is to eat a fresh orange, which the mother cannot afford. As in many cartoons about toys, each of the dolls and stuffed animals the mother has made comes secretly to life when humans are not looking. But that evening, as the girl sleeps, the mother wraps many of them, including Duffy, and apparently sells them. The dolls escape from the live action delivery truck into the streets of Paris, where they scatter in many directions. Lost, Duffy scampers about town and at one point even urinates on a policeman's shoe. The combination of back projection and clever editing strategies, some right out of 1920s French avant-garde cinema, inserts Duffy and the gang into the bustling diegetic space, where he grabs an orange and sets out on the journey home to the poor girl. After dark, a bizarre, nightmarish alternate world comes alive, including scary toys and dolls, but also animal skeletons rising from garbage cans. Cruelty abounds in Starewich's storytelling and an unsettling amount of bestiality is retained in his animals. A riotous and cruel batch of characters torment Duffy and try to steal his orange, but in the end Duffy returns home to toss slices of orange into the girl's waiting mouth just as the sun rises. Eric Schneider argues that *The Mascot* is built around "the simple theme of a search for goodness and generosity in the modern world" (Schneider 2000: 6). And this modern world is indeed filled with cruelty and

Figure 3.3 Duffy, the mascot, lost in the city. *Fétiche mascotte/The Mascot*, produced and directed by Ladislas and Irene Starewitch, 1933.

unpleasant actions. In *The Mascot*, one clown character dies when a car runs over his head, and the multitude of haunting figures that come out at night are much more threatening and mature than Sid's gruesome creations in *Toy Story*. But Duffy survives and comforts the poor, sickly girl (Figures 3.3 and 3.4).

The Duffy Mascot films became a short series of five films, each repeating Starewich's narrative pattern, with naive characters descending into a violent,

Figure 3.4 Duffy's haunted evening. *Fétiche mascotte/The Mascot*, produced and directed by Ladislas and Irene Starewitch, 1933.

surreal alternative world, often during the night, only to resurface into normalcy by the end. For the second film, Duffy works in a circus. He even marries in a 1935 installment, then in *Fétiche en voyage de noces* (*The Navigator*, 1936) the happy couple takes off on a steamer for their honeymoon, which is destroyed by a villainous monster who calls up a wild sea storm that eventually sinks the ship. However, Duffy and his wife manage to fight their way to a beautiful tropical island and a happy ending. Along the way, Starewich inserts his characters in a number of sequences and settings that recall underwater sequences in Georges Méliès as well as classic silent ship scenes from films such as Chaplin's *The Immigrant* (1917) and Keaton's *The Navigator* (1924). The final installment continues the couple's aquatic adventures with *Fétiche chez les sirènes* (*Mascot and the Mermaids*, 1937). However, World War II interrupted their production schedule and for a decade the Starewiches failed to release any newly completed films.

Among their more successful post-World War II films, *Fleur de fougère* (*The Fern Flower*, 1949), based on a tale by nineteenth-century Polish writer Jozef Ignacy Kraszewski, follows a boy who ventures into the forest on the night of the summer solstice, in search of a fabled magic fern flower. Once in the woods, he encounters a number of bizarre and menacing creatures living among the underbrush. Trees reach out at him, pine cones and mushrooms sprout faces and sing. The boy steals the magic fern flower, which, much like Aladdin's Lamp, grants his every wish. The boy is turned into a prince, with a charging horse. A castle filled with servants springs up for him. To give the impression of running or riding long distances, Starewich's landscapes rotate beneath the characters' feet, though only occasionally does the camera reframe or pan to follow the action. Though the camera remains rather static, the young prince in particular moves gracefully with smooth movements. All the animals and plants are capable of speaking in this strange fantasy world, and Starewich includes many tangential musical and comical numbers to highlight a vast array of figures in motion, from silly stuffed frogs to dancing maidens. There is also a Cinderella subplot about a visiting Princess who leaves her shoe behind. However, the boy finally returns home to his farming family, as his fantastic kingdom disappears with the dawn. All that is left for him is his handsome steed, behind which he now happily plows the fields. In an end that befits *The Wizard of Oz*, everything was as if a dream, and the remnants of his Cinderella are last seen as a cluster of clouds passing overhead. *The Fern Flower* won a prize for Best Children's Film at the Venice Film Festival.

Simon Pummell notes that Starewich's stories are built around strict binary oppositions, including life vs. death, human vs. animal, and fantasy vs. realism: "Yet his films . . . face both ways as they look into the history of cinema. They presage the increasingly composite cinema which the digital age may bring; but their uncanny quality for us is that, within cinema, they embody and celebrate an essentially pre-cinematic culture of folklore and animism" (Pummell 1996: 125). Historian Raymond Maillet agrees that Starewich is truly influential: "A poet and artisan, inventive as well as ingenious," Starewich can be credited with "many technical innovations put to service by his fertile imagination and animation at the highest level" (Maillet 1983: 95). Beyond granting dead insects, stuffed animals, and dolls personality and allegorical significance, Ladislas Starewich made them seem nearly as alive as the trained animals of live action cinema, but with much more characterization. Yet beyond his craft and storytelling, he is highly significant as an exemplary independent animator who survived on the fringes of the French national cinema from the silent era until the 1950s. Unfortunately, however, the Starewiches and their stop-motion animation have not always received the credit they deserve. Even Bernard Génin labels Paul Grimault's *La Bergère et le ramoneur* (*The Shepherdess and the Chimneysweep*, 1952) as the first French animated feature film, rather than *The Tale of the Fox*.

Ladislas and Irene Starewich, along with Emile Cohl and Lortac, helped establish and embody the mode of production that dominated French animation throughout the century. Starewich proved yet again that a small-scale production model fit best for the niche genre of animation. Faced with the absence of commercial studio production or distribution support for animation, Starewich struggled to maintain his own very personal cinema of undercapitalized movies. *Cahiers du Cinéma* laments that Starewich's work is that of a devoted auteur-artisan, from concept to camerawork to post-production, the likes of which one too rarely finds today (Orléan 1998: 78).

This production model paralleled avant-garde live action practice of the 1920s and 1930s in France and helps demonstrate once more how distinct the conditions, content, and styles were in French animation from the studio-made American cartoons of the same era. However, while some of Ladislas Starewich's family-style mode of production and particular techniques may have resembled aspects of the avant-garde, there were other highly influential filmmakers who helped tie animation firmly within their artistic exploration of the cinema, without reverting at all to fables or children's stories.

Berthold Bartosch's *L'Idée:* A Working-Class Allegory

Berthold Bartosch, another Eastern European immigrant, provides an additional instructive case for the individual animation auteur in 1930s France. He first worked in the Soviet Union and Germany, even helping Lotte Reiniger with her *Adventures of Prince Achmed*, before managing single-handedly to make *L'Idée (The Idea)*, a 24-minute film, in the cramped, makeshift space above the Vieux Colombier Theatre during 1930–1932. Bartosch serves as yet another example of the international nature of "French" cinema and animation in particular during this era. His techniques and themes sprang from European and Soviet models, which he synthesized in truly unique, personal, and even baffling ways. *The Idea* is a leftist project based on a book of chiseled engravings by Frans Masereel, a Belgian artist who also lived in Germany and France. Masereel's *Idea* is a series of images organized around a female savior, a personified "Idea" sent to help transform humanity, but this new concept and presence frighten the corrupt capitalists in power and shock the people who apparently fail to understand her message. William Moritz claims Bartosch's adaptation of *The Idea* is "the first animation film created as an artwork with serious, even tragic, social and philosophical themes" (Moritz 1997: 93) (Figure 3.5).

Bartosch's version begins with a title sequence explaining that men live and die for an Idea, and though others may chase it down, censor it, or try to kill it, it can live on in humanity's spirit and comfort those who are oppressed and isolated. The film then opens with "the Thinker," a serious young man somewhere in front of a window. Outside is the cosmos. As he thinks, his brain seems to become a swirling solar system, superimposed over his head until a naked woman appears. His idea is represented by this naked doll-like figure. He even cuddles her in his arms and caresses her like a baby or tiny lover. The dazzling composite animation celebrates the mind as containing the entire universe, but also suggests the less progressive notion that woman is a creation of man, though William Moritz points out that abstract concepts almost all had "feminine gender in European languages and her nudity, the naked truth, was then an important resistance symbol" (Moritz 1997: 97). The premise is that in an oppressive world where cruel, powerful men control big business, the courts, and the military, woman is a lonely, fragile symbol of hope and humanity. This serious thinker, who resembles a stylized worker right out of Soviet poster art, slides the woman into an envelope and sends her into the troubled world below (Figure 3.6).

Figure 3.5 Masereel woodcut. Copyright Frans Masereel, 1920; reissued by Redstone Press, 2000; used by permission of Artists Rights Society.

Once on the ground, the female Idea is delivered to an office building where the paper cut-out figures of the male bosses are frightened of her. The woman, disappointed, is then clothed by the men, like a paper doll, but she tosses off the coverings and runs naked into the streets. Caught and again clothed, she is put on trial, though now her image becomes softer and soapy; in the diffused light she loses the crisp paper edges. Soon she meets a working-class young man, who resembles the opening thinker, and the stars reappear behind them. Throughout the movie, scene-to-scene transitions involve short scenes of the cosmos. In the center of a town square in front of the factories and before thousands of workers, the young man appeals to the people, with the naked woman beside him. But he is arrested, sentenced to

Figure 3.6   Man contemplates his "Idea." *L'Idée/ The Idea*, produced and directed by Berthold Bartosch, 1932.

death, executed, and his coffin is carried by the crowds. The woman, as a looming white ghostly shape, follows the brave man's plight, and Bartosch relies on various forms of montage, including cutting away to the bosses sleeping soundly and dining at fancy restaurants as the victim's coffin is lowered into the grave. Such alternating montage to reveal the contrast between the classes is also present in Masereel's book, where one page may stand in direct contrast to the following plate.

By the next scene, a scientist or scholar discovers the woman and tries to press her into his book. In a frenetic scene, he distributes handbills of her which fly about and even strike frightened people in the streets (Figure 3.7). However, a politician captures her and confronts her with his glowing icon of money, around which a globe rotates. He seems to be explaining that money makes the world go round and that the State is physically squeezing the workers for profit. Next, armed soldiers march across the screen against the protesting crowds. A battle breaks out in explosive silhouette images that anticipate some of the war scenes in *Persepolis* (Paronnaud, Satrapi, 2007) in their stark, staccato composition and rhythm (Figure 3.8). The bosses' army wins and the woman's head, now a white, lightning sketch-like outline, gradually spins into a star and returns to the cosmos. Though the working class has been crushed, "The Idea" apparently proves immortal and is seemingly whisked back into the heavens, hopefully to appear again somewhere else another day. The original Masereel version ends with the battered woman returning to the Thinker who is busy preparing, sadly, to

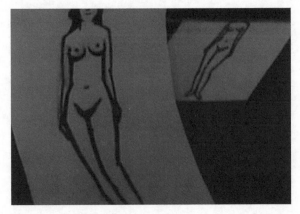

Figure 3.7   The Idea, distributed on handbills. *L'Idée/The Idea*, produced and directed by Berthold Bartosch, 1932.

send another naked woman down to try to reform humanity. A bit like the old tale of John Barleycorn, Masereel's graphic novel concentrates on the brutal treatment of the idea that continues to tempt and trouble the people.

Bartosch was working within a very personal mode of production, building on techniques he had learned over the years but also synthesizing them in new ways. He combined drawings with cut-out paper objects – the characters were hinged cardboard figures – often placed on several layers of glass plates. But he also devised his own methods, including applying soap

Figure 3.8   Troops are sent to fight the Idea and her followers. *L'Idée/The Idea*, produced and directed by Berthold Bartosch, 1932.

to add a blurred look to the often back-lit images. As Robert Russett and Cecile Starr point out, "On the mere technological level the film represents a prodigious achievement – some 45,000 frames, many of which were animated on four different levels simultaneously, often with as many as 18 superimpositions made in the camera" (Russett and Starr 1976: 84). The result is a subjective world, sometimes concrete, other times quite abstract, in soft focus. For instance, characters moving along a street occasionally pass behind objects such as street lights or buildings, but other times they seem almost intangible, as vague white shapes floating across the screen. The woman too is ever-changing. She can tower over men or slip into an envelope. She can be a concrete paper cut-out or a translucent white form through which men and bullets freely pass. Bartosch managed all this working alone with his home-made animation stand lit only by several 100-watt bulbs which required long exposure times for his complex, composite images. Impressed by Bartosch's skill and patience, Alexandre Alexeieff observed that just to animate a cloud for *The Idea* could require four different parts, and these techniques created a unique mix of fantasy and "unrelenting reality": "In such an art he excelled, working – if I may say – like Renaissance painters layer by layer, thus obtaining incredible fineness of tone" (cited in Russett and Starr 1976: 84).

Everything about the production of this uncommon film defied any commercial norms, from its radical, occasionally obscure content to its nightmarish visual style to its unsettling soundtrack. Bartosch was partially crippled from birth and walked with great difficulty, which may help explain the long, solitary hours he put in on his painstaking labor for the two years required to animate this 24-minute film. Moreover, the haunting music was composed by Arthur Honegger. In what may be the first use of electronic music in a motion picture, an "ondes Martenot," or Martenot waves device, similar to a theremin, was used. The machine creates sounds as the operators pass their hands around an electrically charged rod. The eery soundtrack reinforced the otherworldliness of the imagery. By the end, Bartosch's grim expressionist visual landscape, based strongly on Masereel's wood-cutting aesthetic, resembles a cross between *Metropolis* (Lang, 1927) and Soviet constructivist poster art, while it also recalls some of the dizzying effects from Walter Ruttman's *Berlin, Symphony of a City* (1927). Many super-impositions and rapid transitions of the chalk-like figures also resemble Emile Cohl's outlines and caricatures. This is an exotic animated project that combines a wild variety of textures and pacing into a truly unique product with its own rhythm, episodic structure, and frustrating logic.

Unfortunately, Bartosch's socialist allegory was censored and only received very limited distribution in Europe. Yet it continues to impress aestheticians and historians, including Giannalberto Bendazzi: "This is one of the rare films in which political commitment does not conflict with lyricism" (Bendazzi 1994: 39). Alexandre Alexeieff went further in his praise: "Bartosch showed that animation could be poetic, and it is there, I believe, that his influence was unique. It was Bartosch who first dared to give animation the dimensions of great art, trusting it to voice his pain, to lay bare his heart, to tell of his hope for a better future – which he never saw" (cited in Russett and Starr 1976: 89). After *The Idea*, Bartosch made several advertising shorts, including a commercial for André shoes. However, he resented such business. He then set to work on an intricate color animated anti-war film, *Saint Francis: Dreams and Nightmares*, but he and his wife Maria fled Paris as the Nazis approached. A copy of his work in progress, up to 2,000 feet of animated footage, was left with the Cinémathèque Française, but almost all of it disappeared during the Occupation. Later, he worked on several short commercial projects, but ended up painting more than animating. It was not until 1959 that the original negative for *The Idea* resurfaced at the Cinémathèque Française, and Bartosch helped reconstruct the sound and image. His example of an individual stylist working alone on a non-commercial project typifies the frail, artisanal conditions for early sound animation in France and much of Europe. Berthold Bartosch also represents another variation on the sort of avant-garde practice that unfortunately fails to find an audience or a stable financial footing. Avoiding the limits of mainstream, child-friendly cel animation proved over and over to be an impractical, if highly artistic, venture.

Jean Painlevé's *La Barbe bleue*

As with many French filmmakers, Jean Painlevé (1902–1989) approached animation after first exploring a number of creative avenues. Jean was the son of Paul Painlevé, a brilliant mathematician and more importantly a politician, beginning as minister of war in 1917 and ultimately serving as prime minister during the late 1910s and again in the 1920s. Young Jean was supposed to follow in his father's footsteps as a mathematician or become a doctor, but from an early age he was fascinated with animals and skipped school to help the caretakers at the Paris Jardin des Plantes zoo. At the Sorbonne in 1922, he pursued zoology and biology and at the very

Plate 1 Reynaud's Pierrot in *Pauvre Pierrot/Poor Pierrot*, produced and directed by Emile Reynaud, 1892 (DVD by Centre National de la Cinématographie).

Plate 2 Animated spanking "rotoscopes" the filmed event. *Les Métamorphoses comiques/Comical Metamorphoses*, produced by Eclipse, directed by Emile Cohl, 1912.

Plate 3 Fantoche draws himself a new home. *La Maison du fantoche/The Puppet House*, produced by Eclair, directed by Emile Cohl, 1921.

Plate 4 Blue Beard's crusade in *La Barbe bleue/Blue Beard*, produced and directed by Jean Painlevé, 1936.

Plate 5 Blue Beard threatens his Queen. *La Barbe bleue/Blue Beard*, produced and directed by Jean Painlevé, 1936.

Plate 6 The stop-motion Prince Charming in *La Belle au bois dormant/Sleeping Beauty*, produced and directed by Alexander Alexeieff and Claire Parker, 1935.

Plate 7 Grimault's boy clings to the flying ship in *Les Passagers de la Grande Ourse/The Passengers on the Big Bear*, produced by Les Gemeaux, directed by Paul Grimault, 1943.

Plate 8 Grimault's Scarecrow and collaborating cat. *L'Epouvantail/The Scarecrow*, produced and directed by Paul Grimault, 1943.

Plate 9 Desire in the toy store. *Le Petit soldat/The Little Soldier*, produced and directed by Paul Grimault, 1946.

Plate 10 Jack torments the Doll in *Le Petit soldat/The Little Soldier*, produced and directed by Paul Grimault, 1946.

Plate 11 The King and his portrait. *Le Roi et l'oiseau/The King and the Bird*, produced and directed by Paul Grimault, 1979.

Plate 12 The Chimney Sweep and Shepherdess escape. *Le Roi et l'oiseau/ The King and the Bird*, produced and directed by Paul Grimault, 1979.

Plate 13 Grimault's Bird repeatedly humiliates the King in *Le Roi et l'oiseau/The King and the Bird*, produced and directed by Paul Grimault, 1979.

Plate 14 The King's Robot captures the runaways. *Le Roi et l'oiseau/The King and the Bird*, produced and directed by Paul Grimault, 1979.

Plate 15 Anatole plays the spokes. *Anatole fait du camping/Anatole Goes Camping*, produced by Cygne, directed by Albert Dubout, 1947.

Plate 16 A train disrupts Anatole's outing in *Anatole fait du camping/ Anatole Goes Camping*, produced by Cygne, directed by Albert Dubout, 1947.

Plate 17 The Eiffel Tower takes a stroll in *Bonjour Paris*, produced and directed by Jean Image, 1953.

Plate 18 Jean Image offers bright, bold characters in *Bonjour Paris*, produced and directed by Jean Image, 1953.

Plate 19 The Eiffel Tower is tickled by a metro train. *Bonjour Paris*, produced and directed by Jean Image, 1953.

Plate 20 Laguionie's cut-out woman and sea in *La Demoiselle et le violoncelliste/ The Young Lady and the Cellist*, produced by Les Films Paul Grimault, directed by Jean-François Laguionie, 1965.

Plate 21 Static bystanders on the beach in *La Demoiselle et le violoncelliste/The Young Lady and the Cellist*, produced by Les Films Paul Grimault, directed by Jean-François Laguionie, 1965.

Plate 22 Gwen and Rosalie in the desert. *Gwen, ou Le livre de sable/Gwen, or the Book of Sand*, produced by Films de la Damoiselle, directed by Jean-François Laguionie, 1984.

Plate 23 Gwen's townspeople. *Gwen, ou Le livre de sable/Gwen, or the Book of Sand*, produced by Films de la Damoiselle, directed by Jean-François Laguionie, 1984.

Plate 24 Terr's mother, killed by a Draag, in *La Planète sauvage/Fantastic Planet*, produced by Argos Films, directed by René Laloux, 1973.

Plate 25 Tiwa and tiny Terr. *La Planète sauvage/Fantastic Planet*, produced by Argos Films, directed by René Laloux, 1973.

Plate 26 Renegade Oms hide in the wilderness. *La Planète sauvage/Fantastic Planet*, produced by Argos Films, directed by René Laloux, 1973.

Plate 27 Kirikou to the rescue. *Kirikou et la sorcière/Kirikou and the Sorceress*, produced by Les Armateurs, directed by Michel Ocelot, 1998.

Plate 28 Kirikou sinks the sorceress's boat in *Kirikou et la sorcière/Kirikou and the Sorceress*, produced by Les Armateurs, directed by Michel Ocelot, 1998.

Plate 29 Karaba the Sorceress. *Kirikou et la sorcière/Kirikou and the Sorceress*, produced by Les Armateurs, directed by Michel Ocelot, 1998.

Plate 30 Karaba's magic kiss. *Kirikou et la sorcière/Kirikou and the Sorceress*, produced by Les Armateurs, directed by Michel Ocelot, 1998.

Plate 31 Ocelot's hinged Prince figure. Photograph by Richard Neupert.

Plate 32 The frog Prince leaps to kiss his Princess. *Princes et Princesses/Princes and Princesses*, produced by Les Armateurs and La Fabrique, directed by Michel Ocelot, 2000.

Plate 33 Baby Asmar in *Azur et Asmar/Azur and Asmar, The Princes' Quest*, produced by Nord-Ouest Production and Studio O, directed by Michel Ocelot, 2006.

Plate 34 Mixed 2D and 3D cues on Jenane in *Azur et Asmar/Azur and Asmar, The Princes' Quest*, produced by Nord-Ouest Production and Studio O, directed by Michel Ocelot, 2006.

Plate 35 Azur and Asmar face off. *Azur et Asmar/Azur and Asmar, The Princes' Quest*, produced by Nord-Ouest Production and Studio O, directed by Michel Ocelot, 2006.

Plate 36 Skan discovers a heartbeat in Callisto's statue. *Les Enfants de la pluie/Children of the Rain*, produced by Belokan Productions, directed by Philippe Leclerc, 2003.

Plate 37 Revived in the pond, Callisto flirts with Skan. *Les Enfants de la pluie/ Children of the Rain*, produced by Belokan Productions, directed by Philippe Leclerc, 2003.

Plate 38 Princess Akhesa and Tut in a flat, colorful world. *La Reine soleil/ The Sun Queen*, produced by Belokan Productions, directed by Philippe Leclerc, 2007.

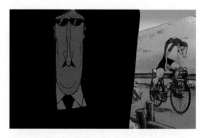

Plate 39 Mme. Souza gives Champion a tricycle. *Les Triplettes de Belleville/ The Triplets of Belleville*, produced by Les Armateurs, directed by Sylvain Chomet, 2003.

Plate 40 Mobster and Champion at the Tour de France. *Les Triplettes de Belleville/The Triplets of Belleville*, produced by Les Armateurs, directed by Sylvain Chomet, 2003.

Plate 41 Souza rents a paddle boat to pursue the ship. *Les Triplettes de Belleville/ The Triplets of Belleville*, produced by Les Armateurs, directed by Sylvain Chomet, 2003.

Plate 42 Girerd's humans resemble the animals. *La Prophétie des grenouilles/ Raining Cats and Frogs*, produced by Folimage, directed by Jacques-Rémy Girerd, 2003.

Plate 43 Mia in Girerd's painterly wilderness. *Mia et le Migou/Mia and the Migoo*, produced by Folimage, directed by Jacques-Rémy Girerd, 2008.

Plate 44 Opening at Orly: past and present in *Persepolis*, produced by 2.4.7. Films, directed by Marjane Satrapi and Vincent Paronnaud, 2007.

Plate 46 *Clik Clak*'s semiotic comedy. *Clik Clak*, produced by SupInfoCom, directed by Thomas Wagner, Victor Emmanuel Moulin, and Aurélie Fréchinois, 2006.

Plate 45 *Oktapodi* and the international 3D look. *Oktapodi*, produced at Gobelins, directed by Julien Bocabeille, François-Xavier Chanioux, Olivier Delabarre, Thierry Marchand, Quentin Marmier, and Emud Mokhberi, 2007.

Plate 47 *Imago* mixes old and new in a timeless tale. *Imago*, produced by La Boîte Productions, directed by Cedric Babouche, 2005.

beginnings of his studies, in 1923, he presented a prestigious paper at the Academy of Sciences. However, the precocious young zoologist was very tied into the contemporary Parisian arts scene. He met many of the leading avant-garde figures of the era and became close friends with Guillaume Apollinaire, Man Ray, Jacques and Pierre Prévert, Sergei Eisenstein, and Jean Vigo, among many others. It was Painlevé who introduced Vigo to the young composer Maurice Jaubert. Painlevé was with Jean Vigo when the young director died and took a famous photo of Vigo on his deathbed.[1] He also helped Luis Buñuel by "wrangling ants" for *Un Chien andalou* (*The Andalusian Dog*, 1928).

Since the age of eight, Painlevé had loved photography. But when he appeared in a movie, *L'Inconnue des six jours* (*The Unknown Woman of the Six-Day Race*, Dubois, 1926), alongside Michel Simon, he became fascinated with André Raymond's trick, time-lapse cinematography and its scientific potential. Painlevé immediately began a film of his own on the sexual reproduction of the stickelback fish. He formed his own company but also the Association for Photographic and Cinematic Documentation in the Sciences. Painlevé would go on to work with scores of scientists, and he specialized in instructional, poetic, scientific films featuring time-lapse and slow-motion, and underwater filming. He helped pioneer the ability to record and present with the camera phenomena which could not easily be perceived, much less studied, with the human eye alone. He went on to produce and direct over 200 scientific films. In 1947, André Bazin praised Painlevé's work as continuing the initial scientific research films of Muybridge and Marey, and their pure aesthetics: "Jean Painlevé occupies a singular and privileged place in French cinema" (Bazin 2000).

Surprisingly, this anarchist scientist would also produce and co-direct *La Barbe bleue* (*Blue Beard*, 1936), a pixilated adaptation of the Charles Perrault fairy tale in vibrant Gasparcolor.[2] Painlevé claims to have wanted to make his version "as far as possible from the spirit of American films," since "it would be useless to compete in a genre where perfection has been achieved" (Hutchins 1938; cited in Bellows and McDougall 2000: 141). The actual animation, involving colorful plastiline, a waxy, soft modeling clay, was accomplished by sculptor and engineer René Bertrand, his wife Germaine,

---

[1] According to Dudley Andrew and Steven Ungar (2005: 357), the severed hands pickled in a jar that appear in *L'Atalante* (1934) were a gift to Vigo from Painlevé.

[2] Criterion released a DVD of Painlevé films in 2009, *Science is Fiction*, which includes *Blue Beard*.

and their three young children, all under 10 years old, within his small studio near Luxembourg Gardens in Paris. Apparently the children's tiny fingers were a great asset for subtle shifts in the malleable little figures. The animation was filmed with an old Pathé camera that was modified by André Raymond and Painlevé to expose individual frames three times, each through a different filter for the three-color Gasparcolor process. Disney too worked with this procedure using specialized Technicolor cameras during the 1930s. The action for *Blue Beard* was written and staged in relation to the 13-minute music and song composed by Maurice Jarre, with lyrics by Jean-Vincent Bréchignac. While the idea and script for the film were initially Painlevé's, he left much of the timing and specifics of the direction to Bertrand. Despite the short length, the filming took nearly three years, often with only 20 frames or so being exposed in a day's work. Patricia Hutchins, visiting the studio during production, wrote for *Sight and Sound* that while Bertrand achieved subtle, natural movements from his figures, it was a painstaking process: "Plastiline can only be worked at night during very warm weather, and its effect of relief has given rise to many difficulties of lighting and perspective, to say nothing of the balance of color and smooth transition from one gesture to another. In the case of panning shots alone, it was necessary to use a studio in miniature with full lighting equipment to scale" (Bellows and McDougall 2000: 142). Moreover, to create sufficiently accurate proportions and gestures on the soft little characters, Bertrand consulted the precise motion studies of Etienne-Jules Marey for guidance and inspiration.

The resulting film, though boldly colored, has a rather choppy plot construction with occasionally jarring transitions, while the movement is always deliberate and a bit jerky. Unlike the subtle expressions from Starewich's marionettes, these clay figures signify with large gestures, such as showing surprise by holding their hands over their faces. Much of the narrative depends upon the explanatory song lyrics but also the audience's advance knowledge of the story. Painlevé's version starts with a book transforming gradually into the grotesque head of Blue Beard, whose mustache writhes like two blue snakes. A pair of children arrive at a chateau to sing the proclamation announcing King Blue Beard's intention to visit and select one of the lovely daughters living there as his bride. As the chorus announces his visit, Blue Beard arrives in the bright yellow courtyard while the mother and daughters watch from behind a glowing stained glass window. The King's entourage delivers luxurious gifts, including a long diamond necklace that undulates up the stairs like another giant snake.

As the chorus sings of his generosity, pixilated elegant dresses walk themselves up and into the castle. Overwhelmed by these rich, animated gifts, one daughter consents and a wedding quickly follows. Next the bride, surrounded by beautiful flowers, swings, singing about trying to forget her ugly husband, whose beard is filled with lice, while the King practices his swordplay nearby and hacks apart his hideous assistants.

When the Saracens arrive to declare war, Blue Beard departs with his army, but not before leaving the new Queen his ring of keys, which resemble a stringer full of fish and warning her not to enter one banned, private room. But in his absence she cannot help but open the forbidden room where she discovers his previous seven wives dead, the floor awash in their blood. The ensuing war incorporates rapid, cheerful music over the chaotic, nearly random shots of violent battles. The unsettling effect resembles some of the discord in Eisenstein's *Alexander Nevsky* (1938) with its audiovisual counterpoint. In *Blue Beard*, heads are ripped off and soldiers skewered, though it is not always clear just who is winning and who is losing (Plate 4). The bright dust of battle kicked up by the mayhem even resembles sand-colored cotton candy, reinforcing the playfulness of the action. But when the triumphant army returns home to colorful fanfare, the wife cannot hide that she used the small key and discovered Blue Beard's villainous secret. However, just as the angered Blue Beard is about to slice his unfaithful wife in two, her brothers arrive quickly to stab him. The film abruptly ends with the written moral: "Curiosity, however enticing, often brings regrets," adding an underwhelming, rather ambivalent tone to the conclusion (Plate 5).

Throughout *Blue Beard*, the quality of animation remains rather uneven. It is unclear that Painlevé and Bertrand would need to study human locomotion to animate these robotic figures. For instance, Blue Beard's gestures are mostly reduced to pointing crudely, and much of his movement comes from simply being turned between frames, so he often rotates back and forth. Rarely does he bend at the joints or step with his legs. Similarly, the bride's mother expresses her shock at her daughter's engagement by simply leaning sideways from the waist. While up to 300 figures were used for *Blue Beard*, most crowd scenes are shot in long shots to give a sense of collective group activity, but fluid individual movement is used sparsely. The set does include a few fine details, including tapestries on the walls and an impressive cathedral-like interior for Blue Beard's castle, but there is a great deal of flicker, especially when the camera dollies in on action. *Blue Beard* serves as yet another instance of French animators searching for a niche project that involves their own cultural history, here a Perrault tale, while simultaneously struggling to avoid copying or even directly competing with the Hollywood model. However, the result looks rather primitive and fails to serve as a new viable aesthetic option for French animators. Nonetheless, Painlevé saw his work as an extension of France's animation history. During his introduction at *Blue Beard*'s premiere, he paid tribute to both Georges Méliès and Emile Cohl as the inventors of animation. Both men had died that year. René Bertrand and Jean Painlevé did not return to animation, but Painlevé did continue as a major figure in scientific documentaries. As with many French filmmakers experimenting with animation, Painlevé's experience seems to have proven too daunting and financially disappointing. However, Painlevé went on to play a central role in the committee to liberate the cinema during Occupation as well as the establishment of the Centre National de la Cinématographie (CNC) immediately following World War II. He is a major, if curious, figure in French cinema of this era.

Alexandre Alexeieff, Claire Parker, and the Pinscreen

If French animation of the early sound era is distinguished by a cluster of often eccentric individuals working outside any formal institution, perhaps no one better represents the triumphs and challenges of this stituation than the two immigrants Alexandre Alexeieff and Claire Parker. Alexeieff (1901–1982) was one of thousands of Russian émigrés who ended up in France during the early 1920s. Alexeieff had quickly become disillusioned with the Revolution and joined the Russian expatriate arts community in Paris where he specialized in set design and painting, working with Georges Pitöeff and the Ballet Suédois, among others, before shifting into illustrating books. Alexeieff specialized in woodcut engravings and etchings, often for poetry books or editions of famous Russian novels, including a three-volume version of *Brothers Karamazov*. For his xylography, Alexeieff often employed a fine stylus to punch and carve hundreds of tiny holes in the wood block to create an impressive wide spectrum of grays. Though his serious subjects and somber tones differed dramatically from the colorful pointillist style of Georges-Pierre Seurat, Alexeieff admired that painter's work, and especially his charcoal drawings (Fragonara 2001: 101). However, he also encountered Berthold Bartosch, another artist exploring the possibilities of engraving and of evoking haunting images, expressionistic lighting, and especially environmental effects such as smoke, snow, and fog.

Alexeieff claims *The Idea* was a great source of inspiration, motivating him to think of other ways to "animate engravings" (Russett and Starr 1976: 85). To a certain extent, Alexeieff would also accomplish the stated goal of Herman Warm, set designer for *The Cabinet of Dr. Caligari* (Wiene, 1920), who had proclaimed that for Expressionists, "the screen must become an engraving" (Eizykman 2001: 141). But, before Alexeieff animated his images, he began by employing still photographs to replace printing off engraved surfaces.

Just how Alexeieff came up with the idea of a pinscreen is unclear, but one day he sent his wife out to the Bon Marché department store (where Emile Reynaud had once sold his praxinoscopes) to purchase 2,000 pins. He inserted them into a small vertical piece of stretched canvas with a layer of wax on the back side to hold the pins firmly in place. By pushing them in varying distances, and positioning a light source at an oblique angle, he could create simulated engravings thanks to the shadows cast by each pin. The first prototype was for single, painterly images that could be photo-graphed. Eventually, Henri Langlois displayed this prototype on the wall at the Paris Cinémathèque's museum. Alexeieff's goal with the pinscreen was to obtain soft edges and a "fuzziness" not easily achieved in conventional engraving or print making, but he also explained that the process allowed him "to eliminate the technical notions of 'silhouette' and 'background' by henceforth achieving pictorial unity" (quoted in Fehman 2001: 153). Happy with the photographs taken from this prototype, his next step was to construct a larger white steel screen, in 1.33:1 aspect ratio, with 500,000 tiny holes for 500,000 pins. The pinscreen would now replace his wood blocks for good and he could add motion, engraving in time. Such a set-up allowed for minutely precise lighting shifts, since the genius of his pin-hole system was that the pins themselves did not comprise the image so much as cast the shadows that would be recorded by the camera. The shadows varied according to the pins' adjustable lengths. For instance, if a cluster of pins are pushed all the way out, that section would appear pure black since they each cast long deep shadows onto one another. When pulled all the way back flush with the surface, the same section becomes nearly white, since only the board itself is then visible, dimpled by pin heads nestled in their holes. A very wide range of gray gradations between those extremes was possible and Alexeieff's mechanical pins and delicately cast shadows are certainly the ancestors of today's computer pixels.

During this transitional juncture in 1930, when Alexeieff sought to shift from static illustrations to moving pictures, he met Claire Parker

(1906–1981) at a screening of an Oskar Fischinger short animated film. Parker was a wealthy, intelligent young student from Massachusetts, studying art in Paris. She was aware of and impressed by Alexeieff's engravings and asked him to take her on as a combination student and apprentice. Soon, Claire Parker became so fascinated by Alexeieff and his new project that she financed the construction of that first motion picture pin board, even paying to support Alexeieff and his family while they all developed the process and created the 8-minute long *Une nuit sur le mont chauve* (*Night on Bald Mountain*, 1933), which took 18 months to complete. This labor-intensive collaboration resulted in what historian Lo Duca labeled "a miracle of patience and taste" (Duca 1982: 37).

Alexeieff's choice of this subject proves much about his personal aesthetics. He sought out a serious "high art" project that would take advantage of the device's marvelous ability to generate gradual transitions from shot to shot and scene to scene while also producing a dream-like softness to every filmed image. He supposedly listened to a recording of Mussorgsky's nineteenth-century tone poem over and over until he planned his entire film in his mind, tagging musical phrases with imagined sequences of moving images. Mussorgsky initially composed "Night on Bald Mountain" to evoke musically tales he had read in a book on witches and sorcery, themes that also fit Alexeieff's own fantasies and interests. For his visual reworking, Alexeieff never drew a preparatory storyboard, so the visuals never really existed in any concrete form before being set-up on the pinscreen, filmed and projected. The pinscreen work ends up resembling Alexeieff's own private dream screen: no physical marks remain on the surface after the filming; the work only exists on the film stock. Despite the project being Alexeieff's personal vision, the resulting mode of production was truly a collaboration in every sense of the word. Claire Parker and Alexeieff experimented with various tools for pressing the pins to achieve the desired shapes and patterns, and while Alexeieff worked one side of the board, Parker worked on the other. Each could push pins toward the other's side in what amounted to a constant creative interaction. Further, the French patent for this first incarnation of the pinscreen was granted in 1935 to Claire Parker, in part because she funded its invention but also because she served as a crucial creative engineer in building the final functional apparatus. She also took control of the lighting and camerawork during most of their pinscreen animation.

Night on Bald Mountain announces its material and conceptual difference from animation norms in its title sequence, which proclaims itself "animated engravings by Alexeieff and Claire Parker." What follows is a dizzying, frustrating, even grim and giddy series of images and fragmentary scenes that combine Bartosch's expressionism with surrealism, and more than a touch of Freudian references and dream imagery. Since the images are dark, blurred, and fleeting, they also owe to symbolism, as if there were a diffusing gauze screen between the camera and the figures. Thus, any written summary of the film tends to simplify its visuals and threatens to fix its effect as too representational and linear. *Night on Bald Mountain* is finally more about texture, tone, and movements even than was Bartosch's *The Idea*. The opening sequence seems to establish a concrete landscape setting as wind blasts clouds past a scarecrow and past the ominous distant mountain. Next, the scarecrow's coat is blown off. As Robin Allan points out, "Everything is in a state of flux as the night of evil spirits takes control. . . . The scarecrow's upright pole and crossed arm pole are now denuded and we are reminded of a crucifix abandoned to the forces of evil" (Allan 2001: 83). However, Alexeieff and Parker then include one of several brief live action pan shots of a craggy ground, apparently set up from miniature table-top models. Returning to the pinscreen, they present rapid chaotic animal scenes of fleeing rodents and a galloping horse. The next quieter section involves a number of nightmarish transformations, including a gorilla morphing into a large stork-like bird that tumbles into a partly human figure whose empty footprints travel across the hills. A child watches in horror and is set upon by ghouls with outstretched arms who seem to descend from menacing clouds. There is a constant blurring of objects as well as their precise spatial relations, as everything is temporary and transient. Screen directions and gravity are both defied. Throughout the action, even the brightest sections of the background reveal themselves as a screen-like grid of holes; there is never a uniform white space within the image, which reinforces the grimness of the setting and lack of clear focus on anything in this haunted visual world (Figure 3.9).

As the fearful onslaught of ghouls continues, a small windmill's wooden blades seem to sprout hands, the moon loops about the frame, and abstract shapes give way to cartoonish villains or witches, apparently witnessed by the boy. Naked, round, mannequin-like humans spin about and battle in the sky in a duel with black creatures as the white horse reappears and races off. This sort of hectic barrage of images reinforces Alexeieff and Parker's play with inversion. Objects, including the horse, shadows, and the clouds, alternate between black and white, much like the dual opposition between the front and the back of the actual pinscreen. They animate so as to refer

Figure 3.9   The pinscreen creates a soft-focus nightmare. *Une nuit sur le mont Chauve/Night on Bald Mountain*, produced and directed by Alexander Alexeieff, 1933.

constantly to their process and apparatus, while taking full advantage of the play of light within their film, just as they must onto their patterns of pins. For a time, there are only grim suggestions of humanoid figures and grotesque faces sliding across the vague landscape, while the fallen horse tries to revive itself and disappoint the buzzards, and explosions rain down small white squares onto the ground. One of the lanky, fleeting black figures crossing the screen supposedly represented Alexeieff's father who had disappeared when Alexandre was a young boy, and Alexeieff always encouraged such personal and Freudian interpretations of *Night on Bald Mountain*. As some of the frenetic action slows, there is a hazy shape that is apparently a church front, and bells can be heard tolling six a.m. as grotesque white statue-like people pray and look to the heavens as the sun rises. In a new establishing shot a fellow stands on a field beneath static clouds until a wipe from the bottom transforms the ground into a lake with a steamship, and then its negative image, the opposite side of the pinboard. Finally, a sailor on board can be seen playing his fife and the movie stops (Figures 3.10 and 3.11).

While the narrative trajectory of many Ladislas Starewich films included a descent into some spooky alternative night world, *Night on Bald Mountain* exclusively concentrates on the nightmare experience, with no bracketing characters or narrative situation. Music and the free play of thought dominate. Moreover, as Bendazzi notes, "A Night on Bald Mountain was,

Figure 3.10   The phantom horse in *Une nuit sur le mont Chauve/Night on Bald Mountain*, produced and directed by Alexander Alexeieff, 1933.

and still is, considered a solution to the old problem of agreement between the music of sounds and the music of images" (Bendazzi 1994: 111). It was not difficult for contemporary viewers to see the sailor playing a flute on a lonely boat retrospectively as a representation of Alexeieff himself conjuring up the troubling, personal series of images that preceded his sudden appearance at the end. But most everything about the content and style

Figure 3.11   Alexeieff's father figure in *Une nuit sur le mont Chauve/Night on Bald Mountain*, produced and directed by Alexander Alexeieff, 1933.

should be ascribed back to two creative minds laboring with pins and light angles, not just his. Yet Alexeieff's own discourse on the film always dominated and he encouraged viewers to connect the feelings evoked from watching *Night on Bald Mountain* to the semi-conscious transitional state as we fall asleep or begin to wake. He also welcomed Freudian interpretations, and by mentioning the inscription of his absent father into this graphic world, Alexeieff openly invited the audience to see *Night on Bald Mountain* as more than automatic writing, but as an extension of Alexeieff's own obsessions, dreams, and fears. The lost child reaching out to phantoms was marked as Alexeieff just as much as the lone static musician who terminates the spectacle, rousing us from his dream world. According to animation historian Pascal Vimenet, "Alexandre Alexeieff is indisputably one of the giants of animation who helped engender the twentieth century. He was a poet who knew ... how to strip this art form down to its metaphysical dimension. His first and most important invention, the pinscreen, became the mirror of his consciousness, a half-awakened projection" (Vimenet 2007: 228).

Parker and Alexeieff's *Night on Bald Mountain* received strong critical support, though it found few opportunities for commercial distribution. It managed to be shown on the bill at the Pantheon in Paris for six weeks and then appeared for two weeks in London at the Academy Theatre. That was the extent of its first run. Importantly, in 1934, Britain's influential John Grierson praised the film's peculiar shadowy qualities with its fluidly dissolving forms: "The film, apart from its technical interest, is an imaginative performance, though difficult to describe. Imagine, however, a Walpurisnacht, in which animated footsteps indicate spirit presences, goblins and hobgoblins appear and disappear and tumble fantastically, scarecrows do a fandango with their shadows on empty hillsides, white horses and black tear across high heaven, and skeletons walk" (cited in Russett and Starr 1976: 90). Such a summary of events may seem just as fitting for a Disney Silly Symphony, but unlike *The Skeleton Dance* (1929) or *The Old Mill* (1937), to say nothing of Mickey Mouse in the Sorcerer's Apprentice sequence in *Fantasia* (1940), *Night on Bald Mountain* actively resisted the world of caricature and popular sensibility, which in turn limited its exhibition options. Parker and Alexeieff were quite disappointed. According to Alexeieff, "We decided to make no more animation films without having distribution in advance: this meant limiting ourselves to advertising films, which had in France a real market but which paid badly" (Russett and Starr 1976: 92–93).

The shift to paid commercial animation allowed Claire Parker to take more charge of content and the production styles. Parker had become increasingly interested in color as well as other forms of stop-motion animation. The Alexeieff-Parker animation studio became something of an extended family business, and even included his former wife, Alexandra de Grinevsky. Over the next several decades, even their commercial projects became increasingly conceptual, moving from concrete stop-motion work for a Nicholas Wine advertisement, *La Belle au bois dormant* (*Sleeping Beauty*, 1935), to creating abstract "illusory solids" by tracing moving lights during the 1950s. Alexeieff's experimental side was constantly balanced by Parker's practicality. Perhaps the most elaborate of the 1930s advertisements was *Sleeping Beauty*. Like the contemporary work by fellow European George Pal, this commercial for Nicholas Wines exploits stop-motion cinematography with miniature models and table-top sets in vibrant Gasparcolor. Based on a script by a young Jean Aurenche, who would go on to write many famous Tradition of Quality French films, and with harpsichord music by Francis Poulenc, *Sleeping Beauty* was a stand-alone short film as well as an advertisement.

Visually, *Sleeping Beauty* owes little to the abstraction of *Night on Bald Mountain*. This stop-motion film is filled with spinning miniature sets and much tracking and panning, perhaps because such physical camera movements were impossible with their previous pinscreen work. In this five-and-one-half-minute cartoon, a rather stiff young prince follows a deer from the woods into a chateau only to discover it is full of characters frozen in place in nearly every room. In the final room is a large book declaring that the spirit of wine (*l'âme du vin*) will revive the beauty. From a series of popping corks arise colorful clouds of smoke and three fairy godmother wine spirits. The chateau with its many sordid intrigues, including stolen kisses and duels, begins to come alive again. Last to be revived is the beautiful maiden on her bed (Plate 6). A kiss from the prince sends the chateau into a festive party mode, and the couple end up cuddling in the garden beneath a cluster of grapes to watch the dancing and fireworks. Despite its short duration and rapid pacing, the overall narrative is difficult to follow and the rhythm of the puppets and scene-to-scene structure rather uneven. Thus, *Sleeping Beauty*, with its story and figures both moving in fits and starts, resembles *Blue Beard* far more than the fluidity and delicacy of Starewich's best work. However, the abstract opening and closing titles certainly recall Oskar Fischinger's films in their complex, colorful patterning.

The Alexeieff team made additional, less narrative advertisements as well. In a commercial for musical instruments, *Opta Empfangt* and *Parade of Hats* (both 1936) for the Sools hat company, objects move without any human or other intervention. Instruments are suspended in a vague empty space and play by themselves, though the thin, manipulative clear puppet strings are often visible, while the colored lights and backgrounds shift. Similarly, the parade of hats passes independently across the screen or rotate in formations and varying colors, as if they were lines of Busby Berkeley's dancers. Another commercial, *Etoiles nouvelles* (*New Stars*, 1937), was made for Davros cigarettes in Belgium and comes closer both to the abstract, dynamic circle films of Oskar Fischinger and the fluid object animation of George Pal, who also made commercials with dancing cigarettes and matches. In the Alexeieff-Parker ad, cigarettes strut about in displays of military precision. As Derrick Knight concluded, "There is no question of mass production with Alexeieff and his collaborators. He has found a way of combining experiment with sponsorship and the collaboration means the sponsor gets a little work of art in the artist's own sweet time" (quoted in Russett and Starr 1976: 97). The ads, with their fanciful transitions and formal patterns, suggest the influence of many experimental European animators. Not until the 1950s and 1960s, after their flight to North America during World War II, where they made *En passant* (1943) for the National Film Board of Canada, and their subsequent return to France, would Alexeieff and Parker expand once again the field of animation with striking experiments and challenging conceptual work. During the early sound era, however, they proved representative of artists who arrive at animation from other media and then struggle to create a personal, alternative product in the absence of state support or developed animation distribution outlets. Their careers also provide another example of how closely advertising and artistic animation were bound together in European cinema of the 1930s and 1940s.

Niche Cartoons: Lyrical *Joie de vivre* and the Surreal *La Fortune enchantée*

Two other immigrants, Anthony Gross from England and the American Hector Hoppin, formed a tiny company, HG Animat, in Paris and managed to create a short film that more subtly attacked the world of contemporary industrialists than had *The Idea*. *Joie de vivre* (1934) was made by a very

Figure 3.12   Joyous women in *Joie de vivre*, produced and directed by Anthony Gross and Hector Hoppin, 1934.

small team but did receive wide distribution. Gross and Hoppin built upon Bartosch's sexist notion of representing freedom and truth via attractive female bodies. *Joie de vivre* features two lovely, long-legged young women in flowing white summer dresses leaping and dancing through a setting initially dominated by electric power plants. Their syncopated entrance, boldly strutting down a sidewalk in cycled drawings past a slightly abstract factory wall, recalls Betty Boop's arrival in *Snow White* (1933) (Figure 3.12). The women dance through the power station; the dangerous power lines become their trapeze ropes, while the jolts of electricity seem to empower their acrobatics further rather than harming these two women-spirits. However, when startled, the blonde drops a shoe, in Cinderella fashion, and the two women flee into the countryside pursued by a handsome young worker on his bicycle. This working-class Prince Charming is simply trying to return the slipper, but the women initially run from him.

Once they believe they have evaded the fellow, the women strip naked and swim, performing water gymnastics until the birds deliver their clothes to them, since the man is getting closer. Here the motif of innocent girls being aided by nature and its small animals anticipates later Disney stories, though Snow White and Cinderella certainly never appear in the nude. Next, all three characters wind up in a train yard where they take over the controls and disrupt the straight tracks and trajectories, twisting and turning scores of trains into a worm-like ballet. Here too, there is a hint of Cohl, as a well-ordered world is suddenly reduced to cartoony chaos. The thin narrative,

Figure 3.13   *Joie de vivre*'s happy ending. *Joie de vivre*, produced and directed by Anthony Gross and Hector Hoppin, 1934.

with no dialogue, ends with the two women riding off into the sky on the young man's handle bars (Figure 3.13). A happy life here seems to require that the women give up their idyllic sisterhood and freedom to be swept off by the one shared man. This cartoon also provides a precursor to French Popular Front art, that brief leftist respite of the 1930s, full of optimism but wary of the rise of Fascism all around. Despite the naive pleasure of the young women, "danger can rise as quickly as the wind. Everything may suddenly turn tragic, but the girls play cheerfully [*s'enjouent*]. All this joie de vivre may just be a dream. . . . But during the dream, they fear nothing and can accomplish anything," according to Florence Miailhe (2007: 74). Much like the heady period of leftist political gains in the 1930s, this joyous romp proves fleeting.

The overall visual style in *Joie de vivre* involves the contrast between the swirling art nouveau lines of the women's bodies and nature, and the rigid constructivist lines and cubist electric grids of civilization. The young man's body too proves increasingly sensual and elastic as he pursues the women. The cartoon becomes a happy, if sexist, Depression-era fairy tale alternative to later, sadder poetic realist films such as *Le Jour se lève/Daybreak* (Carné, 1939), where the bicycle-riding factory worker François (Jean Gabin) does not get to live with either of the two women he loves. It can also be celebrated as a specifically French attempt to break clear of the limiting comic traditions of 1930s cartoon animation (Mitry 1980: 728). Though, as Sébastien Denis points out, *Joie de vivre* offered a rather limited notion of progress and escape, while its decorative style and vague, shallow politics allowed it to be re-released by the Vichy government during the early 1940s (Denis 2007: 111). Regardless, it provides an important glimpse at the eccentric individualism of 1930s French animation, which remained much freer in style and content than American cartoons. In his book on World War II-era animation, Sébastien Roffat observes that *Joie de vivre* "is still extremely enjoyable today; it makes use of humor and fantasy, all the while displaying an elegant graphic style and fluid animation" (Roffat 2009: 99). It is, as Miailhe (2007: 77) explains, the sort of film that invents a new visual language for desire and sensual movement, displaying a freedom only animation could deliver.

If the fluid, lyrical drawings of *Joie de vivre* evoked an erotic Poetic Realism, designer Pierre Charbonnier's *La Fortune enchantée* (*The Enchanted Fortune*, 1936) offered a bizarre hybrid world of live action and animation that built upon a wider range of influences and references from comic strips and avant-garde theater to surrealism and children's books. Pierre Charbonnier (1897–1978) was a successful painter during the 1920s and became friends with Robert Bresson as well as scriptwriter Jean Aurenche in the early 1930s. For Bresson's first film, a short comedy, *Les Affaires publiques* (*Public Affairs*, 1934), Charbonnier served as production designer. He went on to design all of Bresson's films through to *Lancelot du lac* (1974). Through Aurenche and Bresson, Charbonnier met a wealthy patron of the arts, André Palasse. A nephew of Coco Chanel, Palasse owned a house in southwest France that served as a sort of home base for Palasse and many of his artist friends. It was in this house that Charbonnier, Palasse, and friends shot the absurd comedy, *The Enchanted Fortune*. Charbonnier had already made a short film in Belgium in 1931 that combined live action with some animation, *Ce soir à 8 heures* (*Tonight at 8 O'Clock*), featuring his young son Lucien. *The Enchanted Fortune* would also involve children in a slapstick burlesque about counterfeit money, several street kids, a rich girl, and Keystone-like cops in pursuit. Palasse's daughter Gabrielle played the central girl in the movie. The music was provided by another friend, Henri Sauguet, in this pleasantly absurd project built around friends and family, with all the actors from the surrounding community in Corbères.

For the animated portions of *The Enchanted Fortune*, Charbonnier drew figures on clear celluloid that were then placed in front of painted backgrounds. For the live action segments, sets were built in the house and populated by actors as well as life-sized cut-outs, recalling the evocative black and white sets by designer André Barsacq, all long before the use of such mannequins in *Playtime* (Tati, 1967). The entire visual style is constructed around an aesthetic that combines the flat looks of black lines on white paper as well as a surreal dream world. The fanciful sets were primarily built from painted plywood, occasionally with a very forced, artificial sense of perspective. Charbonnier's background as a painter combined with the animated drawings helped him devise an alternative universe in which carefully composed still images spring to life but never approach anything natural. As for costumes, which were also designed by Charbonnier, "they were made from heavy canvas stretched out and painted, which limited mobility because they were so rigid," recalls Gabrielle Palasse (Garnero 2007: 88). The cumbersome costumes resulted in jerky movements that also helped make sure the live actors resembled the stiff staccato gestures of the animated figures. The combination of all these *mise-en-scène* and animation tactics produced a truly unique film that owes to René Magritte's paintings as well as the expressionism of *The Cabinet of Dr. Caligari*, while referring back to slapstick and burlesque comedies, including the king of comedy for surrealists, Charlie Chaplin (Figure 3.14). Yet, while Charbonnier pursued a style owing to various influences, he overtly stated that his visual language here was hopefully something quite new, according to archivist Jean-Baptiste Garnero (2007: 88–89). One other significant and distinctive contribution of *The Enchanted Fortune* is its defiantly silly soundtrack, which contains wordplay and nonsense songs while rendering verbal communication as a childish, dadaist game.

Figure 3.14   Charbonnier's surreal settings in *La Fortune enchantée/The Enchanted Fortune*, produced and directed by Pierre Charbonnier, 1936.

Figure 3.15   *La Fortune enchantée*'s mixed performers. *La Fortune enchantée/The Enchanted Fortune*, produced and directed by Pierre Charbonnier, 1936.

The title sequence for *The Enchanted Fortune* announced that this is a children's tale composed of "burlesque images" by Pierre Charbonnier. In a mix of animation styles that will recur throughout, the cartoon begins with a crude cityscape and a police officer directing traffic. However, an announcement scrolls across the buildings announcing that the city is awash in counterfeit money. The live action police chief, in heavy white make-up and a suit painted in stark black and white, mobilizes his comical cops to hunt down the foul-smelling counterfeit bills (Figure 3.15). While they search the city streets, deep underground the villain Tyro rolls ink onto a 1000-franc pattern on his chest to generate the fake bills. Charbonnier hired two brothers, one heavy, one thin, to play the double character Tyro. Below ground, a burly Tyro dresses like a thug, but once he changes clothes before our eyes he rises up in a fanciful elevator to his chateau where he is a thin, wealthy, family man. The transformation scene involves a hair-dryer which becomes an animated chicken, but also a boxing ball that strikes the round Tyro in the head, thinning him into his public self, as the actors are switched. Above ground, in live action, dinner is served by waiters presenting plywood cut-out food to Tyro and his daughter. Outside, two street urchins, one white, one in black face, serenade the girl and her family for hand-outs, but the father teases the boys by dangling a coin on a string, so the boys, in animation now, hopscotch off down the street.

Inexplicably, in the next scene the burly Tyro is caught by a police officer and hundreds of the 1000-franc bills spill from his jacket, most landing in a vacant lot where the two poor boys are cooking their hobo stew. This scene combining the live boys in front of a painted backdrop and alternating shots of animated bills falling from the sky is quickly followed by the boys being driven in a fancy chariot, tossing counterfeit money to the police chief disguised as a beggar. Next, the boys meet up with Tyro's daughter and attend a movie said to predict the future. Each boy watches himself portrayed as a successful politician, though the black-faced boy's is the "negro version," with the footage running in negative. Back at her chateau, the white boy kisses the girl in animated silhouettes and the jealous black boy fires a cannon that alerts the police, among other gags, and reverses the boxing ball blow to Tyro's head, transforming him back into a villain. Once he chases the animated children down into his workshop they discover his secret. Hundreds of animated police arrive, and the film ends with a ticker-tape procession of the children and police and the recaptured Tyro through the streets. However, an open man-hole allows Tyro to escape in a fashion worthy of Fritz Lang's Dr. Mabuse, mocking the inept police and their self-satisfied ceremony. Its absurdity, musical interventions, and stop-start rhythms also make *The Enchanted Fortune* a perfect complement to René Clair's fanciful, anarchist musical comedies of the early 1930s. As in Clair's comedies there is a constant self-conscious sense of humor in which the characters all seem on the verge of winking toward the camera. *The Enchanted Fortune*, with its uneven mix of slapstick, staginess, and childish animation, offers an unsettling, home-made romp that looks more modern today than many live action French films of the 1930s. While *The Enchanted Fortune* is clearly a product of this creative era in French culture, it nonetheless looks timeless and quite alien. Even in the face of the wild diversity of animation from this early sound period, *The Enchanted Fortune* remains quite extraordinary in both its storytelling and graphic style (Figure 3.16).

Artisanal animators typically distinguish their practice from commercial conventions by exploring new methods for generating movement and rhythm while also exploiting uncommon techniques, graphic styles, and spatial arrangements. Pierre Charbonnier and his collaborators from the worlds of avant-garde theater, painting, and children's literature produced a unique textual collage that stands alone among animation practice in the 1930s, while it strangely anticipates some of the bizarre antics of eventual children's television shows during the 1950s and 1960s. Yet, in part as a result of its experimental mode of production and eccentric story and look, *The Enchanted Fortune* never received national distribution. Its tiny

Figure 3.16 Animated police in parade. *La Fortune enchantée/The Enchanted Fortune*, produced and directed by Pierre Charbonnier, 1936.

distributor, Terramonde Films, only managed to book the 14-minute film in a few theaters and Charbonnier's playful movie fell into obscurity, only being re-released briefly after World War II. It is another example of a stunning dead-end experiment that fits no business model and ends up providing no viable alternative within French animation. Pierre Charbonnier continued to work as a set designer and painter, but never animated again.

As the cases of Ladislas Starewich, Berthold Bartosch, Alexandre Alexeieiff, Claire Parker, and others reveal, 1930s French animation remained the domain of highly specialized individuals and tiny studios on the margins of commercial cinema. Functioning at a lowly capitalized level, without the support of major producers or distributors, animation occupied a space analogous to that of France's famed 1920s avant-garde cinema. Most of these individuals and tiny enterprises vowed to avoid the dominant techniques and narrative formulas of mainstream animation, especially American cartoons. Whether working with stuffed animals, pins and their shadows, ink on paper, or articulated cut-out figures, French animators sought to adopt European graphic arts traditions to the narrative and technical models provided by Emile Cohl and other silent French experimental animators. These filmmakers lived up to the spirit of animation, as expressed by animator Jean Image at the opening of this chapter, since they literally catapulted normally static objects into motion. However, the economic realities of such labor-intensive and unusual products made their work difficult to complete and just as challenging to market to domestic or international audiences. While the conversion to sound brought increasingly institutionalized and standardized practices to American animation, 1930s French animation rejected those trends, including efficient cel techniques, division of labor, and predictable 6- to 8-minute cartoon formats. The result was an even weaker framework for French animators than during the 1920s. With a more fixed exhibition format in 1930s film theaters, such early sound animation was rarely accessible for average spectators, except in the case of animated advertisements or André Rigal's brief cartoon introductions for newsreels. Thus, animators in France continued to experiment with style and content within individualized auteurist production modes during an era when such a strategy offered few rewards. As we shall see in the next chapter, however, several new entrepreneurial animators set out to forge more successful business plans and artistic options, though many of their efforts would not really flourish until government subsidies eventually helped stabilize animation in France decades later. Until then, animation would remain a fragile, quirky, artisanal subset of French film production during the cinema's classical era.

4

Toward an Alternative Studio Structure

Practically speaking, what are the chances for animation in France?
The economic challenges are most significant. Unfortunately, animation
is expensive because of its artisanal nature. It is a luxury that not all
countries can afford . . . . The Centre National de la Cinématographie's
important financial assistance is not adequate to ensure the prosperity of
a viable animation industry. (IDHEC Report, 1956)

After the 1930s, individual animators continued to create a wide
variety of films and to explore alternative techniques. During the Occupation, there were also new conditions for production that affected animation. The Germans imposed the Comité d'Organisation de l'Industrie
Cinématographique (COIC), charged with reorganizing France's film
industry from the top down. Beyond purging Jews and leftists from
positions in film production, COIC set rules to control almost every aspect
of the cinema's business practices. Already in 1940 a decree outlawed double
bills, so cinemas could no longer offer two features for the price of one ticket.
However, COIC's new rules favored inclusion of short films preceding each
feature, which in turn benefited animators. Moreover, American films were
banned after May 1941 (October 1942 in the "unoccupied" zone), so the
historic dominance by Disney, Fleischer, and Warner Bros. cartoons ended,
opening new opportunities for French animators to compete for screen
time. Ironically, COIC imposed a mandate to strengthen all forms of
"French" cinema, including documentary and animation. Their animation
division's goal was to encourage the recruitment and training of a

French Animation History
© Richard Neupert. Published by John Wiley & Sons

new generation of animators, in-betweeners, and technicians. The COIC plan also established a system whereby short films would be distributed nationally, coupled with particular feature films, allowing the cartoons to earn typically 4 or 5 percent of the net receipts of the accompanying feature. This emphasis on new opportunities, even during the darkest days of the Occupation, motivated a number of people to retool their skills for animated cinema. Even the well-known painter and graphic artist Paul Colin, famous for his poster art, formed an influential school for animators in 1941, where he hired Jean Image, among others, to teach their craft. As historian Sébastien Roffat (2009: 110–111) points out, however, the task of revitalizing French animation was enormous because there was only one animation studio in place before the war, Gémeaux, which belonged to André Sarrut and Paul Grimault.

Paul Grimault and the Artist-Owned Animation Studio

As we have seen, there was no studio structure for French animators beyond small entrepreneurial firms that typically followed the model established during the 1920s by Lortac, of depending upon advertising work to help remain viable. Such enterprises also became a training ground, mentoring other artist-animators. Paul Grimault continued this tradition and managed to establish both a small production company and a strong reputation during the classical era and beyond. Grimault and his business partner André Sarrut formed Gémeaux in 1936. However, they remained a tiny niche company. During peak production periods Gémeaux ideally employed a balanced crew of seven animators, seven in-betweeners, and seven artists to paint the drawings onto the cels. While Grimault accepted occasional commercial jobs, including advertisements for L'Oréal and Mazda light bulbs, his ultimate goal in the 1930s was to make shorts to compete with Hollywood imports, especially Betty Boop. As Grimault specialist Jean-Pierre Pagliano points out, "These beginnings bear witness to a strong ambition: to compete with American productions by following original inspirations and within the constraints of his own country" (Pagliano 1996: 10). Grimault always retained a very idealistic, childlike quality within his films, even though his themes did not match the naive storybook optimism of most commercial animation. Grimault began with *M. Pipe fait de la peinture* (*Mr. Pipe Does his Painting*, 1937):

The first film undertaken by Paul Grimault was perhaps, poetically and technically, the most beautiful cartoon scenario one could imagine: M. Pipe lives in a sad area. From his window, on his day off, all he can see is the huge wall of the factory across the street, where he works. It completely blocks his view in all directions. Gradually, he decides to destroy the wall by drawing the world of his dreams on it, an idyllic Polynesian setting. Thus M. Pipe proves his desire to fight reality and in the end, he enters his drawn world. (Chilo 1957: 77)

From this very first example on, Grimault's characters struggle to escape repression, often through creativity, but they never really manage to improve the world around them. There are no Disney endings with a celebration of a new social order. However, the business conditions were also far from Disney's situation, and Mr. Pipe was apparently never fully completed or commercially exhibited.

Throughout its rocky history, Gémeaux found it difficult to turn out consistent, high quality cartoons. Cinémathèque founder Henri Langlois observes that during this era "France would have really benefited from the renewal of animated film. Several valuable French attempts were made during the 1930s to restart animation.... But alas, a national plan for animation would have been needed to overcome all the commercial contingencies." Langlois also mentions that despite their best efforts, Paul Grimault and his Gémeaux confronted stubborn real-world obstacles (Langlois 1986: 294). Tellingly, Grimault made a relatively small number of films, especially for a commercial animator, and many of them were never finished to his satisfaction. Yet he also worked with top talent, especially screen writer Jean Aurenche and then more successfully with Jacques Prévert, who lent a dark poetic depth to Grimault's storytelling. However, Grimault drew inspiration from a variety of sources, including an epic Victor Hugo poem, *Plein Ciel (Clear Sky)*, about a fanciful trip in an airship, which helped shape his own ideas for the meandering tale *Les Passagers de la Grande Ourse (The Passengers on the Big Bear*, 1943). Supported in part by Air France and filmed in Agfacolor, *The Passengers on the Big Bear* chronicles how a young boy follows his dog onto a fantastic boat, an "air ship," the Big Bear, that they accidentally launch into the sky. Its only inhabitant is a fussy robotic butler. After several misunderstandings and adventures, including being tossed overboard, suspended from a rope, and chased by a gigantic eagle, the boy returns to the ship to be rewarded with a nice meal for himself and the dog, and the film ends. Roffat praises *The Passengers on the Big Bear* for its smooth animation and original concept. He argues that in terms of technical quality, this is the first animated French film that can be favorably compared with the best foreign films (Roffat 2009: 152). However, while it contains several trademark characters for Grimault – the big-eyed boy, a feisty bird, an ambivalent robot, etc. – the story remains fragmentary and incomplete, as if *The Passengers on the Big Bear* were part of a longer work that was never finished (Plate 7).

Also completed that same year, Grimault and Aurenche's *L'Epouvantail* (*The Scarecrow*, 1943) was a very professionally animated tale of an ineffective scarecrow who loves birds. It officially shared the new Emile Cohl prize in 1943 with *Callisto, la petite nymphe de Diane* (*Callisto, Diana's Little Nymph*, André Edouard Marty), though the film critics at the competition later unanimously argued *L'Epouvantail* was the clear winner. Cartoons were often interpreted metaphorically during this era, and many celebrated *The Scarecrow* as a timely story about protecting the innocent against oppression and deportation, since it is centered on a nice, bumbling scarecrow who heroically refuses to collaborate with the satanic cat trying to trap the local birds. Thanks to advances from various Occupation government funds, the Crédit National, and even the minister of information, almost all expenses for the film had been covered when Grimault began work on *The Scarecrow*. It even premiered in Berlin. The German officials informed Gémeaux that this was an "excellent and unique" film within European cinema (Roffat 2009: 129–130). Thus 1943 proved a great success for Paul Grimault and his studio, while the story preserved a subtle sense of French resistance at the same time that it helped COIC and the German occupying forces demonstrate their positive effects upon French filmmaking (Plate 8).

For one of his most successful shorts, Grimault worked with Prévert, adapting Hans Christian Andersen's tale of the lead soldier to make their postwar allegory, *Le Petit soldat* (*The Little Soldier*, 1946). Initially, Gémeaux had received a healthy advance through COIC and its financial partner, le Crédit National, in 1944 to begin work on *The Little Soldier*. But the end of the war brought a stop to the earliest phases of animation. With the Liberation, Grimault's co-producer Sarrut was found guilty of scheming with COIC and Nazi forces and publicly censured, though Grimault, who also benefited during the Occupation, received no official condemnations. As he renewed pre-production work for *The Little Soldier*, Grimault re-read the story and engaged Jacques Prévert to help outline their version of the tale. Grimault claims not to have written any script, rather the two men talked it through and made a few drawings to thinly sketch out the plot (Roffat 2009: 165). The result is a cartoon deeply affected by the devastation of World War II. André Bazin (1952: 19) acknowledged its resulting unity of theme and style, while Pagliano writes that in *The Little Soldier*, "Grimault and Prévert found the perfect balance of satire, humor, and emotion" (Pagliano 1996: 18). However, Grimault complained that when he initially pitched his somber tale to financial backers they hoped for a tale closer to Hollywood cartoon norms: "I apparently did not understand that for them animation needed gags, chases, movement! And why not some cream pies as well?!" (Denis 2007: 126). In the end, while it remained more serious than typical cartoons, *The Little Soldier* included some Hollywood-like touches, including a somewhat misleading and quaint babes-in-toyland opening.

The Little Soldier begins with a small village in a gentle winter snow, and a shop full of toys coming to life on their own. A girl doll looks lovingly toward a toy soldier, who winds himself up with his heart-shaped key to perform back flips. However, a large menacing Jack in the Box jealously spies on the pair from his box (Plate 9). A sudden round up of toy soldiers for war, including our helpless hero, gives Jack his chance to harass the girl left behind. After Jack forces the girl into a seemingly endless whirlwind dance, there is a cut to a barren winter landscape (Plate 10). The war has ended and the wounded toy soldier limps back to find the store bombed out, but big bad Jack is still "spinning" the girl. Unable to defend her, the soldier falls and Jack steals his heart key. Strangely, a passing snowman gingerly carries the soldier off and places him in a paper boat in the icy river. The girl grabs the key and chases after him on the ice flow before finally rescuing the sinking, freezing soldier, and reviving him. Meanwhile, Jack, who failed to destroy their love, is caught in a bear trap and attacked by crows. But the sun finally comes out on the reunited couple. Thus the tale, while melancholy and more graphic in its desire and violence than Hollywood cartoons of the era, remains close to American cartoons in its story structure and even style, though it is long at over 10 minutes.

The Little Soldier is exemplary of Grimault's themes as well as his consistent visual style. Though it is ostensibly a children's story, the implications of a handsome young man sent into a battle he does not understand, while the powerful male figure stays home, forcibly seducing the female, hold the mood on a relentlessly serious level. The wartime context lends extra gravity to the sometimes clichéd actions here. The young couple is also typical of Grimault's protagonists, who are often gentle folk who just want to be left alone (Stephenson 1973: 102). As Michel Chilo points out, Grimault is one of the great French storytellers and his characters manage somehow to escape the caricatures of Disney, Walter Lantz, and others: *The Little Soldier*, "an exceptional film, with Grimault at the peak of his art, succeeds at creating pure emotion in original characters without becoming overly sentimental" (Chilo 1957: 79). The visuals, which Lo Duca (1948: 43) labels "cinégraphic," exploit some depth of field but primarily follow continuity editing. Despite the fact that many of the toys, including the soldier, are clearly supposed to be wooden figures, with hinges at the major joints, they are all drawn as if tubes, and bend in a rubbery, cartoony manner. They are painted with bold colors and stand out against their duller settings. Grimault has been heralded as a confident colorist who recalls Paul Klee's palette; he has also been called an architect of movement who combines fantasy and surrealism to build a coherent but reliably strange world (Chilo 1957: 82). *The Little Soldier* won the international prize at the Venice Biennial in 1948 and was distributed in 15 nations around the world. Yet, while Grimault in many ways became one of the most visible and influential animators in France, his cartoons lacked some of the energy seen in Hollywood cartoons that were receiving praise in Europe. As animation expert and archivist Jean-Baptiste Garnero notes, "Even Paul Grimault's *The Little Soldier*, which is a very beautiful film with a universal theme and strong aesthetic, paled next to Tex Avery of the same period, with his gag every second!" (Chauville 2008: 29).

Grimault's protagonists retain round, wide-eyed faces and youthful postures throughout his career, all the way up to *Le Roi et l'oiseau* (*The King and the Bird*, 1979). His characters still look rather modern today, in part because they resemble many comic book figures and even anticipate later limited TV animation, with supple bodies and deliberate, crisp movements. French animator René Laloux also acknowledges Grimault's significance: "While his work looks rather close to the American school in terms of technique and the roundness of the characters, the decors painted in gouache are superb. What is more, Grimault opened the way for more poetic forms of narration in which drama and emotion take the place of comic aggression" (Laloux 1996: 34). Grimault proved inspirational to many French writers, directors, and animators, in part because he won a great number of awards, especially given how few films he actually completed. For instance, Grimault and Prévert's *La Bergère et le ramoneur* (*The Shepherdess and the Chimney Sweep*, 1952) won the animation prize at the Venice Film Festival, though it was shown incomplete, and against their wishes. However, André Bazin (1952: 20) noted that Grimault's feature was more like a short film dragged out, with too little narrative depth. That first version featured the voices of veteran actors Serge Reggiano and Pierre Brasseur, as well as newcomer Anouk Aimée. Much later, Grimault expanded it for a final, longer version, *The King and the Bird*, which took years to complete. *The King and the Bird* incorporated most of the original footage from *The Shepherdess and the Chimney Sweep* as well as the additional sections never accomplished in the 1950s. This revised version won the Louis Delluc Award in 1979. While for Bendazzi, *The King and the Bird* ranks as "one of the finest feature films in the history of animation" (Bendazzi 1994: 156), many critics, including at *Cahiers du Cinéma*, found the tale rather dated and lacking in dramatic or aesthetic interest.[1] It was something of a personal film caught between the two very different eras of its production.

The King and the Bird brought renewed interest to Grimault as well as to the history of animation in France. *The King and the Bird* begins with a long prologue introducing the short, vain, cross-eyed King who lives in an elaborate castle dedicated to himself and equipped with trapdoors to dispose of annoying subjects. The King's only real problem seems to be a large floppy bird who mocks him constantly. When the King's new artist paints his portrait accurately, including the troubling eyes, the king eliminates him and his servants paint in "correct" eyes. This portrait, however, secretly comes alive and begins to lust after the beautiful shepherdess in another painting in the gallery (Plate 11). The shepherdess also comes alive when no humans are around, but she is in love with the chimney-sweep boy in another painting. This pair of young lovers, menaced by the evil, older man, recalls the plot of *The Little Soldier*. That night, the painted King escapes his canvas to pursue the shepherdess, but she and the chimneysweep leap out of their frames and escape across the rooftops. Frustrated, the painted King drops the real King down a trapdoor, becoming the new ruler, now obsessed with finding the girl and punishing the boy. For the rest of the feature, the girl and boy are pursued by the fake King's police, and the bird repeatedly helps them evade capture (Plates 12 and 13). At one point the young pair even discover an underground city populated by oppressed people who have never seen the sun. Eventually, thanks to an enormous iron robot, the King captures the girl, who agrees to marry him if

---

[1] Similarly, Bruno Edera calls the original version "possibly one of the best cartoons ever made in Europe" (Edera 1977: 83).

he spares the boy. However, the bird and other characters they have befriended along the way disrupt the wedding ceremony and rescue the girl. They even take control of the mighty robot, reducing the entire kingdom to rubble and blowing the King off into the night sky. The fortress is destroyed, supposedly leaving a new space for love and liberty, themes already established in earlier Jacques Prévert films (Gasiglia-Laster 1986: 108). Finally, the robot sits on the pile of debris. Strangely, there is no attempt to reward any of the poor people or see them unite to build a new life or town. The shepherdess and chimney sweep are reunited, but the end is dominated by bleak and total destruction, with a curious, ambiguous symphonic flourish on the soundtrack (Plate 14).

The King and the Bird is full of recurring character types from Grimault's oeuvre. There are vulnerable birds in need of protection, a sweet, poor young man, a foolishly demonic figure pursuing a feisty, resourceful young woman, as well as various surreal figures who appear as if from the plot line in another film. Further, what should be a happy ending is undercut by the devastation all around. Visually, Grimault's *The King and the Bird*, like most of his previous animation, remains flat and cartoony. The figures all have bright, clear edges that hold their shape, there are no shadows under foot, and few cues for weight or texture. There is no real difference in the ways skin, cloth, or stone are represented. The intense hues lend a flatness to all surfaces, much like a coloring book, so there are few gradations in shading. However, while some compared Grimault's output to a French Disney, his plots typically lacked classical gag structures or active protagonists. His characters, whether a loopy scarecrow, a toy soldier, a boy who happens upon a ship, or a shepherdess in a painting, remain rather passive. Bad things simply happen to them and eventually the films stop. There are few character goals or defined traits, other than wishing to be left alone, and few large thematic lessons. These are entertaining tales but they lacked the character development and dramatic hooks found in Hollywood cartoons, so had trouble attracting dedicated audiences.

During the 1980s, Jacques Demy, who had initially considered a career as an animator, and even worked briefly for Grimault during the 1950s, helped put together *La Table tournante* (*The Editing Table*). This compilation film combines live footage of Grimault in his studio where he shows scenes from many cartoons across his career and even interacts with some of his old characters. *The Editing Table* is designed to reassert Paul Grimault's role in French film history. Indeed, Grimault deserves credit for a number of key contributions to French animation. Though a rather isolated figure, he struggled to maintain a viable animation company and personal style against great odds. Grimault, who fought to establish a French tradition "in the face of the imperialism of Walt Disney," managed to provide "a universe filled with solitude, danger, sadness, and finally hope" (Le Roy 2007: 275). He is widely respected, yet his characters and stories failed to capture the imagination of the international audience. Many of the next generation of animators, some of whom worked alongside him at some point, including René Laloux and Jean-François Laguionie, readily acknowledge their debt to Grimault, but their stories and styles took them in very different directions. In the meantime, however, there were two other continuing trends among French animators of the 1940s and 1950s.

Transitional Animation: From High Art to Made-for-TV

As part of the wave of encouragement for animation during the Occupation, including "the high hopes for a national renaissance," a society for French imagery launched the Emile Cohl Prize to promote and recognize animation in France, with its first competition in 1943 (Kermabon 2007: 103). While the jury found that none of the nine first entries merited the grand prize, they awarded both Marty's *Callisto, Diana's Little Nymph* and Grimault's *The Scarecrow* for their technical excellence. As Roffat points out, "The goal of the Vichy government had been to create a true French school of animation completely separate from American influence and promoting national art." Apparently, none of the films in competition fully lived up to those ideals (Roffat 2009: 145). Acknowledging the technical value of these two very different films, the jury foregrounded the two trends in French animation of the era: some animators pursued "fine art," artisanal traditions, while others openly sought a more popular and commercially successful route to sustainable filmmaking. While Grimault's cel animation followed the latter, small studio model, André-Edouard Marty was clearly in the high art, individual artist camp. Marty was already 60 years old and well known as a painter, illustrator, and graphic artist when he began animating. He brought with him art deco flourishes from his past career making posters and fashion sketches for his adaptation of the mythical tale of Callisto, the young woman hunter who has sworn a vow of chastity to live alongside Diana, Goddess of the hunt, and her idyllic all-female community.

Callisto is a beautiful, sensitive woman in love with nature. She even feels pity for a deer she wounds with an arrow, so nurses it back to health.

Figure 4.1 Jupiter chases Callisto. *Callisto, la petite nymphe de Diane/Callisto, Diana's Little Nymph*, produced and directed by André Edouard Marty, 1943.

However, one day when lost alone in the forest she is pursued by the lustful Jupiter. The deer Callisto had earlier rescued comes to her aid and the woman rides away from Jupiter (Figure 4.1). Frustrated, the god transforms into a replica of Diana, then comforts and finally seduces Callisto. When Diana learns Callisto is pregnant she sends her away. The single mother raises her baby alone in the fertile countryside that includes more traditional farming families. But one day Jupiter's jealous wife Juno sees Callisto playing with her child and changes them into bears. Distraught, the mother bear and her cub appeal to Jupiter, who tosses them both into the sky where they will live forever as the constellations Ursa Major and Ursa Minor. While this tale seems universal, Marty's adaptation has been interpreted as infused with specific themes prized by Vichy France, including the need for women to remain pure or sacrifice themselves for the community's wellbeing. Sébastien Roffat points out that Marty idealizes Diana's young women via often-nude representations, "in a chaste, artistic style," as allegories for women as created by God, prior to sin (Roffat 2009: 142). Jacques Kermabon agrees: "The Pétain regime's rhetoric becomes most obvious at the moment when Callisto discovers the ideal image of earthly happiness: bountiful fields and a thatched cottage where the wife and child await the farmer returning from his harvest, the scythe resting on his shoulder (Kermabon 2007: 142) (Figure 4.2). Sébastien Roffat goes further: "*Callisto* represents 'the spirit of Vichy,' in its exaltation of love for family and the earth. It extols a wholesome childhood, ardent youth, and a united family.

Figure 4.2   Callisto watches an idyllic human family. *Callisto, la petite nymphe de Diane/Callisto, Diana's Little Nymph*, produced and directed by André Edouard Marty, 1943.

And, the story is told via sung texts composed by Arthur Honegger and Roland-Manuel that respect the government's decrees that the French language must not be distorted" (Roffat 2009: 142). The lyrics exploit very formal language and the male singer's voice booms in a highly pretentious pseudo-operatic style that contrasts harshly with the picturesque tone of the rural imagery.

Thus, *Callisto* marks a clear attempt to create a French animated film that corresponds to the moral dictates of the Vichy government while its visual and audio traits spring from lofty French artistic traditions. There is nothing here that suggests the influence of American cartooning, much less its popular music, and while *Callisto*'s distinct qualities pleased some in COIC, it was less successful with many film critics. Lo Duca, for instance, pointed out that Marty's film resembled ornate, "artistic," calendar art rather than vibrant animation (Duca 1982: 48). Callisto is inspired by a return to classicism and even the print of its opening titles signals its serious cultural context. Marty's graphic style reduces characters to basic outlines, several times resorting to silhouettes and cut-out figures, as when Jupiter, failing to make a leap across a gorge, spins and tumbles like a paper doll into the lake far below. But the movement evokes academic art school conventions, with streamlined bodies, typically sliding sideways across the screen, and a mix of modern athleticism in the women along with classical poses from Greek and Roman mythology and statuary. Upon its release, playwright Jacques Audiberti observed that Callisto was "incredibly graceful and poetic, erotic without shame, limpid yet melancholy" (cited in Maillet 1983: 22). *Callisto* remains a unique, isolated experiment. Marty attempted only one more animated film about the Nativity during the 1960s. He remains much more known for his elegant and often idyllic poster art and fashion illustrations than for his cartooning. But beyond serving as a representative of a new Vichy initiative in jump-starting short film production, he is also another example of the sort of connections between the commercial arts and animation that could exist so easily in France, but were almost unheard of in American animation.

Like Marty, Albert Dubout (1905–1976) came to animation after attending art school and becoming a successful graphic artist and designer. A southerner, he published comical sketches and illustrated books, but is best known today for his humorous figures and joyous posters, including the artwork for Marcel Pagnol's Marius trilogy. His characters are jovial, rolly-polly caricatures who seem to come bounding off the paper. Always interested in animation's potential, Dubout experimented with painting directly on film stock in the early 1930s, but he had to wait for the Occupation before attempting to launch his own cartoon series built around his character Anatole. Beginning in 1942, Dubout worked throughout the war on *Anatole fait du camping* (*Anatole Goes Camping*), but the short cartoon was not completed until 1945 and not distributed until 1947. The soundtrack was recorded by Germany's Tobis-Klangfilm and the color film stock was from Agfa. That a well-known figure such as Dubout required several years to produce a 12-minute cartoon points to the problems in commercial French production, despite all the war-time encouragement from COIC and others. Yet Dubout's work remains engaging and influential, exploiting as it does cheerfully absurd stories. His central character, the scrawny, diminutive Anatole, has a bloated, domineering wife, Margot. This couple serves as one of the key inspirations for Sylvain Chomet's *Les Triplettes de Belleville*, 60 years later. For instance, Chomet's opening sequence features mammoth wives towing their minuscule husbands like handbags. Dubout's Anatole also plays the spokes on a wheel as a harp, anticipating the comical musical routine late in *Les Triplettes de Belleville*. *Anatole Goes Camping* is itself intertextual, recalling influences as diverse as Popeye cartoons and Jean Renoir's *Partie de campagne* (*A Day in the Country*, 1936) (Plate 15).

Dubout's Anatole is a bumbling little figure in a suit and bowler. All the characters in *Anatole Goes Camping* are rubbery caricatures painted on cel with heavy outlines and monochromatic body parts. The visual style extends

Dubout's poster art, but keeps the action firmly in the tradition of coloring book graphics. During this absurd, doomed outing, Anatole and Margot are confronted by a comically rude train that runs without rails, destroying their picnic (Plate 16). Later, Anatole literally blows into a bar, motivating a brawl with the gigantic bully from the train, Sparadra. Finally, Margot's fist ends the mayhem and the couple take their horse and cart back to Paris. Dubout, hard at work trying to launch Anatole as a recurring cartoon series, was simultaneously working on a second episode, using the same central characters. *Anatole à la tour de Nesle* (*Anatole at the Nesle Tower*) sends them all back to medieval times. Margot is a queen looking for a mate and Sparadra and Anatole compete for her attentions. Once more, the playful, cartoony figures pursue silly antics until Margot puts an end to their outrageously excessive attempts to entertain her. However, while Dubout's populist poster art retained a clever, satirical perspective, the Anatole cartoons became rather frantic and childish in both their pacing and themes. After both films were released in 1947, Dubout continued to pitch feature-length animation projects, but his proposals failed to find backers. Dubout remained a popular personality, however, and in 1953 he received the Legion of Honor, proving his value and reputation as a beloved figure within France's visual culture pantheon.

While the Anatole films turned perhaps by accident into childish cartoons, Jean Image (1910–1989) successfully launched a series of animated films for young people. Image, born Imre Hajdu in Budapest, moved between France and England during the 1930s. In London he collaborated with his friend Janos Halasz, who later changed his name to John Halas and revolutionized British animation. Jean Image even made an anti-Nazi cartoon, in which a crazed Hitler devours Poland. Beyond making topical and pacifist films, Image forged a long, successful career animating for children. Unlike many of the animators we have discussed so far, Image managed to bolster his films with ancillary income from spin-off projects, including children's books about his more popular characters and phonograph records of the theme songs. In this way he was influenced by American cartoon marketing. He also established a small-scale animation school as well as Jean Image Productions in 1948. His small studio began work on *Jeannot l'intrépide* (*Johnny the Giant Killer*), which premiered in 1950 amid a strong publicity campaign championing it as France's first color, feature-length cartoon. This story of a boy in an alien world of gigantic insects won the Grand Prix for children's films at the Venice Film Festival. After a strong initial run, including a dubbed English version, *Johnny the Giant Killer* was apparently re-released in a number of unauthorized versions, in part because Image and his distributor failed to register a proper copyright.

Next, Jean Image quickly released a second feature, *Bonjour Paris*, in 1953. For this feature, Image turned familiar Paris and its most famous landmarks into a playground for two pigeons. A poetic, rhyming voice-over, written by producer and eventual TV personality Claude Santelli, and narrated by actor François Périer, replaces the need for sync-sound, and lends a displaced serious tone to the comically naive antics of the characters. Part of the central appeal of the film is also that truly inanimate objects such as the gargoyles on Notre Dame and the Eiffel Tower themselves come alive. The story concerns the two love-struck pigeons who fly from monument to monument, eventually motivating the Eiffel Tower to wander as well, so he goes on vacation, leaving the city. Paris is thrown into comic disarray over his absence, until the pigeons locate the now bored Tower, who seems ready to come back home (Plate 17). Image's cel animation does not pretend to follow in the footsteps of the more artisanal traditions in France, though at one point there is an almost avant-garde sequence with chalk-like lines that illustrate how Gustave Eiffel's little boy tower grew up tall and strong. In fact, Sébastien Denis (2007: 153) asserts that new post-World War II American styles strongly influenced Jean Image, especially the recent output from UPA, whose characters such as Mr. Magoo were more modern visually than the realism of Disney, and whose content differed from the fairy tale and gag structures (Plate 18). Image's rubbery, cheerful, childish characters are richly colored and the settings offer France a new contender in the realm of popular animation. For instance, at one point a lost metro train runs up the Tower, tickling it and sending it into contortions (Plate 19). However, if the visuals fit comfortably within the international look of 1950s limited animation, the story remained less than compelling. Jean Image's tales, a bit like those of Grimault, avoided both familiar fairy tale structures and clear goal-oriented protagonists, preferring meandering, episodic plots. These French feature-length stories could not really compete with the more developed contemporary tales from Disney, such as *Peter Pan* (1950) and *Cinderella* (1951).

Beyond producing and directing these two color feature films and a host of shorts, Jean Image's lasting significance for French animation arises from his transition to television production. He brought crisp, lively images to television, beginning in 1960 with *Les Aventures de Joe*, followed with a long line of new series titles. Initially, his *La Fontaine des trois soldats* (*Fountain of the Three Soldiers*, 1963, 26 episodes) and *Picolo et Picolette* (1963–1965, 26 episodes) were very short shows of 5 and 7 minutes. But at the prices fixed by French television, they had to be made very cheaply with very limited animation, distinguished by few moving parts from frame to frame. Image had to find another mode of production to deliver that much material under such cheap conditions, so switched to using paper cut-outs placed on glass in front of flat backgrounds or even three-dimensional sets. Among his most successful creations, *Kiri le clown* initially ran for 130, 5-minute episodes from 1966 to 1969. The character has since continued to show up in various formats and was revised and produced in a 3D computer animated series beginning in 2005. Over the years, Jean Image Productions led the way in devising and marketing child-friendly characters and adapting its methods to the French marketplace. Along with his wife France Image, who co-authored many projects, Jean Image completed several more features, but their production house depended, and continues to depend, upon the constant demand from television and its thirst for clever child-friendly products.

While Jean Image managed to establish a foothold in both film and television, he remained one of very few success stories. In 1956, a meeting of the International Schools of Cinema was organized by the French national production school IDHEC and held during the Cannes Film Festival. A portion of the sessions was devoted to assessing and reporting on the state of animation. Their summary began by acknowledging that France has played a central role in world cinema, but that the greatest names in animation are still Emile Reynaud and Emile Cohl. The report laments the weak state of animation in 1950s France and points out that while short live action films can be accomplished on small budgets, animated shorts can cost nearly as much as live action features. They also complain that the industry must become more centralized, with collective access to better equipment and studios. The IDHEC committee, composed of animation instructors and professional advisors, warned that without increased government aid and commercial collaboration, the situation would not improve for the foreseeable future. They also ac-knowledged that even the notable successes were few and far between: "One name dominates French animation in recent years, that of Paul Grimault. But it took even him eight years to complete his first feature, *La Bergère et le ramoneur*" (IDHEC 1956: 29). Importantly, Paul Grimault served on the Cannes jury that year in the short film competitions, where Albert Lamorisse's *The Red Balloon* won the best short film, rather than any animated submission.

Among the few bright spots cited in the dossier was Jean Image. The IDHEC group praised Jean Image's *Johnny the Giant Killer* and *Bonjour Paris*: "These two films account for the greatest quantitative effort of the past decade" (IDHEC 1956: 30). That they praise Image for quantity over quality somewhat qualifies their compliment, and they also mention, perhaps as a caution to others, that Image's visual style and anthropomorphic figures resemble Walt Disney's output. However, as their call for increased national and commercial funding demonstrates, the committee was clearly frustrated, in part because the few French successes seemed to owe too much to dreaded Hollywood's example. "Must one copy the successful models from abroad? Or, can one search within national traditions, including newspapers, for comic inspiration that remain more original? Grimault has provided one answer" (IDHEC 1956: 35). Clearly, they were hoping for more pertinent options to appear that also retained the enduring spirit of Emile Cohl. The IDHEC report nonetheless concludes with rather patriotic praise for persistent animators on the front lines: "French artists have come to understand the plastic and poetic possibilities of this marvelous means of expression and are engaged in a difficult fight to match their foreign competitors" (IDHEC 1956: 35). The ongoing struggle to balance national graphic and aesthetic traditions with a more commercially rewarding mission would continue to haunt and challenge French animators for years to come. While many important animators found solid and creative employment during this era, including veterans such as Arcady, André Rigal, and Henri Gruel, a new generation of entrepreneurs would gain significance and point to new business models, including small production houses built around very personal projects for TV and film.

Toward a New Era of Micro-Studios: Laguionie and Laloux

During the 1950s, as the Cannes Film Festival gained increased international attention and marketing strength, advocates for animation, especially André Martin, Michel Boschet, and Pierre Barbin, helped organize special events during the festival. In 1960, they, along with a host of other animators and critics, including Canada's Norman McLaren, launched ASIFA, the International Animated Film Association, in Annecy, France. ASIFA sponsors the annual Annecy International Animated Film Festival, which remains to this day the world's most important animation festival. Annecy is a highly successful venue that includes special seminars for professionals and students alike, as well as nearly non-stop screenings, and prestigious prizes for short and feature-length animation in film and television, as well as student awards. The Annecy Festival has helped increase the visibility of a wide range of animation from around the world. It has also assured that French historians and critics remain central to the aesthetic evaluation of international animation.

In the world of production, Jean-François Laguionie typifies both the excitement and the frustration within French animation of the 1960s and 1970s. Originally involved in live performance and theatre, Laguionie met Paul Grimault in 1963. Grimault provided studio space and helped find financing via French TV's experimental grants allowing Laguionie to make several short films. Thanks to Grimault's mentoring, Laguionie forged a very personal, experimental oeuvre. Laguionie worked primarily with cut-out paper figures, a technique he borrowed from animator Jacques Colombat, initially taping his figures in place for each shot. Gradually, Laguionie added tiny springs, hinges, and magnets. Working chronologically with cut-out pieces poses many challenges and a single mistake can force the re-shooting of an entire sequence, but Laguionie advocates this mode of production. He compares this process to a circus acrobat performing without a net. Moreover, using cut-outs helps escape the potential monotony of cel animation thanks to the use of a wider variety of drawing tools and components, though rather mechanical character movements typically result and animators cannot see their work until it is projected on the screen (Génin 2003: 62). Yet his carefully controlled action and painterly touches manage to lend a great deal of character and atmosphere to these occasionally stiff figures (Noake 1988: 88). In Laguionie's hands, such animation combines a childish simplicity with surreal visuals and a hint at somber mysticism. Laguionie's status was guaranteed when his first film, *La Demoiselle et le violoncelliste* (*The Young Lady and the Cellist*, 1965), won the Grand Prize for short films at the Annecy Animation Festival.

A tale without words, *The Young Lady and the Cellist* presents an early twentieth-century setting in which a man wearing a suit arrives at a beach to play his cello. Meanwhile, a young woman fishes with her net in the surf (Plate 20). As the man plays an ominous piece written by Edouard Lalo, the weather changes – rising waves and a mighty wind push the woman far out to sea. He stops playing (though the music continues non-diegetically), and he hauls his cello into a small boat to attempt a rescue, but he soon sinks. Underwater, he locates the woman, who appears quite relaxed, and the man resumes playing his instrument. Though the sound is distorted, breathing underwater does not seem to be an issue for these two. Rather, the threat comes in the form of a giant crab that carries the woman off and a huge fish that chases the man. Eventually, the two beasts struggle against one another while the man and woman escape from their colorful underwater world, walking up onto a shore populated with static caricatures of beach-goers who seem stunned to see the couple rising from the water (Plate 21). The couple eventually retreats to a spot further down the beach, apparently seeking their own private space. The 9-minute film ends with the cello music trailing out over black leader. *The Young Lady and the Cellist* offers a dreamy world with no real characterization or resolution. The images flow like the music, though there is a strict three-act plot structure as well as strong binary patterns throughout the tale: he loses his cello, she loses her net, each is pursued by a large underwater creature, they enter the sea twice, and so on.

During an era when commercial animation was dominated by television series, Laguionie worked on the margins of commercial animation and was part of a European attempt to retain the individual artistry of the medium. Later, his *La Traversée de l'Atlantique à la rame* (*Rowing across the Atlantic*, 1978) won both the top prize for animation in France and at the Cannes Film Festival. It too employed cut-out figures, combined with bright background drawings, often resembling colored pencil and crayon. At a duration of 21 minutes, *Rowing across the Atlantic* expanded on the sequential structure of Laguionie's earlier films. This melancholy movie takes the form of an allegory: a newly married couple embarks on a long journey, rowing across the Atlantic. They begin happily, relishing the intimate time together, eating and playing music, as if on an endless romantic outing. Along the way, however, years pass and they face a series of hurdles. They battle survivors from the *Titanic* trying to enter their boat, endure stormy waves that resemble elephant tusks, and suffer surreal hallucinations that torment them until they turn violently against one another. Eventually, decades later, they die floating in each other's arms in the water.

Rowing across the Atlantic actually opens with what will turn out to be the end of the story, as a variety of rather static shots reveal an empty battered row boat washing up on a beach. Then the story begins with the happy couple embarking from New York City in their rowboat, "Love and Courage." Despite occasional voice-over dialogue from the man and woman, and some glimpses of their diary, Laguionie makes no attempt to develop character traits or any plausible action. *Rowing across the Atlantic*, like *The Young Lady and the Cellist*, remains a very personal fantasy full of metaphors and obscure dream images, and is strongly marked by the rigid cut-out animation rhythms and a distorted Magritte-like juxtaposition of objects. Languionie steers clear of any classical narrative devices, so that the couple's long journey toward old age and death becomes an existential fact rather than any sort of learning experience. His saga of life as struggle in a small boat remains quite alien from more philosophical journey metaphors, such as Yann Martel's *Life of Pi*. Yet, spectators are welcome to interject their own interpretations into *Rowing across the Atlantic*, which is built succinctly around the ritual of human life as a series of challenges we initially face with optimism before eventually accepting the ineluctable reality of death.

Importantly, in 1979 Laguionie converted a former cloth factory in a village in southern France into a studio, La Fabrique, to begin work on his first feature, *Gwen, ou Le livre de sable* (*Gwen, or the Book of Sand*, 1984). La Fabrique, which took advantage of local financial support, would provide a model for other small-scale animation houses that could be established far from Paris, and benefit from regional arts grants. Laguionie formed what Sebastien Denis (2007: 177) labels a sort of hippie commune that turned into a creative center for exploring new themes and styles. For his shorts, Laguionie had worked mostly alone, so for the feature, he continued to use a tiny initial production team of only six people. While the feature took over four years to complete, its overall budget of roughly $1.5 million was quite low for such a task, and each of the crew members drew the same salary in this cooperative venture. *Gwen*, the tale of an apocalyptic future in which little remains on the earth but vast deserts of sand and a few outposts of humans, was a daring science fiction project, at a time when there were still relatively few European feature-length animated films being produced. Laguionie benefited strongly from the blueprint established by René Laloux during the 1970s. As we shall see, Laloux's *La Planète sauvage* (*Fantastic Planet*, 1973) had proven that a personal, feature-length animated "art film" could be made and find an international audience. Yet Laguionie's feature would not be as fortunate.

In discussing *Gwen*, Laguionie speaks wistfully of the production process as a long journey among friends, adrift in the same boat. Such meandering travels are at the core of his cinema. Yet while *Gwen* may have the basic plot points of a potentially compelling epic drama, the film systematically undercuts most narrative conventions. In a world of the future, after some disaster that may have been caused by the consumer society in the City of the Dead, a mysterious force called Macou appears over the desert at night, dropping enormous household items such as sinks, radiators, and beds.

Macou can also abduct people, so the desert inhabitants hide in wells dug in the sand. During the days, the nomadic people hunt ostriches, harvesting their feathers for food. The narrator, a 173-year-old woman named Rosalie (whose voice is provided by male actor Michel Robin), tells of the day an orphaned 13-year-old girl, Gwen, joined their tribe. Gwen meets a boy, who may, according to Laguionie, be Rosalie's grandson. While Gwen and the boy play one night, the strange white force field that is part of Macou captures him and apparently takes him to the walled, old fashioned City of the Dead. Rosalie and Gwen set out on a long trek to rescue the boy (Plate 22). The people living in the City of the Dead have apparently somehow caused the catastrophe that turned the earth into a land of sand dunes, though it is not clear they know this. Nights, they meet in rituals where two men read the only remaining book, a catalogue of house and garden tools. The people seem to believe it is a sacred text, so their art classes religiously copy images such as watering cans from its pages and the choir chants its product descriptions as part of a ritual. Finally, Gwen succeeds in bringing the boy home. Gwen, the boy, and Rosalie are reunited in the barren desert and the younger pair sets off pursuing yet another ostrich. One of the film's organizing ideas was that Gwen's quest to sneak into the City of the Dead and rescue the boy would be a reversal of the myth of Orpheus, including an ending in which both characters return alive (Plate 23).

Even Laguionie acknowledges that taken globally, the story is not necessarily coherent: "If you try to understand the story from every angle it becomes absurd. . . . Perhaps poetry requires that things remain unclear [just as] landscapes become more poetic with some added fog."[2] Yet, while such avant-garde narratives are common in short personal works, they are certainly unusual for feature-length films. In the tradition of his shorts, Laguionie has included stunning scenes which do not necessarily advance the plot, including the first capture of an ostrich, a fireworks display, or butterflies fluttering about the kidnapped boy. Such scenes also display remarkably different animation styles, from rigid cut-outs to abstract light patterns. The result is a disjointed, picaresque series of scenes, while the amount of time passing between them and the spatial or causal relations are often left obscure. At one point, when discussing three lights they see in the sky, Rosalie teaches Gwen that just because she sees something does not mean it exists. Nothing is certain in Laguionie's worlds. Moreover, the soundtrack, which pairs the simple sounds of the desert people's

---

[2] Jean-François Laguionie, "Presentation," on French DVD supplemental material.

instruments with Pierre Arland's richer non-diegetic compositions, rarely clarifies any single dominant mood, so it is unclear whether the ostrich hunts are joyous or pathetic. A melancholy sense of loss reigns, and the resolution, with the boy returned to his tribe, is left incomplete since there is no apparent celebration and everyone just sets out on a new ostrich hunt. No one is any closer to happiness or security. We assume Macou will still rule the desert. The film is open ended, much like *The Young Lady and the Cellist*, with a couple again heading off away from the viewer.

Yet *Gwen* is a hypnotic experience, conjuring up a unique fictional universe and creating its own strange rhythm. The haunting visuals sometimes include frozen images, like the pages of a comic book, but at other times there is great fluid motion, as in the dancing ostrich neck and fireworks displays. *Gwen* has been praised for "a finely rendered graphic style" with some incredibly smooth movements and lyrical timing (Noake 1988: 93). All Laguionie's films offer strong visual set pieces, dreamlike images, and short scenes that often seem independent of any overarching narrative. In order better to manipulate each image, La Fabrique built its own version of the multiplane camera, with four levels. The crew exploits this device, creating several distinct planes of action and varying focus on specific objects in the frame. Moreover, they adjust the light separately on each plane, often shifting colors and accenting particular portions of the image to generate unnatural compositions. Such attention to constructing the visual frame and setting up shots in which several objects may be competing for the viewer's attention, typifies Laguionie's rare breed of animation.

Despite its visual beauty and poetic approach to science fiction, *Gwen, or the Book of Sand* never found international distribution. After *Gwen*, La Fabrique continued producing shorts and serials for film and television. Jean-François Laguionie directed two features aimed at children and a more general audience, *Le Château des singes* (*A Monkey's Tale*, 1999) and *L'Île de Black Mór* (*Black Mor's Island*, 2004). Neither film managed to find much commercial or critical success, while their visual style proved rather generic, resembling many other television cartoons. However, the obscure, minimal symbolism and carefully sculpted imagery of Laguionie's earlier work would prove influential and find parallels in other European and Japanese science fiction films that would nonetheless labor at constructing more conventional dramatic storylines. Still, as Bendazzi notes, "Laguionie's delicate and elegiac films, made with a rhythm which adapts to the viewers' receptiveness, are deceptively simple." They possess multiple levels of complex ethical and political themes, providing potent meditations on life as well as "a vision of solitude" (Bendazzi 1994: 290).

But it was clearly René Laloux who initially proved France could produce aesthetically and financially successful feature-length animation. From the beginning of his career, Laloux experimented with distorted visions of humanity. During the 1950s, he worked in a mental asylum, teaching painting and theater, but he also managed to collaborate on a 16mm film with his patients, much of it composed of cut-out figures and shadow art. Laloux sold the project to French television. These articulated paper cut-outs, with hinged body parts placed on painted backgrounds, also became the central materials for his subsequent career. In 1960, the 11-minute *Les Dents du singe* (*Monkey's Teeth*), by Laloux and his patients, won the Emile Cohl Prize for best animation. Early in this cartoon, which combines childlike coloring book urban settings with cut-out paper figures, a character enters through a door in a wall, in a shot recalling Reynaud's *Poor Pierrot*. This grotesque cartoon of a dentist who removes healthy teeth from poor patients to implant them in rich customers is rendered in highly expressionistic style. Characters with green faces and stiff elongated hands move about this place made of nightmarish dark skies and interiors that seem to spring from Van Gogh crossed with Kafka. The group project was influenced by Jungian imagery, with plenty of free association, including an avenging monkey on a bicycle.

During the 1960s, Laloux began working with the novelist, post-surreal illustrator, and caricaturist Roland Topor. They continued to use flat, cut-out figures. Part of their motivation for this technique was that it was more economical than cel animation. Moreover, "our graphic training and background drew us toward something beyond the standard graphics of American styled cartoons. . . . We were sort of the New Wave of animation, and for the same reasons as their live action choices: We had limited budgets, but also sought freedom in form and content" (Blin 2004: 41). For their award-winning short *Les Escargots* (*The Snails*, 1965), Topor and Laloux employed rigid cut-out figures that owed to Topor's drawing style, with visible pen marks resembling wood cuttings or etchings. Here, an eccentric farmer cannot manage to grow lettuce, until his tears of frustration magically revive the wilted plants. The only problem is that he must continually devise ever more extreme measures to make himself cry in order to water the vast field. Once the leaves grow to gigantic proportions, however, snails arrive, devour the crop, and become enormous in their own right, wreaking havoc and temporarily destroying the countryside and cities alike. Finally, that crisis passes and the farmer switches to planting carrots, only to attract gigantic rabbits. Thus, much of Laloux's work revolves around comical nightmare scenarios that implicate humanity as the ultimate cause for throwing the world out of balance. Even when the action is whimsical, Laloux's work comes with a warning.

The crowning achievement of Laloux's career was *Fantastic Planet*, which won the Special Jury Prize at the 1973 Cannes Film Festival and was distributed throughout the world. A frightening, futuristic fantasy, *Fantastic Planet* was based on a book by Stefan Wul and adapted with the help of Topor. Set in an alternate universe where humans are kept as tiny pets of the Draag people, the story is an allegory about colonialism, slavery, rebellion, and finally peaceful coexistence. It also proves a synthesis between the worlds of 1970s European comic books and the anti-Disney nature of much international animation of the era. "In France during the 1970s, science fiction was one means of reflecting on the future of our society" (Denis 2007: 176). Laloux's tale, like many science fiction stories popular after May 1968, attacked social rules, complacency, and racism, all in an unsettling, metaphorical setting.

Fantastic Planet begins with a shocking scene in which a young mother, clutching her baby, is abused and killed by a huge blue hand, which turns out to belong to a Draag child, a race of humanoid giants on a distant planet (Plate 24). Tiwa, the sympathetic daughter of the ruler Shin, adopts the minuscule baby Om (for the French *homme*, man) and names him Terr, after his home planet, Terre, or Earth. As Terr grows he learns the Draag language and other valuable facts from Tiwa's instructional headphones (Plate 25). Meanwhile, the Draag people spend great amounts of time meditating, during which a small image of themselves drifts off in a bubble. These mystical moments suggest a dreamy out-of-body, drug-like experience. Eventually, Terr, tired of his captivity, escapes the city and discovers outposts of wild Oms. Welcomed by a beautiful Om girl, he helps their group survive, even as the Draags launch an attack to kill off the wild Oms (Plate 26). From an abandoned rocket factory, the Oms manage to build two small space ships to escape to the nearby Fantastic Planet, where they discover that the Draag meditation bubbles arrive and dock, becoming heads on giant naked bodies as part of their reproduction process which also somehow energizes their other Draag bodies on their own planet below. From their phallic little rockets, the Oms shoot a small stream of something that breaks up the bodies, yielding terror and chaos on their home planet below. Finally, the rational leader Shin convinces the Draags and Oms they must live together and the movie ends rather abruptly but happily, with the assurance that the Oms ultimately thrive on their own natural, Earth-like planet while the Draags evolve into a more peaceful people. *Fantastic Planet* combines ecological and pacifist themes with futuristic sci-fi motifs and action-adventure genre traits. Beyond combining popular discourse with art film conventions, its significance also lies in its critical success. Winning the prize at Cannes marked a major achievement for both France and the animated feature.

Fantastic Planet arrived during an era when feature-length animation worldwide was in a slump. It had been five years since *Yellow Submarine* (Dunning, 1967). Ralph Bakshi's *Fritz the Cat* (1972) and *Heavy Traffic* (1973) were among the most successful alternative features, while Disney's $15 million *Robin Hood* did well internationally, selling 3.8 million tickets in France alone. *Fantastic Planet* was a moderate success at the box office, thanks in large part to its prize at Cannes, with 800,000 tickets sold in its French first run. Despite selling many fewer tickets than the mainstream *Robin Hood*, *Fantastic Planet* was one of the most successful European animated features since *Yellow Submarine*, and proved inspirational to many international, independent animators. Working closely on the storyboards with Roland Topor, Laloux ended up producing the film over a period of nearly four years in Prague, at a studio that would later be named for Jiri Trnka. The film was a French-Czechoslovakian co-production, completed thanks to former New Wave producer Anatole Dauman. Already in 1970, the cost of animating in Eastern Europe was dramatically lower than in Western Europe.

Topor preferred to remain in France, so Laloux was often the only French person in the Czech studio, working with a core production team averaging around 25 people. For *Fantastic Planet* Laloux refined many of his earlier techniques: "The characters were drawn on very thin sheets of Bristol [paper], painted in colored ink and then cut out with scissors. Thus, each cut shape represented a fraction of a second on screen, in opposition to the usual cut-out figures with articulated limbs that could be moved between each shot like mannequins" (René Laloux, quoted in Blin 2004: 49). The resulting characters move much more smoothly than articulated cut-outs, though they are never as fluid as conventionally drawn cel characters. There is still a perception of the figures as moving paper, especially since they feature heavy dark outlines and generally slide across the background paintings, or occasionally slip behind other paper objects in the foreground. The final print was composed of 1,073 distinct shots.

Fantastic Planet provides a strong test case for adult comic book/*bande dessinée* aesthetics in European animation, with Laloux transforming Topor's static illustration style into the cinema. "Its form and poetic charm lie in the contrast between the cruel naivety that results from Topor's expressionistic drawings and the lyrical *mise-en-scène* by Laloux" (Blin 2004: 44). Admittedly, not everyone would label the outcome as lyrical, since it retains a rather heavy-handed, sometimes plodding, narrative structure, and the music becomes repetitive, striking poignant accents even when none seem warranted. Yet, Laloux and Topor were consciously striving to avoid many commercial animation clichés: "Our goal had been to escape the ghetto of the art house movie theater without falling into the eye-catching demagoguery of a Walt Disney" (Blin 2004: 65). Their work fits firmly within the history of French animation which constantly struggled to define its own stories and styles in opposition to international competition and conventions. All the animators mentioned up to this point contributed to France's network of varying strategies and shaped the renaissance in animation that was to bridge the centuries. Grimault, Laguionnie, and Laloux provided valuable lessons in production, aesthetics, and marketing that would serve as instructive guidelines for the future of French animation.

5

French Animation's Renaissance

Fortunately the [relative absence of animation from film histories] began to improve somewhat during the 1980s when a number of auteurs, thanks to their unflagging determination, managed to begin animating very personal feature films and thereby drew attention to their own work and to French animation in general. (Predal 1997: 576)

Le Cartoon Plan

While a number of important French productions appeared over the decades, animated cinema remained a marginalized, under-funded wing of France's national cinema. For Western Europe as a whole, maintaining a steady output of commercially viable animation, and especially feature-length animation, had proven impossible. Moreover, by the 1980s, when national television stations were scheduling increasing numbers of inexpensive American and Japanese imported cartoons for children, serious concerns were raised about the loss of European traditions in the face of an accelerating media invasion that amounted to a new form of cultural imperialism. For instance, thanks in large part to the new video rental and sales market, Disney's Buena Vista became the largest distributor in France and much of Europe. Independent animators, film critics, government media officials, and television and film industry insiders alike began to call attention to Europe's slipping hold on children's fare and the lucrative field of multimedia animation. Globalization and the approaching challenges of expensive, emerging computer animation technologies became central to debates on the aesthetic, ideological, and economic viability of national and regional animation. Small national cinemas, with limited domestic audiences, could not easily compete with Japan or the US, which had the advantage of large-scale home audiences and vast international distribution

French Animation History
© Richard Neupert. Published by John Wiley & Sons

networks. Most commercial animation was produced and distributed by huge multinational corporations. The general opinion was that Europe had already lost the feature animation race before it could even begin to compete. The few successful European TV cartoons were often farmed out to South Korea for the bulk of the actual animation, while many talented animators trained in Europe were leaving for jobs in the United States and Canada.

By the mid-1980s, the perception of a crisis looming in television and cinema motivated the European Union Commission's Media Program to call for proposed solutions: "Faced as it is with the expansion of new technologies, the European audiovisual industry must develop original productions to match outside competitors and must promote its productions throughout the extended market of the entire Community" (European Communities Commission 1986a: 49). The Commission called for increased distribution agreements and co-productions within Europe. The two-year studies would culminate in high profile events during 1988: "Whereas the audiovisual media are among the chief means of conveying information and culture to the European citizen and contribute to the strengthening of individual European cultures, as well as the European identity. . . . We welcome the agreement that 1988 should be declared European Cinema and Television Year" (European Communities Commission 1986b: 52). During 1988, the European Union's Media Program acknowledged "concern at the lack of competitiveness of the European cinema industry," and the need to "promote films for children and young people" (European Communities Commission 1988: 44). Clearly, animation was right in the middle of such concerns: if children were raised primarily on non-European content, then "European culture" was at risk, and as those young audiences grew up they would be ever more likely to continue seeking television and cinema content from the United States and Asia. None of this boded well for the future of European national cinemas. Animation's fate was a warning sign for future difficulties in live action film production.

In 1988, Europe only accounted for 8 percent of the world's commercial animation, a figure that also reflected a serious lack of crucial infrastructures. Europe needed more specialized professional training, funding for large-scale projects, access to up-to-date production facilities, and increased exposure to international audiences. The French journal *Cinémaction* argued that four major factors were working against Europe's traditional modes of animation production. European animation suffered from unfavorable market prices, high unemployment forcing skilled workers to leave, distribution networks that favored highly capitalized super-productions, and a technological disparity that put smaller producers at a disadvantage (Levasseur 1989: 207). Pressure for modernization of the animation industry thus came from many directions at once, including those worrying about loss of a cultural identity all the way on down to animation students looking for competitive training and steady employment.

The European Commission's Media Program proposed a "cartoon plan" calling for national governments and private industry alike to work toward common models for teaching animation, especially with the incorporation of new technologies, as well as cooperative ventures in production, financing, and distribution (Génin 2003: 27). The assumption was that if each nation could find ways to build up its own cinema and television industries while integrating as much as possible its methods and goals with other member states, Europe would arise as a powerhouse for traditional and new media. Attracting and holding the youth market would be a high priority for ensuring the future health of these culture industries. But European neighbors also had to break down trade barriers and work toward multilingual final products.

Most national cinemas were already quite aware of the problems, and France, thanks to its forward-looking Centre Nationale de la Cinématographie (CNC), was actively grappling with the challenge. But this European Union call to arms got the attention of business and government leaders alike and can be credited with concrete advances and cooperation in a wide variety of areas across Europe over the next decade. The first successes came in national television animated series, while the expansion of feature-length animation would take longer. During the 1990s, roughly 80 percent of international animation was made for television. France managed to make the biggest advances and today it is the third largest producer of animation in the world. Yet, in the realm of motion picture animation, France managed to continue its long history of artisanal, independent projects. Its phenomenal recent success in feature-length animation owes to new schools, new technologies, and government aid, but also to a strong cluster of daring small producers and distinct individual animators. The expansion in French animation cinema did not come at the expense of its particular national history or its modes of production. France's animation today is a direct result of its past practice.

Michel Ocelot's Alternative Mode of Production

The most important French animator since Emile Cohl may be Michel Ocelot. Ocelot proved that personal feature films could indeed be made, and quite profitably, for the European market without copying Hollywood's formats or techniques. However, his success also depended upon a series of important producers. Ocelot began animating in the 1970s, and his *Les Trois inventeurs* (*The Three Inventors*, 1979) proves an important early glimpse into his distinct style and lyrical fantasies. Ocelot employed cut-out white lace for his figures in this episodic series of cinematic attractions, and the texture as well as the outlines prove stunning, thanks in large part to the lighting, which casts shadows between the thin paper and the background surface. Later, his *La Légende du pauvre bossu* (*Legend of the Hunchback*) won the French César for best short animation in 1982. In 1988, at the beginning of the "cartoon plan" era, Michel Ocelot benefited from his friendship with Jean-François Laguionie, who allowed Ocelot to make a series of cut-paper short films at La Fabrique studio. Ocelot's project was for eight films of roughly 11 minutes each in a series for television that might someday also be released as a single film version.

The series was initially called *Ciné Si* (and distributed narrowly in English as *Cinema If* and *We are the Star*). The premise is that a boy and girl meet occasionally in a former film studio with an old technician. There, they plan out short narratives, research the subject matter, select and create costumes, often with help from bizarre machines, and then the boy and girl perform their newest "dress-up" prince and princess drama each session. According to Ocelot, *Ciné Si* was accomplished "without money, with two fixed Bolex cameras, several sheets of glass, drawing paper, and a couple lights from the hardware store" (Lorfèvre 2005: 5). Ocelot cut paper figures from black construction paper and attached small hinges and wires to their joints for articulated paper marionettes that could be re-used over and over and moved between frames. He placed the characters, and their elaborate set objects, on back-lit glass, creating silhouettes against colorful backgrounds. The hinges were invisible to the camera. Ocelot was returning to the cut-out paper techniques of France's past as well as Lotte Reiniger. Unfortunately, after a very limited run on television, and a few film festivals, *Ciné Si* initially attracted little attention, though one episode, "The Princess of Diamonds," was nominated for a César award. As we shall see, however, *Ciné Si* enjoyed a second life later, following the amazing success of Ocelot's first feature film, *Kirikou et la sorcière* (*Kirikou and the Sorceress*, 1998).

Though Michel Ocelot was born in southern France, he spent an important part of his childhood in Guinea, West Africa. For his first feature, he adapted a popular African folk tale which allowed him to refer to this key portion of his life, and the setting allowed him to combine interests in African art and primitivism. Similar to director Claire Denis, Ocelot is continually fascinated with relations between France and its former colonies. Kirikou is a newborn boy who immediately sets forth to help his village, which has fallen under the spells of an evil sorceress who apparently devours all the men who dare confront her. The minuscule Kirikou springs from his mother's womb with full speech and great cunning. He exploits his tiny size and uncanny intelligence to combat a wide array of beasts before discovering the secret to Karaba the Sorceress's evil motives. Kirikou cures her by removing a nail sunk deep in her spine and as a result sets all the captive village men free, while he himself grows into a handsome young man thanks to Karaba's appreciative and magic kiss. *Kirikou and the Sorceress* proved quite challenging from many practical perspectives and particularly for locating potential producers and distributors, since Ocelot's protagonist was a naked African boy surrounded by topless African women. A large part of the ideal audience would be children and families. Distributors in Great Britain and the United States, for instance, resisted the movie due to fears of censorship problems. There was also the potential backlash from culture critics complaining about the nudity but also pedophilia concerns. As *Variety* later reported, "This is one pic the religious right won't be lining up to see" (James 2005: 11). Further, not everyone on the left would approve of the film either, especially since it is made by a white European male depicting naked Africans who are often superstitious and narrow minded.

Fortunately, Ocelot managed to convince producer Didier Brunner to take on the project. Brunner points out that there was no practical model for distributing a movie such as *Kirikou and the Sorceress*, and Michel Ocelot had no established track record at this point. Further, compared to live action, animation has higher initial pre-production expenses (Brunner 2007). Brunner obtained an advance from the CNC for 10 percent of the $4,000,000 budget and another 15 percent from Canal +, but he also sought funding from various international and regional sources. "Eventually, one could say that *Kirikou* is a film largely funded by institutions," including the Belgian ministry of culture and Eurimage, among many others (Ciment 2000: 80–81). Ironically, what would become the lead example of "French" feature-length animation required financial investments and talent from beyond France's borders. After a two-year search to secure financing, Ocelot required four years to complete the animation. *Kirikou and the Sorceress* proved instructive and inspiring on many levels for European animators, in part because it provided a new blueprint for a viable option in international co-productions that nonetheless maintained a personal style. In the end, there were eight co-producers and five nations involved in the production. The voices for the original version and Youssou N'Dour's music were recorded in Dakar, while the animation was completed in Paris and Angoulême, Brussels, Budapest, Luxembourg, and Riga, Latvia. Ocelot likes to recount that, "One of the most beautiful aspects of the production was that this village of African women was animated by a team of women on the Baltic Sea.... These white Baltic women adopted this village of black women" (Ocelot 1998: 126).

Ocelot expanded and adapted the African story, adding plot points from folk tales he had heard over the years, including an Alsatian tale of a boy confronting a monster in a cave, which motivated Kirikou's battle to restore a spring. The mode of production involved creating a combination storyboard and script for the eventual 1,200 shots; he calls this stage the "scénarimage" since it mixes sketches, dialogue, music, and technical cues. Ocelot traveled regularly between all locations, but he also worked closely with seven lead animators. Everything was drawn out in 2D, though one artist actually constructed his character in a 3D computer program, then drew it out by hand in 2D. While the character drawings feature some detailed markings, most tend to be rendered in a flat style, with minimal colors, dark lines to denote muscles or body parts, and heavy outlines. Much of the rigidity of Ocelot's earlier silhouette cut-outs remains in the drawn animal and human bodies of *Kirikou and the Sorceress*. The characters move more deliberately than naturally. The dark brown characters resemble figures from a coloring book, while the clean, mildly abstract graphic style fits the subject matter of a children's folk tale.

By contrast, Ocelot wanted the setting to be spectacular in terms of species of plants, soil, and terrain: "I advised the designers that each plant in the forest should be a masterpiece, botanically accurate, with Egyptian stylization, coloring from Henri Rousseau, with each petal and leaf carefully made iridescent" (Ocelot 1998: 93). The resulting visual style is a startling mix of mostly monochromatic human and animal figures inserted in front of richly detailed and colored backgrounds. Each plant is drawn with extreme precision and careful color gradations (Ocelot, personal email). Thus, while the wild boar resembles a piece of construction paper, the fields he runs through are made more fully rendered with fine-grained details and careful volume cues. Further, Ocelot occasionally uses motion blur on his backgrounds, creating a tension between the fixed outline of characters and the colorful abstraction of the environment. When Kirikou runs to rescue the children in a boat, the forest is reduced to streaking speed lines, but once he leaps in the boat and cuts a hole in the bottom, his surroundings appear to be a series of parallel surfaces rather than the sides of a three-dimensional boat interior. Repeatedly, the viewer's attention is drawn to the surface of the screen and the artifice, and rarely do perspectival cues generate a plausible diegetic visual space (Plates 27 and 28).

Narratively, *Kirikou and the Sorceress* has much in common with children's books and folk tales. Here, as with all Ocelot's subsequent work, the tales employ bits and pieces of traditional fairy tales that are then rewritten into original, very personal stories: Ocelot mines the world of fantasy tales for the materials to forge his own unique narratives. He is a master of employing intertextual bricolage to generate a striking new product (Gudin 2005: 153). *Kirikou and the Sorceress* is arranged as a series of incredible adventures involving the tiny, newly born Kirikou, and could easily be adapted to a cartoon series. After telling his mother he is ready to be born, and then cutting his own umbilical cord, Kirikou immediately speaks forcefully of saving his village. In scene after scene, he outwits Karaba's strange robot "fetishes" (who turn out to be the transformed men of the village). He restores the village's water from a blocked up spring, saves the children from being kidnapped by the sorceress's fantastic boat, outfoxes the wild boar, and locates his grandfather in a magical cave. The grandfather explains to Kirikou how Karaba was attacked by a group of men who drove a large poisonous thorn into her backbone. This harrowing sequence is presented in a completely distinct visual style, as a grotesque slide show with saturated red and black imagery. The thorn torments her but also gives Karaba magical powers. Kirikou cleverly steals Karaba's jewelry to lure her into the forest, then drops onto her back, ripping the thorn out with his teeth. Cured, Karaba rewards him with the kiss that frees him from the child's body. Kirikou magically transforms into a young man and a perfect match for the stunning Karaba (Plates 29 and 30). Kirikou convinces the village that Karaba is now a friend (and that he himself is indeed the toddler Kirikou, now magically grown). The film ends with the celebration as all the men return and Kirikou and Karaba embrace. The village is returned to peace thanks to many happy reunions, while the whiny old man who has been in charge of the community is replaced by the strong young men of a new generation. It is a story of a child's resourcefulness and value as well as proof of renewal at the hands of young, sexually charged men.

Finding distribution for the unconventional *Kirikou and the Sorceress* proved difficult, but the small firm Gebeka agreed. The movie opened to rave reviews among the French press, which painted a picture of Ocelot as a sort of artisan come to save European animation. Ocelot, working away in his tiny Studio O, was their Geppetto, Kirikou was his Pinocchio. Initially, producer Brunner had calculated he would need to sell 300,000 tickets in France, but eventually *Kirikou and the Sorceress* sold 1.5 million tickets, which is a very strong showing for any film, much less an animated feature about a previously unknown character with no star voices. Ocelot's movie went on to win multiple animation and children's film festival awards, but most prestigious was the Grand Prize at Annecy. Sales on DVD have further reinforced the reach of Kirikou, who also appeared on many ancillary products as well as on stage in a live musical production in which Kirikou the child is portrayed by a puppet. However, the only distributor willing to buy the rights for the United States was the small African specialty company, Artmattan, which made only nine 35mm copies of the dubbed version. As *Variety* reported, "All agreed that the debut film by helmer Michel Ocelot . . . was enchanting and beautifully animated. There was just one problem. Its thimble-sized hero . . . was as naked as the day he was born, as were his friends" (James 2005: 11).

Ocelot's cultural value was launched with *Kirikou and the Sorceress*, a truly unique and personal project. One blog sponsored by France's CNC observers, "We had to wait for 1999, with the release of *Kirikou and the Sorceress*, for a breach to open our minds and public opinion allowing us to become interested once more in French animation, a full 20 years after *The King and the Bird*" (CNC 2004). Quickly after this success, Gebeka, the distributor for *Kirikou and the Sorceress*, suggested Ocelot gather some of his previous shorts for a special theatrical release, to capitalize on Kirikou's fame. Ocelot decided to rework *Ciné Si* for its own re-release. Thanks to support from *Kirikou*'s producer Didier Brunner at Les Armateurs, Ocelot digitally scanned most of the earlier artwork from six of the episodes: "We did not really change anything. The image remained the same physical shadow theater, pieces of paper, and back light. We simply blew it up from 16mm to 35mm and re-mixed the soundtrack" (Ocelot, personal email). The result, *Princes et Princesses* (*Princes and Princesses*, 2000), helped solidify Michel Ocelot as a central figure in the renaissance of French animation. This unusual project was also celebrated for avoiding the dominant commercial norms and returning to one of the most artisanal forms of animation, cut-out figures. Working within an already marginal niche of the film industry, animation, Ocelot radically exploited techniques from the days of magic lanterns and Chinese shadow silhouettes, making them new again, while obliterating conventional narrative space, since the flat silhouettes and their settings rarely created any coherent depth or volume cues.

The bracketing narrative device of *Princes and Princesses*, with the characters planning out their shows, foregrounds that this is a movie about representation, narration, and animation. The movie also exploits frames within frames, doubling the fictional activity. The self-conscious style was also a practical solution to Ocelot's original predicament of telling animated stories with almost no budget. By devising a story of characters like himself, innocently animating tales for their own pleasure, the production ends up justifying perfectly its own eccentric, home-made look. The six tales are quite different in their fictional settings, including ancient Egypt, medieval Europe, Hokusai's Japan, and even a futuristic science fiction story with rocket ships, but they share several basic plot devices in which one character must demonstrate spunk and cunning to reach their goal. The articulated paper figures prove quite compelling, thanks in large part to the vocal work of the actors and the saturated colored backgrounds. Further, the characters are built from numerous pieces with hinged body parts, and the dragon in one tale is constructed from scores of small cut-out discs, each connected with tiny hooks invisible in the projected print (Plate 31).

The opening and final tales reveal the cleverness of Ocelot's story structures. "The Princess and the Diamonds" features the girl as a princess held captive on a throne in a meadow by a strange spell. Any man who wishes to save and marry her must quickly gather the 111 lost diamonds from the grass to rebuild her necklace. However, if they cannot perform this task before the hour glass runs out they are turned into ants. After a gruff older man fails, the handsome young prince tries his hand, and since he had been nice to the ants earlier, they help him locate the diamonds and reassemble the necklace. He not only wins the hand of the appreciative Princess, but his success magically releases all the other men from their curse as ants. As with Kirikou's exploits, a selfless young man liberates a woman and releases older men from a dastardly spell. The tale is accented by a hot pink sky and pulsating points of white light for the diamonds, all accompanied by lyrical music, which help compensate for the inherent limitations of black silhouette characters.

In each of these tales, intelligence and humility win out over brashness and power, and usually the losing force is strongly marked as overly confident and patriarchal. But the final, comical episode, "Prince and Princess," provides a new twist on the pattern. It opens with the girl wishing for another story in which she can play a princess. The boy exclaims, "Again?!" but the man explains that they have not yet exhausted all possibilities. The internal narrative for this last tale begins where some others end, with a happy, beautiful young couple. However, after promising each other their undying love, the couple is put to a strange test. As soon as they share a first kiss, the Prince is transformed into a frog. He immediately demands she kiss him anew to change him back. However, though seconds earlier the Princess had sworn there was nothing she would not do for him, she is disgusted at the notion of kissing a frog: "I could take you to the pond," she offers. But the frog leaps up to kiss her lips and she turns into a slug. From this point on they continue to kiss, and each time one of them changes into yet another creature, including a butterfly, giraffe, pig, elephant, and even a whale. These clever transformations allow Ocelot to show off the fluid movements and acrobatics of his cut-out creations (Plate 32).

The final transformation, however, brings things nearly full-circle, as the Prince is turned into the Princess: "How horrible! I am you!" he protests. Another kiss is needed. However, the stunned Princess, now a cow, is not sure whether she should "kiss a girl," but she relents and she changes into the Prince. Rather than risk any further wicked changes, she decides they should stop while they are ahead, since as a heterosexual couple they can now marry and live in the castle, something impossible for them as cow and pig. When he protests, she explains: "I'll go hunting while you wait by the fire, embroidering." Though the Prince is outraged, she assures him he will learn to be a princess just as she had to. The topper is that now she, in the body of the prince, is more sexually assertive and leans in to get a kiss just as the iris closes in.

With this quick resolution, the audience is left wondering whether the next kiss is a rash act that might change them further or whether this gender switch is permanent. The humor here, as in much of Ocelot's work, comes from his overturning usual stereotypes. But there is also no return to the bracketing situation with the man and the boy and girl. The film simply stops, offering no closure effect of seeing the original boy and girl back safely in their studio, and thus the final episode challenges the film's own narrative structure. The characters are left in the wrong bodies but with their own voices. Throughout the film, each "actor" had worn many disguises, and some stories were about the success of pretending to be what one is not. Yet, this cross-gender finale only works because spectators by now grant that these flat silhouettes "have" a correct body. Across *Princes and Princesses*, viewers have come to recognize and repeatedly feel empathy for these minimally rendered characters, even as they engage in role playing. Finally, Ocelot's film comically proves Murray Smith's (1995) claims that the embodiment of characters is a crucial stage in our identification with their traits and stories. (For more on animated bodies and Ocelot, see Neupert 2008).

Princes and Princesses not only proved successful in its first run but it also performed well for the home video market, with over 200,000 DVDs sold. Ocelot's unusual release was seen as yet another sign of a resurgence of auteurist animation. One reviewer even pleaded openly for families to support Ocelot's work: "Here is a film that all children should see, and accompanied by their parents, for pity's sake! Because if adults remain as institutionalized in the Disney-fied aesthetic, how can we expect that our children will ever be interested in anything other than commercial Hollywood?" (Mercier 2001). Further, there was a sense that Ocelot was a national rallying point for creative artists. At the Annecy animation festival, Ocelot was asked whether he was strongly influenced by Laguionie: "If he had any influence it is mostly in the sense . . . that we were French animators and not ashamed of it. He never dreamed of imitating the Americans, nor did I." The interviewer concluded that "Michel Ocelot understands well how to resist Uncle Sam's annual assaults by practicing an animation steeped in beauty and tolerance, nourished by tales from the world over" (Gatto n.d.).

Michel Ocelot and Benedicte Galup followed this production by returning to the Kirikou franchise with *Kirikou et les bêtes sauvages* (*Kirikou and the Wild Beasts*) in 2005. UNESCO even hosted a special screening, with Kirikou saying hello in 12 languages, for a "children only" showing at Cannes. Nearly 50 nations bought distribution rights to the sequel and it sold even better in the theaters and on DVD than had its predecessor. Its first run attendance reached 1.8 million in France. The large audience was due in large part to families with small children. Most animated features draw roughly 20–25 percent of their ticket sales from children under 10; for *Kirikou and the Wild Beasts*, young children accounted for 40 percent of the box office. In this version, the grandfather, glowing in his white robe within the blue cave, narrates further tales of triumph from tiny Kirikou's past:

"The story of Kirikou and the Sorceress was too short. We did not have time to relate all he had accomplished." He announces there were many "beautiful and good deeds" by Kirikou and that his brave actions must not be forgotten. Thus, rather than serving as a conventional sequel to the original, *Kirikou and the Wild Beasts* offers a sort of flashback to deliver more of the child Kirikou's valiant acts. "[The] animation, like dialogue and narration, is simple and direct. Messages of the value of teamwork, pride in shared labor, self-reliance and resourcefulness are nicely embedded into compact, suspenseful adventures" (Nessleson 2005: 49). The plot structure not only parallels the episodic *Princes and Princesses*, it also recalls *The Adventures of Popeye* in that it revisits key moments from Kirikou's past and recycles some scenes. *Kirikou and the Wild Beasts* begins with Kirikou having nearly drowned while fixing the water source for the village and reinserts footage from *Kirikou and the Sorceress*, but it also includes new information on how the village profited from his actions. *Kirikou and the Wild Beasts* concentrates more on the good will between Kirikou and his people, who now trust him and work with him in this tale, though the village elder is still revealed repeatedly to be cynical and wrong-headed. Further, Karaba is much more passive in this episode, as Kirikou repeatedly reveals that she is not behind all the village's miseries and there are often other enemies, including stealthy wild beasts beyond her control. The glory of Africa as a beautiful land filled with gentle people and helpful, exotic animals and birds is also celebrated. There is much dancing and singing in this version. The young children even work together with Kirikou to save their poisoned mothers. Yet, while *Kirikou and the Wild Beasts* extends the story of Kirikou's triumphs, and exploits additional computer-aided techniques, it was *Azur et Asmar* (*Azur and Asmar, The Princes' Quest*, 2006) that revealed Ocelot's storytelling and style had taken a huge leap forward, expanding his own range while broadening the field of European animation.

For *Azur and Asmar*, Michel Ocelot switched to Nord-Ouest Productions, with Christophe Rossignon as producer. Rossignon had produced many live action successes, including *La Haine/Hate* (Kassovitz, 1995), *Irreversible* (Noé, 2002), and *Joyeux Noël/Merry Christmas* (Carion, 2005). Thanks to Kirikou's success, they had luck pre-selling Ocelot's new project, and its budget eventually reached 10 million euros. Moreover, since Kirkou had become a popular character for children's books and games, the French publisher Nathan signed on early to release a book based on *Azur and Asmar*. Thus, while Ocelot was at work on this film, he had a broader team of producers signing advance deals and plotting out marketing than had been possible with *Kirikou and the Sorceress*. For distribution, rather than the more specialized animation house Gebeka, Ocelot signed with Diaphana which had handled *Les Triplettes de Belleville* (Chomet, 2003) and scores of live action films. Clearly, *Azur and Asmar* was being produced and marketed more along the lines of a mini-major production, which exceeded the opportunities open to most other European animated features, except perhaps Aardman's *Chicken Run* (2000) and *Flushed Away* (2006).

Azur and Asmar begins with two babies, blonde and blue-eyed Azur, and Asmar, of Arab descent, being breast-fed by Asmar's mother, Jenane, who is Azur's wet-nurse. When she later tries to teach them language, she has trouble convincing Azur to address her as "Nanny" and Asmar to call her "Momma." The boys see no difference between themselves, so she is nanny and mother to both. Jenane also tells them a tale of a fairy princess, a Djinn Fairy, who is imprisoned far away in her native homeland, and must be rescued one day. Both boys vow from an early age to find and free the Djinn Princess, as Jenane's tale fires their fascination with the mysterious and magical Orient. As they grow, the boys squabble and fight, much like competitive brothers, and Azur's haughty noble father becomes increasingly worried about Azur's association with Jenane and her son. At one point when the boys are fighting, covered in mud, he has to ask, "Which of you is Azur?" The father sends Azur away for schooling and cruelly dismisses Jenane and Asmar. Years later, the grown Azur leaves his Western European home to cross the seas to Jenane's exotic distant land, somewhere in the Middle East. There he must hide his blue eyes from the superstitious locals, so feigns blindness, and is guided about by a comical ex-patriot, Crapoux. Along the way Azur cleverly discovers two of the fabled three keys necessary to save the Djinn fairy (Plate 33).

Once Azur locates Jenane and the now hostile Asmar, the story shifts to the competing young men riding off to save the Princess. Ocelot inserts them in an amazing Oriental land reminiscent of *Prince Achmed*. After harrowing, fantastic challenges, including getting past a ferocious red lion, the two learn that they must work together to win the prize. Azur has two keys while Asmar possesses the third, essential, key. Azur and a badly wounded Asmar finally enter the protected cave, free the Djinn Princess, and are each rewarded with love. The beautiful Arab Djinn Princess finally selects Azur for her mate, while her blonde cousin, the Fairy Elf Princess, chooses Asmar. The story's symmetry and themes of cross-cultural toler-ance have come full circle. Jenane and Asmar, who were destitute when thrown out of Azur's home, are now the richest people in her homeland.

Azur, once wealthy, had to beg to survive in their land. And, while Azur's father was a widower and Asmar's mother was single, the sons are both in happy couples that are interracial and intercultural. Ocelot's story exploits many European stereotypes while also presenting a revised Orientalism that emphasizes the Middle East as a matriarchal land offering great promise to Azur, the sensitive (non-colonialist) European.

Ocelot had once heard a true anecdote of a man from Britain who rediscovered his former nanny in Lebanon 30 years later, and she took him in as if he were her own son, though they could barely communicate. For *Azur et Asmar*, he retained the language conflicts by refusing to subtitle the Arab dialogue: "There are many languages in the world and no subtitles. I want people to accept this diversity" (interview, film DVD). While *Azur and Asmar* touches on cultural conflicts between West and East, as well as immigration, which are all very contemporary issues, it is simultaneously a universal fantasy, employing many plot points and character oppositions from the world of fairy tales. The story involves masquerades, including that of a young princess who secretly slips outside her castle to see "real" life, arduous travels far from home that cross seas and deserts, a mystical quest, and challenges of mind and body that test the young men's valor. It offers a colorful rite of passage for both boys. Asmar tames a magical, multicolored bird, while Azur wins over the scarlet lion with a roar all his own. In the end, it turns out the Djinn Princess, imprisoned in her glass chamber deep in a mountain cave, has had many opportunities to be freed, but none of her would-be saviors impressed her until now. Much like Ocelot's earlier tale of the princess and the diamond necklace, and Karaba cured by Kirikou, the Djinn Princess can now leave her throne and enjoy her body, moving freely.

Azur and Asmar retains one symbol common to Western Orientalist narratives, in that the European male must penetrate the Oriental woman's chamber and metaphorically unveil or "expose" her before possessing her (Shohat 1997: 33). However, Ocelot tempers that conventional trope by allowing the Oriental princess, and her blonde European cousin, to select which man they wish to marry. The women grant the men part of their power and their kingdoms. Another important Western epic theme is that Jenane admits to the Princess that she is merely a wealthy merchant and that neither of her sons is a real prince. The Djinn Princess declares that the men's brave and selfless conduct makes them princes, so they are indeed worthy mates for royalty (for more on this theme, see Jones 1993). Thus, the fable of two boys raised as brothers, separated as youths, and reunited in early manhood, ends with their happiness assured, thanks to the enlightened noblewoman. The two intercultural couples, moreover, are said by Azur's sidekick Crapoux to announce "the future."

Ocelot's fanciful, carefully structured story is built around rich binary oppositions. Yet the visual style also contains many productive contrasts. While the figures are built in computers, with access to 3D, most of the film, including the backgrounds, nonetheless preserves a hand-drawn, 2D aesthetic. Much more than *Kirikou and the Sorceress, Azur and Asmar* creates a vibrant tension between flatness and depth. Alain Bergala points out that Ocelot seems to be exploiting a sort of pre-Renaissance visual layout, with two incompatible perspective systems in the same film. Ocelot agrees that *Azur and Asmar* recalls the fifteenth century when the illusion of depth and realistic lighting cues were voluntary. Further, Ocelot points out that artists of Persia were unconcerned with monocular perspective, and he too is not interested in creating three-dimensional imagery for most elements. His characters may shift their bodies as they walk, but the clothing remains one flat color and surface: "On the clothes, I suppressed all the lighting cues, as I am not obsessed with fabrics. I kept delicate modeling for faces and hands ... I only want minimal cues ... I use the 3D with a light touch" (interview, film DVD). The characters retain some of the flatness of silhouettes and are typically staged in profile. Ocelot not only continues his distinct style of creating characters who resemble paper cut-outs, but he also prizes clarity in the image. Everything is drawn out first as detailed storyboards in small frames like comic strips, so he sketches every gesture and expression simply and retains that economy of line during the entire production (Plates 34 and 35).

The figures in *Azur and Asmar* are thus presented in bold, uniform colors. Though the facial gestures are controlled by sliders in 3D software, the faces and bodies retain a 2D look. Ocelot has never approved of conventional, mainstream 3D visuals, so he reserves 3D modeling for only occasional details, such as Jenane's exotic jewels. For the most part, despite the access to 3D software, the depth cues in *Azur and Asmar*, like those in *Kirikou and the Sorceress*, spring primarily from overlap between foreground and background objects, while the characters generally move horizontally across the screen in one flat plane of action. Ocelot has also famously stated that characters look better in profile; straight on, he claims, they resemble potatoes. The combination of storybook settings (including medieval Europe and the Orient, wild seas, barren deserts, fantastic creatures, and vibrantly colored fairies) with strong, appealing characters, made *Azur and*

Asmar another major success for Ocelot and French animation. It sold 1.5 million movie tickets in France during the fall of 2006. For context, *Cars* (Lasseter, 2006), which enjoyed a much more extensive advertising campaign, performed slightly better the previous summer, selling 1.9 million tickets.

Comic Book Aesthetics and Niche Studios

Michel Ocelot's success provided a production model for other French animators, as a small, but unprecedented cadre of animators began to produce feature films in France. During the summer of 2003, Philippe Leclerc's *Les Enfants de la pluie* (*Children of the Rain*) premiered at the Cannes Film Festival, though it never found a broad audience. Appealing mostly to comic book and science fiction fans, it sold 200,000 tickets in France. The film was produced by Belokan and MK2, with most animation by Hahn Shin studios in South Korea. Adapted from a novel by Serge Brussolo, and illustrated by the celebrated graphic artist Philippe Caza, *Children of the Rain* chronicles two enemy cultures that were formed when an ancient community, represented by a dragon, was cut in two: the clan from the desert, the Pyross people, have a feudal slave society and die if water touches them, while the peaceful, vegetarian Hydross tribe loves water and prizes music and dance. The Pyross are ruled by Razza and his cruel war-culture. During the dry season their knights, riding dinosaurs, scour the desert for hot sun stone crystals that serve as money and power sources in their kingdom. They also smash the Pyross cities, because the Pyross people must hibernate during the dry season, so they disguise themselves as statues, awaiting the rain to reanimate them (Plate 36). By contrast, during the rainy season the Pyross hide at home while the Hydross romp in the water. Eventually, a young Pyross foot soldier, Skan, whose parents both died because of Razza, falls in love with a Hydross princess, Kallisto. Skan and Kallisto learn from each other: he teaches her the value of fire while she teaches him to trust her people and follow his heart. Eventually, with help from a renegade band of Hydross hiding in the desert, Skan and Kallisto enter the Pyross fortress where Skan kills the evil Raza who turns out to be the fabled "Thief of Souls" wizard keeping the two halves apart. Skan thereby liberates both communities at once and the two sides of the smitten dragon are repaired. Further, the "impossible love" between Skan, child of the sun, and Kallisto, child of the rain, restores balance and harmony, curing the world with their union.

Children of the Rain conforms to a number of conventions and even clichés of European fantasy comic books: there are mythical themes, with dragons and an ancient prophecy, medieval icons including knights, dungeons, and tests of courage, but also lessons of youthful truth and love winning out over deceit and ignorance. The scene-to-scene plot structure also owes to classic graphic novel construction: alternating sequences showcase the conflicting value systems in this divided world. For instance, while the oblivious Skan and Kallisto flirt playfully beside a calm pool of water, his friends are staked out in the burning sand to die. The efficient, coherent graphic style also reflects a comic book layout, with the angular red-skinned Pyross in their brutal sand empire, contrasted with the round-faced turquoise Hydross, whose world owes more to art nouveau vine patterns. The animators used 3D to render the aquatic world of the Hydross and to plot out camera positions. However, the stiff, halting figures seem to have stepped recently off the static pages of a comic book, as if they are not quite competent at walking yet. There is no attempt to simulate realistic muscle action or to suggest bodies in motion, shifting their weight. In this stylized world, where every object bears a fateful, metaphorical significance, none of the figures move naturally or seem to have a life force all their own. Characters are outlined by strict contour edges, not unlike cut-out figures. Despite occasional strong shadows, there are few volume cues in *Children of the Rain* and no texture differences between surfaces. For instance, when Skan stands against a building, there are no markers to suggest his skin is made of a material that is any different from the wall. Similarly, the pond of water surrounding Kallisto resembles her skin. Characters quite literally match their surroundings (Plate 37).

Children of the Rain is rather typical of the modes of production of much European animation. The layout and storyboards were all directed by Philippe Leclerc and his team in France, where the music was also composed, while the actual animation, including the final digital compositing, where the decor, colors, painted figures, camera movements, and sound are combined in the computers, was accomplished in South Korea. The clever script, evocative soundtrack, and poetic visuals of *Children of the Rain* generate a cluster of rather complex central figures whose actions are determined by destiny and family histories. The fantasy successfully synthesizes comic book traditions, primarily determined by Caza's personal style, with cinematic norms of animation which use 3D to assist with what still remains a 2D animated world. Leclerc more recently directed another fantasy drama set in an alien era, *La Reine soleil* (*The Sun Queen*, 2007), which features a very crisp, bright visual style full of strong contrasts, to serve the setting of sunny, ancient Egypt. Based on the book by Christian Jacq, the film follows the rambunctious young Egyptian princess Akhesa (Ankhesenpaaten), who is unhappy living with her father, Pharaoh Akhenaten. She sneaks off with young Prince Thout (or Tut, the future Pharaoh Tutenkamen) on a dangerous voyage to find her exiled mother, Queen Nefertiti. In the spirit of *Children of the Rain*, the youths, who remain somewhat childish but also intelligent and resourceful beyond their years, manage to challenge the patriarchs and overturn the rigid rules put in place by scheming adults. Once again, much of the world is split in two, symbolized by the dry sunny realm of the Pharaoh and watery haven of the Queen mother Thanks to their budding romance, the young couple eventually bring about the end of injustice, ensuring a fair and culturally rich world.

For *The Sun Queen*, Leclerc and this team emphasize the exotic locale, presenting a hot sunny environment alternating with deep blue and purple for nights full of danger. The overall color palette may be more striking than that of *Children of the Rain*, with bright, saturated hues, yet both films share divided worlds and massive architectural constructions and statuary that emphasize the pompous, vain side of pageantry that comes with tyranny. Backgrounds and buildings tend toward simplified computer generated forms, including the triangles, rectangles, and cones that make up Sun City, while props such as palm fronds are treated as large flat shapes with a single color green, as if cut from construction paper. The boat on the river is typical: it is composed of only two browns, has a pure white sail, and the burning sky above is one bright yellow. Similarly, there are few texture cues between skin, sand, or clothes. However, with its theme songs, a comical cat side-kick, and perky voice work, and a plot revolving around a headstrong young princess trying to save her family and people, *The Sun Queen* is a project designed to copy aspects of Disney's trademark tales. Despite an expensive advertising campaign, this feature failed to find a large audience and only received limited theatrical releases internationally. This mix of personal style and popular genre cinema conventions failed to point the way for commercial feature-length animation projects, revealing once more the difficulty of finding a viable formula to compete with the American model (Plate 38).

Another major figure from 2003 proved to be Sylvain Chomet. His *Les Triplettes de Belleville* (*The Triplets of Belleville*) became a strong force in the revival of European animation. Chomet first gained a following with his short, *La Vieille dame et les pigeons* (*The Old Woman and the Pigeons*), which won the Grand Prize at Annecy in 1997 and was nominated for an Academy Award. That 23-minute film establishes many of the eccentric character models and cultural stereotypes that later populate *The Triplets of Belleville*. For instance, *The Old Woman and the Pigeons* opens with poorly framed snap-shots being taken beneath the Eiffel Tower accompanied by voices-over from American tourists: "Poor little Junior is hungry; you don't want to go to no French restaurant do you? . . . They eat weird stuff like horse and donkey and cheese from a goat." These bulging pear-shaped characters made of rolling fat are prototypes for the later inhabitants of Belleville. However, subsequent scenes also lampoon the French, including the lanky, suspicious gendarme, who could be Jacques Tati's cousin. His wandering character connects the disparate scenes. In one small park he hungrily watches an elderly woman feed the fat pigeons fine pastries. That night, the poor officer eats a meager dinner in his depressing flat.

The action in *The Old Woman and the Pigeons* accumulates rather than following any generic plot line. The policeman dreams of the old lady feeding him, while the pigeons stand around and watch. The next day he captures a number of pigeons, plucking them to make a huge pigeon outfit from their feathers. Dressed as a pigeon, he shows up at the woman's apartment where she welcomes him into her home and serves him a table full of food. After repeated visits, the officer gains weight and begins to move with pigeon-like gestures and dance steps. Eventually, this glutton bloats like the American tourists. The old lady attacks him with shears, apparently deciding to eat her gigantic fattened bird, though he escapes, falling out her window. The film ends with a return to some Americans, now apparently at home watching their own super-8 footage of the Eiffel Tower. In their footage, the policeman, now thin and stripped of his shirt, hops about among the begging pigeons, while the former tourists turn their conversation back to the awful things the French eat. Other than the opening and closing scenes with English-speaking tourists, there is no language spoken in the film. As in Tati's cinema, sound effects and an occasional accordion replace dialogue on most of the soundtrack. Chomet's cartoony figures and settings provide distinctive cultural caricatures and distorted settings, all of which will be expanded in his first feature.

Initially, Sylvain Chomet had a contract for another short film with Didier Brunner of Les Armateurs. However, gradually Chomet came to realize he could combine several of his plot lines into a feature. *Kirikou and the Sorceress* had just come out, earning strong profits for Les Armateurs and proving the potential value of unusual animated features. *The Triplets of Belleville* was made for roughly €8,000,000, which Brunner raised from a wide variety of sources, 19 in all, from a number of countries. Within France there were regional funds such as the region of Charente, home to the animation hub Angoulême, but other investors included Belgian, Canadian, and British companies and institutions, such as the BBC. The story, which owes heavily in spirit, sound effects, and humor to Jacques Tati, to whom it is dedicated, loops from a nostalgic, 1950s-era Paris working-class neighborhood of Belleville across the Atlantic to the big, bad city of Belleville and back. But it also owes to cultural and artistic traditions from Canada, where Chomet had worked for Disney, as well as to Belgian comic traditions, American cartoons, and French music, TV, and movies. As the *New York Times* review proclaims: "For all its irony and technical virtuosity, *The Triplets of Belleville* most effectively seduces us with the ambience that emanates from its rich allusions to a known or reimagined past. . . . Individual frames are bursting with cultural references, sight gags, wordplay and graphical sleight of hand – too many to keep track of but they give the film a dreamlike aura" (Clements 2003). Fortunately for Chomet and Brunner, the risks taken on *The Triplets of Belleville* paid off handsomely, and it even received a nomination for an Academy Award, though it lost out to *Finding Nemo* (Stanton, Unkrich, 2003), another film about a kidnapped son and an eccentric relative who must travel a great distance to rescue him.

Chomet "wrote" the film primarily in storyboards, a process that recalls Michel Ocelot's "scénarimage." Initially there was to be a voice-over, but that was abandoned for a Tati-like soundtrack built from poignant sound effects and music, just as in *The Old Woman and the Pigeons*. *The Triplets of Belleville* opens with a surreal, Fleischer-like sequence, in sepia, as if it were an old, scratched newsreel or variety show now seen on a black-and-white television. Grotesque spectators, primarily made up of gigantic, marshmallow-like wives and minuscule husbands, show up for a live radio show built around the three singing triplets belting out their "Swinging Belleville Rendez-vous." During the song, caricatures of several real entertainers take the stage, including Fred Astaire, whose shoes rebel and devour him, and Josephine Baker, whose topless routine transforms the little old men into monkeys, clutching at her banana skirt. The triplets then disappear for over

30 minutes of screen time, as the plot shifts to a short, elderly woman with a club-foot, Mme Souza, and her grandson, Champion, several decades later. They are watching the re-runs of the triplets on television within their isolated house on the edges of Paris. From photos in Champion's room one can gather that his parents have died and Champion is now Souza's responsibility. She buys him a puppy and makes repeated efforts to find the boy a happy pastime, before she discovers his love of bicycles and racing, which may be tied to an old photo of his parents, happily posing by their bike (Plate 39).

In one of the many amazing scene transitions in Chomet's film, there is a shift from the ecstatic, plump, young Champion riding his red tricycle in circles in his little garden, to a montage of the home as seasons pass and the city, with its cranes, buildings, and electric poles, encroaches upon their space. An elevated commuter train trestle eventually pushes up against their home. On a stormy night, with the wind blowing their *Jour de fête* (Tati, 1949) wind vane, the dog Bruno, now fat and old, barks out his window at passing train passengers. Years have passed in seconds and the future is rather dismal. We discover Champion, now an exhausted stick of a man, biking through the rainy streets, while Souza keeps the cadence on her whistle, following behind on the old tricycle. She is training him to be a racer. Back at home she exercises his muscles with a push lawn mower and vacuum. After another fanciful transition, through the dog's black-and-white dream, the film seems to come out of a dark tunnel into sunny southern France where Champion is riding in the Tour de France. Souza and Bruno follow in a van. However, two thugs, shaped like black rectangles, abduct Champion and two other riders and take them off to America aboard a stylized ocean liner. In pursuit, Mme Souza rents a paddle boat and she and Bruno follow across the ocean in a poetic scene that allows Chomet to toss them about on impressive waves (Plates 40 and 41).

In bustling Belleville, the impoverished Souza is taken in by the eccentric aging triplets, who seem to survive only on frogs they blow up in the marsh. Souza even becomes part of their new act, performing music on household objects; she plays bicycle spokes. Souza also tracks Champion down to a mysterious bicycle gambling club in the French Wine Center. The bikers, fueled by red wine, pedal fixed bikes while looking at movies of French roads projected on a screen. The absurdly satirical action and exaggerated caricatures in Belleville are reminiscent of the graphics of 1960s Mad Magazines. Eventually, the triplets and Mme Souza manage to spring the bikers free and outsmart the ridiculous French gangsters, as Champion pedals them all off to freedom on his racing contraption. They slowly move off like a parade float slugging steadily out of town. In the final shot, Champion, now older, is watching TV and turns to say his only words: "It's over grandma." Bracketed by the beginning and ending television scenes, *The Triplets of Belleville* comes full circle, and reinforces its alternative story structure. Unlike most Hollywood features, this is not the tale of an "I think I can" child who conquers all odds to succeed. The lonely boy does not grow up to become the success his name suggests. Champion is not a hero, and he is more like an object than a character. If there is a protagonist, it is the grandmother. Her actions drive the plot and return the son. However, there is little character development, and the slow, lumbering dog gets more screen time than most other characters. Chomet's episodic tale defies norms of character motivation and unfurls with a unique rhythm and sense of humor all its own.

The lack of dialogue not only makes *The Triplets of Belleville* more dreamlike, but it also puts more pressure on the functions of the image and music. Chomet's designs make full use of clever visual cues to guide our attention, including the distinctive character shapes and the emphasis on eyes and seeing. The extreme nose on Champion helps the audience recognize him in the grown, gaunt biker, though he had last been seen as a chubby boy, and the flat black blocks of the gangsters can be detected at a distance in any setting. Moreover, Souza's mood and psychology are reflected through a number of subtle cues, including the way she snaps her glasses and what she chooses to observe. During the Tour de France, for instance, she looks through a telescope to catch a fan handing Champion a water bottle. That action nearly slows to a freeze frame as Champion turns to the fan, in apparent appreciation. The next shot of Souza, clutching the telescope to her chest and blinking, suggests her pride and satisfaction. The sound effects, including the click of Souza's glasses and the clomp of her big shoe, work with the music and the clever visual efficiency to reinforce the film's surreal rhythm. According to Chomet, "Since I come from BD [*bande dessinée* or comic books] and a school advocating caricatural realism, I wanted to transpose those traits onto the movie screen" (Pasamonik and Alion 2003: 40). He creates an evocative but playfully satirical world.

Chomet's fanciful style reveals his willingness to return to the essence of animation: objects readily shift and change before our eyes. De Gaulle's face on a newspaper, glimpsed in the train, can suddenly come alive as it is rapidly transposed onto a television screen in a nearby apartment. A pot full of tadpoles can morph into the face of the moon. Chomet foregrounds animation's magical ability to reduce referential objects to a few lines, only to breathe life back into those nearly abstract sketches. The obvious marks of narration and surprising ellipses in *The Triplets of Belleville* call the spectator's attention to the surface of the image and the narrator's clever manipulation, finally challenging the audience actively to perceive and comprehend the time, space, and action. This movie is as much about the glories of animation as it is about an eccentric, dedicated grandmother. In Chomet's cinema, the process is part of the product. For instance, during the "Making of" for the French DVD supplements, Chomet demonstrates how animators work with both hands. With the right hand, he draws the characters in their environment, with the left hand he flips through the previous pages to see how each sketch moves in relation to the others: the right hand creates the space while the left hand creates time. That act of simultaneously creating space and time is constantly on display in *The Triplets of Belleville*. Further, the graphic style of the film retains cartoony thick dark lines around most characters and props, preserving the look of an artist's ink on paper. Everything, including the mechanical objects such as bicycles, passenger ships, and the elongated cars and skyscrapers of Belleville, seem to be hand-drawn, even though 3D CGI is central to the process.

Part of Chomet's distinct visual look arises from his particular application of computer animation techniques. Typically, 3D software programs assume one wants a crisp, clean image. However, Chomet and his team wanted to preserve some of the pencil effects and hand-drawn feel despite the use of computers. The animators began with 2D drawings and combined them with 3D, but they also used an additional program during digitization that would restore some of the softness and lack of focus to the environment. For instance, in creating the Tour de France sequences, initial black-and-white models for Champion and other characters were accomplished in 3D, then individual frames were printed out for the animators to redraw in 2D before they were scanned back into the computers where color and other lighting effects were added. The computer-assisted animation lends important advantages for many aspects of the visual world of *The Triplets of Belleville*, including the virtual camera movements and rack focus effects, the spinning bicycle spokes, the undulating streets of Paris in the rain, and the fluid movement of the shifting waves during the ocean crossing. The combination of 2D aesthetics with 3D modeling yields a very rich and functional environment for Chomet's fascinating array of characters.

The surreal aspects of *The Triplets of Belleville* function on every level, from the sudden shifts in setting and tone, including the dog's black and white dreams, to the rich array of fascinating characters. The triplets themselves were actually based on earlier sketches Chomet had made of African-American basketball players he observed in the parks of New York City. Long, drawn-out fellows with seemingly endless arms were transformed into the lanky singing sisters, Blanche, Rose, and Violette. Given the film's title, one joke is that the triplets are not more central to the plot, though their strange lifestyle dynamiting ponds for frogs and licking frozen frog-sicles certainly establishes them as crucial to the comically bizarre milieu of Chomet's fictional universe. Their musical performance plucking on refrigerator shelves and squeezing eery sounds from a vacuum provides another break from the action of Souza's pursuit of Champion's trail. Suddenly, however, it is at their cabaret performance that Bruno picks up the scent for the rescue and the story can move forth. The plot, like the hobbling gait of Mme Souza, careens about in a wildly chaotic fashion, while the characters encountered along the way, from the Tour de France van driver to the paddle boat operator to the sweet, bloated Belleville boy scout, each seem to deserve their own feature film. Even the crazy gendarme from *The Old Woman and the Pigeons* makes a brief cameo appearance among the roster of characters populating this strangely melancholy world.

Chomet's meandering story, with its surprisingly endearing caricatures, combined with his evocative visual style and intricate soundtrack, provided yet another convincing example of France's distinctive renewal in animation. *The Triplets of Belleville* became an international art house hit, selling 800,000 tickets at home, an estimated $14 million worldwide, and half of that from the USA alone. Importantly, none of France's recent successful films followed the Hollywood formula of building from a comical gag structure. Sebastien Denis explains that while a graphic sensibility is very developed in France, the visual gag is not: "Far from sharing the visual efficiency of American cartoons, they develop an 'intellectual' form of animation" (Denis 2007: 187). Instead, what is striking about French animation is its unique tone, often combining serious elements with caricature. Unlike fast-paced, impatient Hollywood cartoons, the French are not afraid to slow the action down where needed. Hence, in international markets, *Kirikou and the Sorceress* and *The Triplets of Belleville* were seen as quite exotic and unexpected films. Both, however, were products of a long history of animation, well-known in Europe, that nonetheless helped strengthen France's cultural image around the world.

A number of important figures helped prepare for and continue France's recent wave of offbeat feature-length animation. In 1984 a small artisanal studio, Folimage, was founded by Jacques-Rémy Girerd in Valence in southern France; it expanded in the 1990s and specialized in producing cartoons for children. Among their successes was the ecological series, *Ma Petite planète chérie* [*My Little Planet, Dear*, 1999]. Not unlike La Fabrique, Folimage brings together a small cadre of animators to work on shared projects. For instance, Michael Dudok de Vit's *Le Moine et le poisson* (*The Monk and the Fish*, 1994), produced at Folimage, was nominated for an Oscar and won the French César for short animation. Folimage markets itself as "a center for frame-by-frame creativity where almost anything is possible. It's a magical place, built up gradually thanks to the will, the talent and the imagination of around a hundred artists and technicians." Folimage added its own animation school in 1999. Their first feature, Girerd's *La Prophétie des grenouilles* (*Raining Cats and Frogs*, or *The Frog Prophecy*), was released in 2003. It is a variation on the story of Noah's ark and the flood. In Girerd's version, a farming family, warned by an intelligent network of frogs, manages to save their small zoo by converting their barn into a floating ship. Adrift on the flooded earth they also have to fight off threats by rapacious alligators. Everyone on the ship must learn to respect one another and work together, including the hungry tiger and the skittish chickens, in this quirky, pacifist drama.

While the fable is clearly aimed at children, the movie does not talk down to them, and it includes mature touches such as bugs having sex, characters drinking pastis, and a deceptive "mother" turtle who turns out to have a penis. Nonetheless, visually this film retains an array of cartoony characters, including the round old sailor Grand pa, who could be Popeye's descendant, his joyous Caribbean wife, the little girl Lili with her orange and yellow hair, and the comic book animals standing on their hind legs. There is no attempt to make a lion move any differently than a turtle or a human; all the characters' motions are slightly jerky, as if they were made from paper cut-outs. Further, everything looks as if it were drawn with crayons or colored pencils. Many surfaces, including wooden walls and the frog pond, are created from uneven crayon marks. Black lines outline all characters, the sky resembles mottled construction paper, and the old man's beard hangs from his face like a paper white scarf. Other than occasional shadows under foot, there are few detail cues for volume or texture. Jacques-Rémy Girerd's cheerful characters and witty dialogue are reinforced with a breezy comic style featuring good natured caricatures, saturated colors, and a strong, evocative soundtrack, including vocal work from veteran actors Michel Piccoli and Annie Girardot. Girerd followed *Raining Cats and Frogs* with a $12 million feature, *Mia et le Migou* (*Mia and the Migoo*, 2008), about a young girl who travels to South America in pursuit of her father. *Mia and the Migoo* retains a peppy rhythm and warm, friendly character drawings that recall the girls in Hayao Miyazaki's *My Neighbor Totoro* (1988). The background painting of the environment emphasizes the beauty and power of nature, but also incorporates a great deal of colorful abstraction, with many shots that seem to offer loving tributes to Van Gogh. *Mia and the Migoo* continues Girerd's concerns with the environment and the value of cooperation and tolerance. It sold over 400,000 tickets in France and enjoyed strong DVD sales as well (Plates 42 and 43).

Contemporary French Animation: 2006 and Beyond

Thanks to companies like Folimage, French animation continued to strengthen, reaching a peak in 2006. That year was also a high point internationally. According to Stéphane Le Bars, director of the French animation trade organization SPFA, 26 animated features were released worldwide in 2006; 45 percent were American, with Japan and France tied at 20 percent each. Further, animated features accounted for 15 percent of France's box office that year. Among France's entries were *U* by Serge Elissalde and Grégoire Solotareff and *Renaissance* by Christian Volckman. These two movies targeted distinctly separate core audiences. *U* is a coming of age drama about a whiny dog-like princess named Mona. Sad, lonely Mona is suddenly befriended by a magical unicorn-girl, *U*, who serves as her guardian angel, best friend, and analyst. Eventually, a dashing male cat Kulka and his gypsy musicians, known collectively as the "wéwés," camp out in the nearby forest. Once Mona grows up a bit and falls in love with Kulka, *U*'s work is done. Sadly, she shrinks down to almost nothing and floats off toward the moon, unsure where she will appear next. While *U* and Mona will miss one another, *U* must disappear so she may help other little girls grow up as well. Kulka and Mona, hand-in-hand, decide to tour the world together, and the tale comes to a bittersweet close. It is a fable about a self-centered girl's moodiness and growing pains; she must learn to trust in others to be happy. But *U* also displays a rather odd sense of humor, thanks to its playfully exaggerated characters.

U's lively soundtrack foregrounds the jazzy guitar music by Sanseverino, who also provides the laid-back vocals for dreamy Kulka the cat. Other voices include veteran actress Bernadette Lafont, with Isild Le Besco as Mona. Visually, the film nearly pulsates to Sanseverino's rhythms. Solotareff and Elissalde craft a casual, colorful world populated by good-natured caricatures. Drawn with felt tip pens to emphasize the hand-made quality and provide saturated colors, the images are scanned into computers but retain a painterly look, rather than any obvious digital effects. Hardly a single straight line is to be found. The color palette is dominated by red, blue, and yellow, and characters seem to flow rather than walk in this vibrant setting. *U* sold a respectable 250,000 tickets in its first run. According to *Variety*, "*U* is a trippy, comical but also very gabby fable about a faintly canine creature's transition from misunderstood girlhood to first stirrings of romance ... peppered with sly visual references, from Rembrandt to Jean-Luc Godard by way of Magritte" (Nesselson 2006: 45). Solotareff and Elissalde's endearing graphic style provides another extreme option for French animators seeking to preserve their own personal visuals in the face of the necessary stylistic coherence of a commercially viable feature-length film. Thanks to *U*'s peppy music and fresh, comic book characters with their long, heart-felt conversations, this fairy tale of a young girl growing into her own avoids most of the traps of Disney's children's fare while presenting an engaging alternate universe as distinct as that in *The Triplets of Belleville*.

A very different alien world is presented by *Renaissance*. A stark black and white science fiction film set in the Paris of 2054, *Renaissance* is aimed at sci-fi fans among teenagers and young adults. This movie was begun as a high concept project. Animator and motion capture experimenter Marc Miance had seen a black and white 3D demonstration at Monaco's Imagina festival in 1998. Next, Miance, actor/director Christian Volckman, and producer Aton Soumache made a short film, *Maaz* (1999), inserting Volckman into a surreal, expressionist 3D setting. That experience motivated them to find a feature-length topic to exploit CGI, motion capture, and high contrast black and white 3D images. They chose *Renaissance* since it combined film noir aspects of Raymond Chandler with a bleak futuristic plot in the vein of Philip K. Dick novels. Other influences include German Expressionism, Hollywood crime dramas, Japanese anime, graphic novels (especially Frank Miller's monochromatic *Sin City*), and the haunted retro-science fiction of *Blade Runner* (Scott, 1982). The entire production team was young; all were in their 20s. IBM helped develop some of the CGI techniques and also participated in the marketing, and *Renaissance* found early support from Citroën among others (the streamlined cars all sport the Citroën logo). The distribution and marketing plan began early, eventually expending three years and 1.5 million euros (Rouvillois 2007). *Renaissance* was a daring project. The film's harsh, often abstract style resembles an inky graphic novel in motion, but it also risked alienating viewers with its relentless onslaught of nightmarish, dark imagery. The new technology allowed them to populate 90 different virtual locations, bringing movement and the pacing of a thriller together with extreme graphic novel sensibilities. Like Richard Linklater's *Waking Life* (2002) and *A Scanner Darkly* (2006), *Renaissance* pushes the frontiers, and definitions, of computer animation.

Renaissance begins with the kidnapping of a beautiful young researcher, Ilona, an employee of the vast mega-corporation Avalon, which controls many aspects of life in Paris of the future. A tough cop, Captain Karas, is brought in to rescue her. Karas, in the tradition of hard-boiled detectives, ruffles the feathers of all authority figures, befriends and beds Ilona's older sister, Bislane, and manages to chase down the man behind the kidnapping, Dr. Muller, a former Avalon researcher and Ilona's mentor. In the process, Karas gets suspended from the force, gains help from a former friend, Farfella, now head of the mafia, and learns that Avalon was secretly researching immortality. Muller, whose little brother had a deadly childhood disease, managed to find the key to longevity, which has kept his pathetic brother alive. But, he has imprisoned Ilona because she had stumbled on the secret process. Muller has realized immortality can only harm humanity, since life without death has no meaning, and he is now trying to save the world by keeping the secret from Avalon. Muller dies, and as soon as Karas rescues Ilona he realizes he must kill her and cover up the whole project (Figure 5.1).

The setting is a hybrid of traditional Paris landmarks and futuristic glass infrastructures, including bridges and sidewalks, that seem designed for constant surveillance. It is a world of screens and reflective surfaces that privilege voyeurism. Further, the fanciful camera angles fragment Paris via extreme points of view. For instance, a low-angle shot from a subterranean passage in front of Notre Dame reveals pedestrians seeming to walk across the face of the cathedral, stepping on the statues. Holograms pop up regularly, and even identity cards come to life as virtual video screens. Volckman inserts many dazzling transitions between shots, taking full advantage of the potential of CGI to exceed the page-to-page rhythm of a graphic novel. The sequence of Ilona's kidnapping provides a dizzying

Figure 5.1   Ilona and the graphic novel aesthetic in *Renaissance*, produced by Onyx Films, directed by Christian Volckman, 2006.

display of this dynamic, exhibitionist world. Part of her abduction is reflected in the eye of her dead dog. As Ilona is grabbed, her purse falls to the ground, tossing out her identity card so that her video photo is activated. The camera cants and zooms in to the card, isolating her videographic face, then begins to zoom out on a virtual wall of projected faces from identity cards just like hers, as a police officer walks behind them. The camera pans and dollies left to follow this character through a hallway at the police headquarters for Section K, the kidnapping specialists, and onto a sort of balcony where other officers look at a curved video screen to monitor a SWAT team approaching a building. During the zoom to the front of the building a lap-dissolve and beep signal that we have crossed from the virtual screen to the "real" event. There is a suspected kidnapped victim inside, but it is not Ilona's case. Rather, Captain Karas is introduced here as he single-handedly kills the team of heavily armed kidnappers, despite being ordered by his superiors to "fall back." His daring success gets him assigned to Ilona's high priority and dangerous case (perhaps as a set-up to silence him for good).

The busy mixture of motion-capture, frenetic camera movements, and extreme shot scales and angles, creates an alien world in constant flux. *Renaissance*, in the tradition of *Blade Runner* and *Robocop* (Verheoven, 1987), is suspicious of a future controlled by the wrong people and a totalitarian corporation. The emphasis on striking imagery also parallels the visual traditions of graphic novels and Japanese manga. However, the visuals also struggle to provide enough variety that the stark black and white does not become too visually oppressive. In one shot, near the Eiffel Tower, Karas descends into a subway, not realizing his partner Pierre, above him at ground level, is being attacked by men in invisibility suits. Seen through the glass "ground," Pierre and others appear gray rather than the usual black silhouettes. The perverse "dance" of Pierre in the distance responding to blows from invisible thugs, while the oblivious Karas walks off in the foreground, helps open up the forced limits of this bizarre monochromatic world. One of the more fascinating settings involves the strange bubble "cell" where Ilona is detained by Muller and his brother. Ilona is kept in what looks like a snow globe that can magically expand as she moves through its dream-world forest and meadows. Such scenes in bright locations with some gray tones, along with the occasional fades to white, provide brief respites for the eyes, in contrast to the many inky dark shots that force the viewer to scan the few white lines for spatial cues before recognizing characters moving through complex black environments. The reliance on black, white, and only occasional grays, yields what may be the most limited visual range in the history of feature films. The sole visual exception to the black and white restrictions are brief saturated color drawings by Muller's genetically altered brother, who twice uses bright crayons to draw flowers while guarding Ilona in her virtual forest.

As the Eiffel Tower scene illustrates, Volckman exploits glass surfaces in his shot compositions, often avoiding standard continuity editing, and especially shot reverse shot conversations, by composing figures in depth or via sometimes jarring reflections. For instance, at the end, when Karas lies to Bislane, claiming Ilona ran away safely, their two-shot is doubled, with the second rendering of them inserted in the distance, as if a reflection or a combination of two perspectives on their conversation on some video monitor (Figure 5.2). In this world, one never knows who is watching. Only Karas finally proves he can stay slightly ahead of all the confusing, often misleading, appearances and misrepresentations. He is "old school" and works on impulse and hunches, though too many people end up dying around him thanks to his brash methods. However, visually, Karas is hardly equivalent to *Blade Runner*'s more psychologically complex Detective Deckard. Karas is more a type than a character, despite the earnest voice work by Robert Dauney (and Daniel Craig in the English version). And throughout, an unsettling tension results from the sketchy characterization and the finely detailed bodily movement. According to Markos Hadjioannou, "The impact the characters make on the audience is not strong enough to override their graphic quality." They seem "bodiless" (Hadjioannou

Figure 5.2   Karas and Bislane are doubled in the frame. *Renaissance*, produced by Onyx Films, directed by Christian Volckman, 2006.

2008: 129). With international first-run earnings of only $1.8 million, or roughly 10 percent its budget, *Renaissance* never achieved the sort of box office success that its cutting-edge mode of production and futuristic thriller plot line seemed to warrant. However, it provides an instructive experiment for others to ponder as digital artists continue to explore how to combine CGI, performance capture, and animation.

   While *Renaissance* is a concept package to mimic the *bande dessinée* aesthetic, *Persepolis* is a direct adaptation of Marjane Satrapi's popular graphic novel, based on her own life growing up in Iran and eventually moving to Europe. *Persepolis* too is drawn primarily in black and white, but offers pulsating contrasts and haunting, stark imagery that help avoid the oppressive darkness of *Renaissance*. Not only is *Persepolis* a very personal project for Satrapi, its mode of production follows many of the conventions of France's small-scale animation houses. This is an intimate project created by a devoted team of friends and acquaintances. Satrapi's four-volume graphic novel series was published in France, beginning in 2000. The episodes follow Marjane Satrapi, born in 1970, as she grows up in tumultuous Iran among a wealthy, educated, leftist family. The first volume recounts parts of her family history, including the imprisonment of her grandparents under the Shah and the death of her uncle under the Islamic regime. Next, a teenaged Marjane witnesses the excesses of the growing repression at home and the war with Iraq, until her parents decide to send her to Austria for her education, far from the growing dangers in Iran. The third installment recounts Marjane's difficult time maturing in Europe.

While relatively free, and surrounded by the bounties of Western European society, she suffers from culture shock, searches for meaningful friendships, but mostly endures a sense of isolation and frustrated rebellion. Finally, lost, sick and homeless, Marjane returns to Iran for the fourth volume. Back in Iran, the 20-something Marjane continues to feel alienated, realizing she will always live between two cultures no matter where she is. After sinking into suicidal depression she regains her bearings, dates again, and even marries, before deciding she will never adapt to life in Iran under Islamic rule. A newly divorced Marjane leaves home a second time, with the blessing of her parents and grandmother, all of whom encourage her to remain true to her values as a liberated woman of the world.

The books found a strong following and were translated widely around the world. The universal theme of a girl coming of age in a seemingly impossible environment was coupled with the timely, critical glance into the troubled history of Iran, first under the Shah, then during the Islamic Revolution. Young Marjane even debates God and Karl Marx, looking for answers to the sorts of impossible questions that frustrate every smart child. Marjane Satrapi's haunting yet occasionally comical tale brought new insight to readers in the West who could easily feel alignment and eventually allegiance for this critic of Iran's repression. For many in the West, she seemed just like the girl next door, with normal desires to dance, flirt, and let her hair blow in the breeze, but she was trapped in a land that denies such basic human liberties. Satrapi and her friend, graphic artist Vincent Paronnaud (who also works under the pen-name Winshluss), reworked the 365-page series into a movie script, taking advantage of cinematic devices, including evocative voice-work, camera movement, music, and even jump cuts, in an effort to transform the graphic novel into a new sort of more cinematic text. The music was composed by Olivier Bernet, Paronnaud's friend and longtime musical collaborator.

Persepolis was the first film by producers Marc-Antoine Robert and Xavier Rigault, both of whom had full-time day jobs in the industry. They had just formed their own company, 2.4.7., and Robert was a friend of Satrapi's. But, they were hesitant to undertake a black and white animated film as their first feature. Rigault gained confidence in the project when shown a famous letter from François Truffaut at the time of *Confidentially Yours* (1983), listing all the important films shot in black and white. They also realized Satrapi's story was pre-sold and the film's radical 2D monochromatic look could be a productive marketing angle. Further evidence of the project's potential came soon after, when American producer Kathleen

Kennedy, best known for her ties with Steven Spielberg, contacted Marjane Satrapi, interested in the movie rights to *Persepolis*. Kennedy became an associate producer, securing the American distribution contract with Sony before the film was even completed. Marc Jousset, another of Paronnaud's acquaintances, was brought on as art director, while Pascal Chevé helped animate as well. Jousset and Chevé each have their own small animation studios. The entire film was completed in France for 6 million euros, or roughly half that of a contemporary big-budget live-action feature such as *Tell No One* (Canet, 2007).

While the graphic novel *Persepolis* opens with Marjane as a school girl, comically indistinguishable visually from her classmates because of their head scarves, the film begins in the present, with Marjane as a grown woman carefully donning a veil in the Paris Orly Airport. The movie is bracketed with scenes of her character preparing for a flight to Tehran she will not take, and finally leaving the airport in a taxi, pretending to the driver she has just arrived from Iran. Apparently, as a home-sick exile, there were times the real Satrapi would go to the airport to watch Iranian flights arrive and depart. This reflexive narrative device makes the entire film a series of flashbacks while underlining the fact that as an expatriate, Satrapi, like so many others, never really feels at home anywhere. The past has formed her character, and continues to dominate her life. The movie's present-tense scenes of Marjane at the airport are drawn with muted colors, while the long flashbacks remain in black and white. Each of the original four volumes is adapted in roughly 20-minute sequences, with a return to the narrative instance in Orly occurring in the center of the film, when young Marjane leaves for Austria and again when she returns home, exhausted, to her parents in Iran.

The graphic novel too contained frequent first-person narration within the comic book frames, such as "This is me at age 10, in 1980," and later, "My mental transformation was followed by a physical metamorphosis." Satrapi and Paronnaud's insertion of the animated internal narrator, alone, sadly thinking back on how she got here, creates a very personal and engaging mental subjective depth. Further, in addition to seeing Satrapi's animated adult figure, the audience now hears "her" voice, spoken earnestly by Chiara Mastroianni. The soundtrack helps bring new life and richness to her characters, though the bracketing narration lends a pervasive sense of melancholy to the entire narrative for this thoughtful, often brutally honest autobiography. Yet this representation of the referential Satrapi is distanced and refracted, first, by Satrapi's own caricatural drawings in the graphic novel, second, by the team of animators giving movement to her images, which include Marjane at five different ages, and third, by the imposition of a voice that is not hers. It is a reworked, abstracted sort of self-portrait. (For more on self-portraits and cinema, see Grange 2008.)

The title sequence of *Persepolis* establishes connections with Iranian culture, from the gently floating jasmine flowers later associated with the grandmother, to a small fountain that recalls the Iranian short cartoon, *Lili Hosak* (Fard-e-Mghadam, 1992). Early on the narrative strategy connects Marjane's personal plight with the history and context of her extended family and Iran itself. *Persepolis* has many internal narrators. Her father provides young Marjane with a mocking account of the British role in the rise of the Shah, that is presented in the film via paper cut-outs that resemble clumsy versions of Laguionie's hinged marionettes. Later he will describe the shocking executions by the current Islamic government. Family friends released from prison recount harrowing tales of their torture. The grandmother tells Marjane about the Shah's cruelty to their family, and Uncle Anoush explains his exile, return, and imprisonment to young Marjane so that the family's history will never be lost. He soon returns to prison where he is executed. Satrapi's texts thus become a tribute to her family, all of whom lost so much while enduring Iran's unfortunate plight.

Stylistically, *Persepolis* returns to the traditions of 2D animation, with every character hand-drawn and then a team of tracers, using felt tip pens, transferred those outlines onto paper. Satrapi herself drew out the model sheets for each of 600 different characters, and often performed their roles, which were videotaped, to help provide as much information as possible to the other animators. The animated humans generally move deliberately rather than smoothly, and they retain thick black outlines, while the overall look retains some of the fanciful graphics of the books, including speed lines and stark black silhouettes. The film even bends the women Guardians of the Revolution who confront young Marjane about her "punk" outfit into black snake-like creatures that exceed the satire possible in the novel. Marjane pleads with them for mercy and her face becomes isolated like a tiny white form against the seamless black of their long robes and her head scarf (Figure 5.3). *Persepolis* also makes strong use of scene-to-scene transitions, often allowing the extreme fades and wipes to black to punctuate and comment on the action, as when the Shah's black tanks shut out the image, followed shortly by another transition to black as protesters reach for their fallen comrade. Frightening glimpses of war are also presented with severe shot compositions, as in the pulsating cannon blasts and bombing runs, and explosions that render the countryside a desolate wasteland, like

Figure 5.3   Caricature and culture clash in *Persepolis*, produced by 2.4.7. Films, directed by Marjane Satrapi and Vincent Paronnaud, 2007.

a bleak etching. While Satrapi has said in interviews that she was influenced by German Expressionism and Italian Neorealism, two other movements that followed devastating wars, the images of battle and social conflict also seem influenced by socialist poster art as well as the crowd scenes of Bartosch's *The Idea.*

Yet, there is much that is light-hearted in *Persepolis.* Early on Mr. Satrapi spins Marjane around the room to celebrate revolt against the Shah, and her smiling face and the accompanying fade to white establish this sensation as a sort of paradise lost that the maturing Marjane may never quite find again. Young Marjane feels most liberated in her room playing air guitar to Iron Maiden (though in the book she also loves Kim Wilde's "We're the kids in America.") When Marjane is in love with Marcus in Europe, for instance, the happy theme music suggests her fulfillment as they toss snow balls in the shadow of Mozart's statue, and roll into springtime together amid butter-flies and flowers. However, happiness is shortlived in Marjane's life. One day she bounds gaily over to Markus's apartment to surprise him with a bag of croissants (Figure 5.4). She floats up the stairs, past its heart-shaped railing, only to discover him in bed with some blonde, at which point the nasty, dark side of Marjane's world returns with a vengeance. Her character will not propel herself happily through the air again until much later in Iran. There she will finally pull herself out of her depression, leaping into her own version of an exercise video to the tune of "Eye of the Tiger," including Mastroianni's comically forced karaoke version of the song. That rhythmic scene provides a cinematic punch, reinforcing Marjane's resurgence of confidence and rebellion.

Figure 5.4 Marjane's brief happiness. *Persepolis*, produced by 2.4.7. Films, directed by Marjane Satrapi and Vincent Paronnaud, 2007.

Still, the crisp lines, smiling faces, and bright settings when Marjane is happy provide only fleeting relief to the overwhelming sense of loss that dominates the film. Perhaps no moment is more poignant in combining all Satrapi's themes and visual strategies than the opening airport sequence, which ends with its transition into Marjane's memory. A sad, distracted looking Marjane hunches over in her seat at the terminal, a white line of cigarette smoke climbs up, as the camera dollies in and the setting's color values shift darker, isolating Marjane and her red jacket in the dark gray frame. A voice-off calls "Marji, stop running," and a black-and-white young Marjane bounds into the frame. The grown Marjane watches her briefly but soon looks off screen right, bored, while the camera pans rapidly left to follow the joyous child run off to meet a family friend at the airport (Plate 44). The voice-over of Marjane the narrator begins the tale, explaining that as a happy child she cared only about French Fries and Bruce Lee. Initially, her mother and grandmother appear as mere silhouettes against the windows of the Tehran airport, but Satrapi's memory will now develop them visually and thematically into complex characters as the story, which Marjane seems to conjure up reluctantly, carries her back to her own beginnings in this personal, often uncomfortable, remembrance of things past.

However, by the end, with the closing bracket of the grown Marjane, there is still a great deal that is unsettled about her character. The story does not lead up to the contemporary Marjane as a successful writer and artist, which would not only valorize her own life choices and provide a happier ending, but would also reward her ancestors' sacrifices and advice. Instead, the final airport scene simply ends with black-and-white Marjane arriving from Tehran, alone, accompanied by tragic-sounding music, then the sequence dissolves to the present with Marjane in muted color, riding off in a taxi, but looking back over her shoulder at the end of her narrated story. The sky is dark and menacing on this rainy evening, and retelling the story has apparently brought no sense of bright hope or new self-knowledge. Marjane is again in transit, pretending to the cab driver she has just landed. She is always playing some role. After the film fades to black there is a return to the grandmother's voice explaining how she places jasmine flowers in her bra to smell fresh. Also in voice over, the young Marjane finds this superb; flowers accompany the end titles, along with the sad musical refrain. The film's intricate memory structure ensures that a somber melancholy remains firmly in place.

Marjane the narrator has relived her tale but it has not delivered her into a productive present. The past still dominates. Thus, somewhat in the spirit of Harvey Pekar's *American Splendor*, *Persepolis* becomes a sort of working cure for Satrapi's character to muddle through and share her personal traumas by presenting herself as a series of drawn characters, caricatural auto-portraits in a sort of visually exhibitionistic diary. It is a powerful use of animation that also anticipates *Waltz with Bashir* (Folman, 2008) just a year later. Further, like *Waltz with Bashir*, *Persepolis* quickly gained attention as a political statement. Among its awards, including a Special Jury Prize at Cannes, *Persepolis* won the Freedom of Expression Award from the National Board of Review. Yet, it was also denounced as an example of Islamophobia by Iran. The Farabi Foundation sent a letter to the French Embassy in Tehran complaining that *Persepolis* presented an "unrealistic attack on the achievements and results of the glorious Islamic Revolution." The representations of God as well as the portrayal of alcohol were particularly singled out, and the Iranian government's lobbying convinced the Bangkok Film Festival to drop *Persepolis* from its line-up. Clearly, the representations of Marjane and her family resemble the sort of Middle Easterners with whom Westerners feel most comfortable: they value Western-style education and cultural liberties, American popular music, and even European food, wine, and culture. As Ruhel Hamid observes, "The consequence is that the film presents a more clichéd and predictable perspective on the events portrayed. It becomes a rather tepid celebration of Western tolerance and a warmed-over indictment of Islamic fundamentalism" (Hamid 2007: 61). During a time of increased cultural and political tensions between Islam and the West, as well as a rethinking of the Iran-Iraq war, it is not surprising that *Persepolis* attracted a great deal of attention. *Persepolis* earned over $22 million worldwide, drawing $9 million in its first run in France, and $4.5 million in the USA. Marjane Satrapi's elegant adaptation proved yet again that European animators, and their adventurous producers, could compete internationally with unique, personal, and sometimes surprisingly unconventional content.

Some 20 years after the "Cartoon Plan" was initiated by the European Union, France had managed to provide a steady stream of original, award-winning, feature-length animation. Other European nations were also actively contributing to an ongoing renaissance in television and motion picture shorts and features. Scores of viable animation studios have sprung up across Europe, often banding together, as was the case for *Kirikou and the Sorceress*, on large motion picture or television projects. Importantly, the annual Annecy Film Festival was no longer dominated so decisively by Japanese and American products. While some projects clearly aim at the anime, Disney, or Pixar audiences, many of the more innovative features from France have escaped replicating their competitors' strategies. There may not be a precise "French look," or national animation style, but the best of French animation retains its quirky auteurist stories and styles, rather than adopting dominant, international CGI conventions. As Sébastien Denis explains, France has remained faithful to traditions of 2D animation, as *Kirikou and the Sorceress*, *Raining Cats and Frogs*, and *Black Mor's Island* (Laguionie, 2004) prove. Further, it has also shown a determination to retain an artisanal mode of production, a trend that has continued from the days of Paul Grimault through Folimage and La Fabrique right up to today's latest features (Denis 2007: 188). Michel Ocelot acknowledges France's longstanding traditions in cinema as a factor in the renewed aesthetic strength of animation there, but he also credits excellent government funded schools as well as regional support of the arts and culture for both the rewarding production and reception of French animation (Zahed 2009).

6

Conclusion
French Animation Today

From the days of its origins right up to the most recent productions, animated cinema has developed a wide variety of techniques and plastic arts experiences that combine technical innovation with aesthetic innovation. . . . Animated films bring their marks of construction to the screen. They deliver a play of grains and filters, modeling with clay, fragments of paper, or even the textured surface from a pinscreen, foregrounding materials in the process of transformation, and the implementation, the mise en oeuvre, of plastic operations. They renew themselves with their links to sources and references to the labor of drawing, painting, engraving, sculpture, and assemblage. (Barrès 2006: 161)

Clearly, Europe's "Cartoon Plan" of the late 1980s took root most successfully in France. Already, beginning in 1983, the popular *Inspector Gadget* television series, a co-production between France, Canada, and the US, had proven French animation was an international force. France's production has consistently strengthened ever since, with its crowning achievement being the steady stream of award-winning animated features. Today, France's output for motion picture and television consistently ranks among the world's top four producers of animation, alongside the United States, Japan, and South Korea. Economically, however, French animation continues to rely upon the generous financial aid opportunities granted by the CNC and other European, national, and regional incentives since the international playing field is so uneven. While theatrical box office earnings for animated features exhibited in Europe have been roughly equivalent to ticket sales in the United States, averaging around 1 billion dollars annually

French Animation History
© Richard Neupert. Published by John Wiley & Sons

over the past five years, the bulk of that revenue still goes to American films. According to *Screen Digest*, "Typically, the best-rating animated films in Europe are the US releases, so that with the exception of an occasional local hit, the bulk of the box office in Europe is accounted for by US films" (*Screen Digest* 2009: 365). Nonetheless, though French animated features generally earn much less globally than *Ratatouille* or *Ice Age 3*, they also cost far less to produce, averaging less than 10 million euros, which then allows for much higher potential profits. A strong regional showing is adequate for a relatively successful first run. Exhibition deals with French television and DVD sales also provide very strong returns for animation, though the extravagant marketing from Disney and DreamWorks consistently cuts into France's own percentage of DVD revenues. Yet it is worth noting that these market conditions hold for live action movies in Europe as well as cartoons. Regardless, compared to all other European nations, France is the animation leader in both national production and international co-productions. Importantly, two of the five nominees for the 2010 best animated shorts at the American Academy Awards were French, with *Logorama* (François Alaux, Hervé de Crécy, and Ludovic Houplain), the satire on commercialism and culture in the US, taking the Oscar.

French animation aesthetics have also proven resilient, with a balance between continued respect for the past, as evidenced with their 2D graphics, artisanal techniques, and themes involving social justice and personal exploration, and an upgrading to new technologies and contemporary tastes. Digital technologies have generally been adapted to France's long-established traditions rather than creating a clean rupture with previous practices. Even some digital effects these days harken back to the earliest experiments in animated pictures, replicating cycled gestures, flickering effects, and simple overlap to mimic paper cut-outs. Marey's first motion studies breaking down real and rapid movement into fixed series of sequential, even overlapping images are regularly replicated throughout mass media today in television coverage of sports, such as the replay representations of the stages mapping out a figure skater or downhill skier's performance. French animation itself retains a persistent devotion to a comic book aesthetic rather than adopting wholesale the drive toward the conventional 3D hyper-realism. A significant factor in France's recent visual and narrative style has been the continued influence of important internship and mentoring programs at exceptional micro-studios such as Folimage, and the rise in private and public animation schools, including the university at Marne-la-Vallée, just east of Paris in the shadow of Disneyland, as well as the high-profile Gobelins, among others.

Gobelins, "L'école de l'image," or school of the image, is funded by the Paris Chamber of Commerce and Industry and has become one of the more visible French programs with a consistent and highly popular presence at the Annecy International Animation Festival each year. Recently, one advanced student group project, *Oktapodi* (2007) by Julien Bocabeille, François-Xavier Chanioux, Olivier Delabarre, Thierry Marchand, Quentin Marmier, and Emud Mokhberi, garnered a great deal of international attention, winning student animation awards at Annecy, SIGGRAPH, and beyond, as well as an Imagina Award in Monaco and an Academy Award nomination. *Oktapodi* is a fast-paced "calling card" cartoon that emphasizes its creative team's talent and commercial potential. The concise story follows a pair of octopuses after one is plucked from his or her tank and driven to market by a comically inept delivery man, while the second octopus sets forth on a rapid-fired rescue. This two-and-one-half-minute short has no need for dialogue, depending instead upon crisp character animation and functional continuity editing to express emotions and motivations. By the end, just when the octopuses are reunited, a sea gull plucks the lead octopus and the poor pursuer must catapult itself into the sky on yet another rescue mission. *Oktapodi*'s gag-to-gag structure owes much to the hectic pacing of a Tex Avery cartoon. The visual style mixes Pixar-like character animation in bright colors and convincing 3D CGI, including motion blur, with a very brief 2D mental subjective scene of a cook butchering the poor octopus. This mix of 2D and 3D caricature continues the French penchant for making reference to long-held traditions even while updating their content and technology to contemporary global standards (Plate 45).

Another short, rapid-paced Gobelins class project is *Cocotte Minute* (Thibault Berard, Sylvain Marc, Loïc Miermont, Amandine Pécharman, Nathalie Robert, and Romain Vacher, 2006). *Cocotte Minute* exploits exaggerated character animation, with rubbery figures, staccato gestures, quick pacing, and sudden, even disorienting camera movements and editing flourishes. *Cocotte Minute*'s 3D CGI retains a cartoony aesthetic as a group of nearly identical, chanting, French chefs set up a race through their kitchen between one fat chicken and one skinny chicken before killing and cooking them. Within less than 90 seconds, *Cocotte Minute* flings its thin protagonist, all eyes and spindly legs, from its happy dream of a country home, to a life-or-death race past cleaver-toting chefs, and blasts it through the roof in a rocketing pressure cooker. The bright, clean animation combined with flash pans and motion blur anticipate some of the frantic kitchen scenes from *Ratatouille* (Brad Bird, Jan Pinkava, 2007), and much of Gobelins' output seems to have one eye on Pixar's style while also concentrating on long-held European themes and tastes. For instance, *Blindspot* (Johanna Bessière, Oliver Clert, Nicolas Chauvelot, Cécile Dubois-Herry, Yvon Jardel, and Simon Rouby, 2008) may be set in an American mini-mart, but it features caricatures that resemble Sylvain Chomet's distorted humans, despite their CGI construction. The thief looks like a bird, the cashier is a bloated, round blob stuffed in her glass booth, and the hunch-backed elderly woman, mistakenly arrested for the murder and robbery, resembles a 2D comic strip caricature, with her head down where her chest should be. Yet the more realistic 3D toys in the shop recall early Pixar figures. As with the other Gobelin shorts, there is no dialogue, only Tati-esque sound effects and music and plenty of comic irony in a quick, condensed plot structure.

However, Gobelins is hardly alone in setting the pace for new French animation. Appropriately, there is even an influential school teaching animation and special effects called the Ecole Georges Méliès in Orly. The winner of the 2006 Grand Prix at the prestigious Imagina 3D Awards in Monaco was *Clik Clak* (Thomas Wagner, Victor Emmanuel Moulin, and Aurélie Fréchinois) from Supinfocom (école SUPérieure d'INFOrmatique de COMmunication) in Arles, one of the top digital animation schools in the world. In *Clik Clak*, a pair of playful robots communicate via sounds in an empty white world where every noise emits a written word, often forming silly variations on common expressions ("L'appétit vient après la pluie en mangeant le beau temps" or "Appetite comes after the rain, eating nice weather"). The movie is an exemplary demonstration of cinematic semiotics. *Clik Clak*'s robots encounter a boy and teach him to be quiet, avoid speech, and only make sound effects like them. For a time this game works, but eventually the boy sneezes, and, in what may be a tribute to Winsor McCay's *Sammy Sneeze*, the explosive racket and a shout from the child disrupt the robots, sending them over a precipice to their destruction. Supinfocom has campuses in Valenciennes, Arles, and now India, proving the ambitious reach toward a globalized future for French animation (Plate 46).

Another top program is the Ecole Supérieure des Métiers Artistiques (ESMA) in Montpelier. One of their recent student productions, *Hugh* (Mathieu Navarro, Sylvain Nouveau, François Pommiez, and Aurore Turbe, 2008), adapts an old Apache American legend about how the sky used to be too low, so the native children rigged up huge poles to push it up, freeing birds to fly, trees to stand tall, and adults to walk upright for the first time. To this day, the stars in the night sky mark the spots where the poles touched the sky. This creative project makes use of both 2D and 3D computer techniques. Students from ESMA also created *Replay* (Anthony Voisin, Zakaria Boumediane, Fabien Félicité-Zulma, and Camille Delmeule, 2008), a post-apocalyptic story about an athletic single mother returning to her son in their industrial bunker home after scavenging. The boy, intrigued by the sounds of children playing on an old tape recorder she has found, sneaks out to a deserted school yard where he encounters imaginary children conjured up from the tape he is playing. He removes his protective oxygen mask to play with these phantom children. The mother, racing to find him, soon discovers the boy dead in the barren playground. *Replay* begins like a video game about a resilient woman, but ends like an elegiac Japanese anime movie, fore-grounding loss, sadness, and grief (see Napier 2005: 275–276). In 2010, another ESMA student film, *Get Out* (Charlotte Boisson, Julien Fourvel, Pascal Han-Kwan, Tristan Reinarz, and Fanny Roche), won the best student and university prize for ESMA at Imagina. Beyond its fanciful mental subjective CGI, *Get Out* features poetic and philosophical dialogue between a frustrated doctor and a troubled mental patient who will not leave his padded cell. It builds into a comically unsettling yet lyrical cartoon with a surprise ending. These ESMA films are rather representative of the output from French animation schools, which encourage a variety of graphic traditions for short narratives that balance visual gag structures with often philosophically or ethically complex themes.

The variety of stories and styles coming from France continues to rival all other nations. While Canadian animation of the 1980s earned a reputation for some of the world's most diverse and innovative produc-tions, France may well deserve that designation now. Beyond the student films combining traditional 2D with cutting-edge 3D tactics, the body of short and feature-length commercial French animation is indeed remark-able as well. For instance, Cedric Babouche's *Imago* (2005), a French-Belgian co-production, presents a softly colored, melancholy tale of a boy whose pilot father died when his plane crashed into the boy's favorite tree. As a youngster, nestled in that tree, he imagines flying alongside his father, but then in a touching 90-second montage, the boy goes from entering his childhood home alone, to moving from grade school to college to marriage to parenthood, to old age as he enters his home alone, this time as a widower. This sequence provides a condensed storyline not unlike the passing montage in Pixar's *Up* (Docter, Petersen, 2009) and *Imago* even ends when the old man takes another small boy to the cliff where his father had died. Babouche also makes use of very painterly 2D animation, including gouache, paper cut-outs, and other 3D CGI effects. The boy, with simple, open facial features, recalls coloring book children and could have been one of the children running about on the farm in *Raining Cats and Frogs*, yet the tale quickly turns quite abstract, switching to a mature, contemplative tone worthy of Hayao Miyazaki before the brief sense of bittersweet acceptance and closure at the end when the old man tosses his old toy airplane into the wind off the cliff in a resigned but hopeful gesture (Plate 47).

Other recent examples of innovative French projects include *Fear(s) of the Dark* (2007), co-produced by Prima Linea Productions, of *U* fame, along with several Belgian companies. This compilation of nightmare and horror-themed shorts springs from graphic novel and comic strip traditions and features art director Etienne Robial and animator Marie Caillou, among others. Caillou's episode follows a hospitalized Japanese school girl's traumatic memories and hallucinations, as a sadistic doctor repeatedly drugs the frightened girl Sumako, forcing her to return to her horrible nightmares. Caillou's anime pastiche exploits CGI for a flat, paper cut-out aesthetic that relies as much on European graphic arts as it does on Japanese manga conventions. In keeping with the overall concept behind *Fear(s) of the Dark*, Caillou's film is almost all black, white, and gray, save for brief blood red accents. This film is about representation and line drawings and foregrounds the essence of animation and the particular visual style of each artist. Beyond being representative of the ongoing 2D graphic novel traditions of French animation, *Fear(s) of the Dark* fits recent industrial trends since it benefits from financial support from the European Union's Media Programs as well as the region of Poitou-Charentes, home to the animation hub of Angoulême. France's exceptional support for animators, via national, regional, and commercial means, ensures a large, highly capable, and well-trained pool of young talent poised to continue and even accelerate the pace of award-winning French animation into the near future. In addition to continued consistencies as well as ongoing experimentation in the graphic and narrative styles of French animation, their modes of production follow a path toward synthesizing small, even intimate production houses with increasing commercial options for distribution. Beyond balancing their production between television and motion picture animation, many new micro-studios have expanded in the field of computer graphics, with some companies even beginning in the niche realm of digital special effects before expanding into stand-alone animated narratives.

Pierre Buffin's firm, Buf, begun in Paris during 1994, has worked on digital effects for art films by Eric Rohmer and music videos by Bjork, as well as international blockbusters featuring main characters with names such as Batman, Harry Potter, Neo, and Spider-Man. But they also made a short film, *Même les pigeons vont au paradis* (*Even Pigeons Go to Heaven*, Samuel Tourneux, 2007), a dark, comic tale about an old fellow who tries to outsmart both the church, which is trying to sell him a machine to reach heaven, and the grim reaper. As in an Ingmar Bergman movie, salvation may be an illusion, but death is a certainty. *Even Pigeons Go to Heaven* earned an Academy Award nomination. Thanks to their own 3D CGI software and excellent track record, Buf next moved into the production of several feature-length animated projects, including Luc Besson's Arthur films. Many other newcomers have recently followed the models of Folimage and La Fabrique by establishing their micro-studios in southern France. The 3D CGI firm Bakery Animation is in the tiny southern town of Gemenos. Bibo Animation, based in Nice, made the short *French Roast* (Fabrice Joubert, 2008), which was nominated for an Academy Award, and then began working on their first feature, *Un monstre à Paris* (*A Monster in Paris*). Another animation company, Nice's Action Synthèse, specializes in producing for the children's market via features such as *The Magic Roundabout* (2005). The pool of young animating talent, regional support, and the attraction of a relaxed lifestyle in southern France have helped retain French animators while simultaneously spurring national production in television, motion pictures, and computer games.

The dramatic increase in the number of animation schools, the rise in French production, and the keen national recognition and international attention its animation has received, have all helped jump-start new historical and critical work within France during the past decade. Happily, in addition to the many new research projects chronicling French animators and their contributions, French film archives are increasingly dedicating themselves to providing screenings of newly restored prints as well as high quality transfers for DVD collections and Internet access. While French scholars, archivists, and audiences alike have always proudly celebrated their incredible long line of prestige, auteur cinema, they have also increasingly begun to investigate the previously marginalized artisans of animation, referring more and more to "the two Emiles," Reynaud and Cohl, alongside Louis Lumière and Georges Méliès. A nation always conscious of its rich cultural heritage, France is actively reevaluating the past practices that helped prepare the aesthetic, technical, and industrial foundations for its contemporary triumphs in animated cinema.

In France, as in every national cinema, animation today is a marker of cultural vitality, and the ultimate signifier of a healthy animation industry remains the feature film. The strong French infrastructure assures a continued string of distinctive commercial as well as quirky auteurist features in the near future. It is fitting, in fact, to close with a brief review of Sylvain Chomet's second feature, *The Illusionist* (2010), since *Variety*'s very positive assessment echoes many of the themes of this book, connecting current practice to historical intertexts: "The pic [*The Illusionist*] is a thrilling exercise in retro aesthetics, from the pencil-and-watercolor look to the 2D animation that harks back to mid-1960s Disney (especially *101 Dalmations*) and the delicate lines and detailed background of Gallic animator, Paul Grimault" (Felperin 2010). Chomet's feature, like the best of French animated images over the past 150 years, proves creative connections to all the arts, to national themes, to historic styles, while it also foregrounds its artistic craft, its marks of production, as it animates the inanimate in challenging aesthetic and narrative ways. Other recent features, including the commercially successful *A Monster in Paris* (2011), Laguionie's reflexive *Le Tableau* (2011), and the post-colonial *Zarafa* (Rémi Bezançon and Jean-Christophe Lie, 2012), prove that French feature-length animation continues to gain strength while preserving a rich variety of stories and styles. Finally, a full 100 years after Emile Cohl, animation has become economically important, aesthetically vibrant, and culturally crucial to France's persistently impressive national cinema.

References

Abel, Richard (1984). *French Film*. Princeton: Princeton University Press.
Abel, Richard (1994). *The Ciné Goes to Town*. Berkeley: University of California Press.
Albera, François (2007). "Emile Cohl, dans sa ligne: de la blague au trait." *1895* 53: 241–257.
Allan, Robin (2001). "Two Nights on Bald Mountain." In *Alexeieff: Itinéraire d'un Maître – Itinerary of a Master*. Ed. Giannalberto Bendazzi. Paris: Dreamland, pp. 79–97.
Andrew, Dudley, and Steven Ungar (2005). *Popular Front Paris and the Poetics of Culture*. Cambridge, MA: Belknap Press of Harvard University Press.
Auzel, Dominique (1998). *Emile Reynaud et l'image s'anima*. Paris: Dreamland.
Barrès, Patrick (2006). *Le Cinéma d'animation*. Paris: L'Harmattan.
Bazin, André (1952). "La Bergère et le ramoneur." *Cahiers du Cinéma* 16 (October): 18–20.
Bazin, André (2000) [1947]. "Science Film: Accidental Beauty." In *Science is Fiction: The Films of Jean Painlevé*. Ed. Andy Masaki Bellows and Maria McDougal. Cambridge, MA: MIT Press, pp. 144–147.
Béatrice, Léona, and François Martin (2003). *Ladislas Starewitch, 1882–1965*. Paris: L'Harmattan.
Bellows, Andy Masaki, and Marina McDougall (Eds.) (2000). *Science is Fiction: The Films of Jean Painlevé*. Cambridge, MA: MIT Press.
Bendazzi, Giannalberto (1985). *Le Film d'animation*. Trans. Geneviève Vidal. Paris: La Pensée sauvage.
Bendazzi, Giannalberto (Ed.) (1994). *Cartoons: One Hundred Years of Cinema Animation*. Trans. Anna Taraboletti-Segre. Bloomington: Indiana University Press.

French Animation History
© Richard Neupert. Published by John Wiley & Sons

Bendazzi, Giannalberto (Ed.) (2001). *Alexeieff: Itinéraire d'un Maître – Itinerary of a Master*. Paris: Dreamland.

Blin, Fabrice (2004). *Les Mondes fantastiques de René Laloux*. Chaumont, France: Pythagore.

Braun, Marta (1992). *Picturing Time: The Work of Etienne-Jules Marey*. Chicago: University of Chicago Press.

Braun, Marta (1995). "Movement and Modernism: The Work of E.-J. Marey." In Marion Leuba, *Marey: pionnier de la synthèse du mouvement*. Beaune: Musée Marey, pp. 83–89.

Brenez, Nicole (2007). "Fantasmagorie: un aboutissement." In *Du praxinoscope au cellulo: un demi-siècle de cinéma d'animation en France*. Ed. Jacques Kermabon. Paris: Centre National de la Cinématographie, pp. 20–29.

Brunner, Didier (2007). "The Animated Feature: Future Prospects." Conference, Annecy Animation Festival, June 13.

Carroll, Noël (1991). "Notes on the Sight Gag." In *Comedy/Cinema/Theory*. Ed. Andrew Horton. Berkeley: University of California Press.

Cayla, Véronique (2007). *Du praxinoscope au cellulo: un demi-siècle de cinéma d'animation en France (1892–1948)*. Paris: Centre Nationale de la Cinématographie.

Centre National de la Cinématographie (2004). "Princes et princesses." CRAC; accessed August 24, 2006 at www.questiondimage.com.

Chauville, Christophe (2008). "Retour vers le futur: rencontre avec Jean-Baptiste Garnero." *Repérages* 61 (Summer): 28–29.

Chilo, Michel (1957). "Paul Grimault, l'inventeur." *Cinéma* 57 (April): 77–82.

Christie, Ian (1994). *The Last Machine: Early Cinema and the Birth of the Modern World*. London: British Film Institute.

Ciment, Gilles (2000). "Kirikou, Kom, et après?" *Positif* 472 (June): 80–81.

Clements, Marcelle (2003). "Oui, It's a Cartoon, Non, It's Not for Your Kids." *New York Times* (November 2); accessed April 5, 2010 at www.nytimes.com/2003/11/02/movies/oui-it-s-a-cartoon-non-it-s-not-for-your-kids.html.

Cohl, Emile (2007). "Les Dessin animés et à trucs!" *1895* 53 (December): 301–305.

Cosandey, Roland (2009). "Töpffer, Lortac et Cavé, *Histoire de Monsieur Vieux-Bois* – en trois tableaux." *1895* 59 (December): 55–71.

Courtet-Cohl, Pierre, and Bernard Génin (2008). *Emile Cohl: l'inventeur du dessin animé*. Sophia-Antipolis: Omniscience.

Crafton, Donald (1990). *Emile Cohl, Caricature, and Film*. Princeton: Princeton University Press.

Crafton, Donald (1993a). *Before Mickey: The Animated Film 1898–1928*. Chicago: University of Chicago Press.

Crafton, Donald (1993b). "Emile Cohl and American Eclair's Animated Cartoons." *Griffithiana* 47: 169–179.

Crary, Jonathan (1992). *Techniques of the Observer: On Vision and Modernity in the 19th Century*. Cambridge, MA: MIT Press.

Crisp, Colin (1993). *The Classic French Cinema, 1930–1960*. Bloomington: Indiana University Press.

Dagrada, Elena (1990). "Through the Keyhole: Spectators and Matte Shots in Early Cinema." *Iris* 11: 95–106.

Denis, Sébastien (2007). *Le Cinéma d'animation*. Paris: Armand Colin.

Denslow, Philip Kelly (1997) "What is Animation and Who Needs to Know?" In *A Reader in Animation Studies*. Ed. Jayne Pilling. Sydney: John Libbey.

Duca, Lo (1948). *Le Dessin animé*. Paris: Prisma.

Duca, Lo (1982). *Le Dessin animé: histoire, esthétique, technique*. Paris: Editions d'aujourd'hui.

Dulac, Nicolas, and André Gaudreault (2006). "Circularity and Repetition at the Heart of the Attraction." In *The Cinema of Attractions Reloaded* Ed. Wanda Strauven. Amsterdam: Amsterdam University Press, pp. 227–244.

Edera, Bruno (1977). *Full Length Animated Feature Films*. New York: Hastings House.

Eizykman, Claudine (2001). "Cinéma épinglé or the Appearance of a Sensation." In *Alexeieff: Itinéraire d'un Maître – Itinerary of a Master*. Ed. Giannalberto Bendazzi. Paris: Dreamland, pp. 139–149.

European Communities Commission (1986a). "Action Programme for Film and Television Productions." *Bulletin of the European Communities Commission* 4, 19: 49.

European Communities Commission (1986b). "European Cinema and Television Year." *Bulletin of the European Communities Commission* 11, 19: 52.

European Communities Commission (1988). *Bulletin of the European Communities Commission* 11, 21: 44.

Fehman, Guy (2001). "Alexandre Alexeieff, Virtual Virtuouse or Film as a 'Cosa mentale.'" In *Alexeieff: Itinéraire d'un Maître – Itinerary of a Master*. Ed. Giannalberto Bendazzi. Paris: Dreamland, pp. 151–161.

Felperin, Leslie (2010). "The Illusionist." *Variety* (February 16); accessed March 10, 2010 at www.variety.com/review/VE1117942211.html.

Fondation Vevey(n.d.). "Histoire de Monsieur Vieux-Bois: Töpffer et le cinéma"; accessed June 25, 2009 at www.images.ch/publications/Töpffer.pdf.

Fragonara, Marco (2001). "The Etched Image of the Dream." In *Alexeieff: Itinéraire d'un Maître – Itinerary of a Master*. Ed. Giannalberto Bendazzi. Paris: Dreamland, pp. 99–113.

Furniss, Maureen (2007). *Art in Motion: Animation Aesthetics*. Eastleigh, UK: John Libbey.

Garnero, Jean-Baptiste (2007). "La Fortune enchantée." In *Du praxinoscope au cellulo: un demi-siècle de cinéma d'animation en France*. Ed. Jacques Kermabon. Paris: Centre National de la Cinématographie, pp. 84–91.

Gasiglia-Laster, Danièle (1986). *Jacques Prévert*. Paris: Séguier-Vagabondages.

Gatto, Robin(n.d.). "Michel Ocelot, enchanteur de l'animation à la français." Online at www.filmfestivals.com, pp. 1, 4.

Génin, Bernard (2003). *Le Cinéma d'animation*. Paris: Cahiers du Cinéma.

Grange, Marie-Françoise (2008). *L'Autoportrait en cinéma*. Rennes: Presses Universitaires de Rennes.

Gudin, Christine (2005). "La Genèse des contes de Michel Ocelot." *CinémAction* 116 (June): 146–155.

Guido, Laurent (2007). *L'Age du rythme*. Lausanne: Editions Payot.

Gunning, Tom (2000). "Introduction." In Laurent Mannoni, *The Great Art of Light and Shadow: Archaeology of the Cinema*, Trans. Richard Crangle. Exeter: University of Exeter Press, xix–xxx.

Gunning, Tom (2006). "Attractions: How they Came into the World." In *The Cinema of Attractions Reloaded*. Ed. Wanda Strauven. Amsterdam: Amsterdam University Press, pp. 31–39.

Hadjioannou, Markos (2008). "How Does the Digital Matter?" *Studies in French Cinema* 8, 2: 123–136.

Hamid, Rahul (2007). "Persepolis." *Cineaste* 33, 1 (Winter): 61–63.

Hope-Jones, Mark (2009). "An Exceptionally Sly Fox." *American Cinematographer* 90, 12 (December): 70–80.

Hopwood, Henry V. (1970) [1899]. *Living Pictures: Their History, Photo-Production and Practical Working*. New York: Arno Press.

Hutchins, Patricia (1938). "A Clay Blue Beard." *Sight and Sound* 7, 26: 74–75.

Image, Jean (1979). *Le Dessin animé*. Paris: Solar.

Institut des hautes études cinématographiques (IDHEC), 1956 (1956). *Le cinéma d'animation dans le monde: troisième rencontre internationale des ecoles de cinéma* [during the Cannes Film Festival]. Paris: IDHEC.

James, Alison (2005). "Some Nix 'Kirikou' Pix Due to Nudity." *Variety* (December 26): 11.

Jenkins, Charles Francis (1970) [1898]. *Animated Pictures*. New York: Arno Press.

Jones, Catherine M. (1993). *The Noble Merchant*. Chapel Hill: University of North Carolina Press.

Joubert-Laurencin, Hervé (2008). "Emile Cohl et le virus fantasmagorique." In *Emile Cohl*. Annecy: L'Oeil, pp. 139–143.

Kaenel, Philippe (2007). "Une esthétique du bricolage: la caricature d'Emile Cohl aux beaux-arts." *1895* 53 (December): 58–72.

Kermabon, Jacques (2007). *Du praxinoscope au cellulo: un demi-sìecle de cinéma d'animation en France*. Paris: Centre National de la Cinématographie.

Knight, Derrick (1976). "Alexeieff's Advertising Films." In *Experimental Animation: Origins of a New Art*. Ed. Robert Russett and Cecile Starr. New York: Da Capo, pp. 96–97.

Lacassin, Francis (2007). "Quand *La Vache qui rit* devançait *Félix le chat* et *Mickey la souris.*" *1895* 53 (December): 211–225.

Laloux, René (1996). *Ces dessins qui bougent.* Paris: Dreamland.

Langlois, Henri (1986). *Henri Langlois: Trois cents ans de Cinéma.* Ed. Jean Narboni. Paris: Cahiers du Cinéma.

Léger, Fernand (1965). *Functions of Painting.* Trans. Alexandra Anderson. New York: Viking Press.

Le Roy, Eric (2007). "Paul Grimault." In *Du praxinoscope au cellulo: un demi-siècle de cinéma d'animation en France.* Ed. Jacques Kermabon. Paris: Centre National de la Cinématographie, pp. 275–277.

Leslie, Esther (2002). *Hollywood Flatlands: Animation, Critical Theory and the Avant-Garde.* London: Verso.

Levasseur, Lionel (1989). "Crise du dessin animé européen: Mutation ou déclin?" *Cinémaction* 51 (April): 202–210.

Loné, Eric (2007). "Les Aventures des Pieds Nickelés." *1895* 53 (December): 324–325.

Lonjon, Bernard (2007). *Emile Reynaud: le véritable inventeur du cinéma.* Polignac: Editions du Roure.

Lorfèvre, Alain (2005). "J'ai découvert que j'étais un sorcier." *Cinebel* (December 7): 5.

McMahan, Alison (2006). "*Chez le photographe c'est chez moi*: Relationship of Actor and Filmed Subject to Camera in Early Film and Virtual Reality Spaces." In *The Cinema of Attractions Reloaded.* Ed. Wanda Strauven. Amsterdam: Amsterdam University Press, pp. 291–308.

Maillet, Raymond (1983). *Le Dessin animé français.* Lyon: Institut Lumière.

Maillet, Raymond (Ed.) (1982). *Le Dessin animé français: 100 ans de création.* Paris: Musée-Galérie de la Seita.

Maltin, Leonard (1987). *Of Mice and Magic.* New York: Penguin, Plume.

Mannoni, Laurent (2000). *The Great Art of Light and Shadow: Archaeology of the Cinema,* Trans. Richard Crangle. Exeter: University of Exeter Press.

Mercier, Marie-Claude (2001). "Le Fabricateur d'images." *Cadrage;* online at www. cadrage.net

Miailhe, Florence (2007). "*Joie de vivre.*" *Du praxinoscope au cellulo: un demi-siècle de cinéma d'animation en France.* Paris: Centre National de la Cinématographie, pp. 72–77.

Mitry, Jean (1967). *Histoire du cinéma 1 (1895–1914).* Paris: Editions universitaires.

Mitry, Jean (1980). *Histoire du cinéma 4 (1930–1940).* Paris: Jean-Pierre Delarge.

Mitry, Jean (1997). *The Aesthetics and Psychology of the Cinema.* Trans. Christopher King. Bloomington: Indiana University Press.

Morin, Edgar (2005). *The Cinema or The Imaginary Man.* Trans. Lorraine Mortimer. Minneapolis: Minnesota University Press.

Moritz, William (1997). *"Bartosch's The Idea": A Reader in Animation*. Edited by Jayne Pilling. Sydney: John Libbey, pp. 93–103.

Myrent, Glenn (1989). "Emile Reynaud: First Motion Picture Cartoonist." *Film History* 3: 191–202.

Napier, Susan (2005). *Anime: From Akira to Howl's Moving Castle*. New York: Palgrave.

Nessleson, Lisa (2005). "Kirikou and the Wild Beasts." *Variety* (December 6): 49.

Nessleson, Lisa (2006). "U." *Variety* (November 13): 45.

Neupert, Richard (2008). "Kirikou and the Animated Figure/Body." *Studies in French Cinema* 8, 1: 41–56.

Newnham, Grahame L. (2009). "Lortac – Animator Extraordinaire." Accessed May 14, 2009 at www.pathefilm.freeserve.co.uk/95flmart/95lortac.htm.

Noake, Roger (1988). *Animation: A Guide to Animated Film Techniques*. London: Macdonald Orbis.

Ocelot, Michel (1998). *Tout sur Kirikou*. Paris: Seuil.

Orléan, Matthieu (1998). "Le Monde magique." *Cahiers du Cinéma* (February): 78.

Pagliano, Jean-Pierre (1996). *Paul Grimault*. Paris: Dreamland.

Pasamonik, Didier, and Yves Alion (2003). "Sylvain Chomet de la BD à l'animation." *Storyboard* 4 (June, July, August): 39–42.

Patte, Caroline (2007). "O'Galop. " In *Du praxinoscope au cellulo: un demi-siècle de cinéma d'animation en France*. Ed. Jacques Kermabon. Paris: Centre National de la Cinématographie, pp. 304–305.

Predal, René (1997). *50 ans du cinéma français*. Paris: Nathan.

Pummell, Simon (1995). "Of Rats and Men." *Sight and Sound* (May): 61.

Pummell, Simon (1996). "Ladislaw Starewicz: Cut Off their Tails with a Carving Knife." In *Projections*, 5. Ed. John Boorman and Walter Donohoe. London: Faber and Faber, pp. 119–125.

Reynaud, Paul, and Georges Sadoul (1945). *Emile Reynaud: peintre de films, 1844–1918*. Paris: Cinémathèque Française.

Robinson, David (1991). "Introduction." *Griffithiana* 43 (December): 8–18.

Roffat, Sébastien (2009). *Animation et propagande: les dessins animés pendant la seconde guerre mondiale*. Paris: L'Harmattan.

Rouvillois, Arnaud (2007). "The Animated Feature: Future Prospects." Conference, Annecy Animation Festival, June 13.

Russett, Robert, and Cecile Starr (1976). *Experimental Animation: Origins of a New Art*. New York: Da Capo.

Sadoul, Georges (1949). *Histoire du cinéma mondial des origines à nos jours*. Paris: Flammarion.

Sadoul, Georges (1962). *Le Cinéma français (1950–1956)*. Paris: Flammarion.

Sadoul, Georges (1972). *Dictionary of Films*. Trans. Peter Morris. Berkeley: University of California Press.

Schneider, Eric (2000). "Entomology and Animation: A Portrait of an Early Master, Ladislaw Starewicz." *Animation World Magazine* 5, 2 (May); online at www.awn.com/mag/issues5.02/5.02page/schneiderstareqicz.php3.

Screen Digest (2009). "Global Animation Industry Thrives: Steady Output of Box Office successes in US and Europe." *Screen Digest* (December): 365.

Shohat, Ella (1997). "Gender and Culture of Empire: Toward a Feminist Ethnography of the Cinema." In *Visions of the East: Orientalism in Film*. Ed. Matthew Bernstein and Gaylyn Studlar. New Brunswick, NJ: Rutgers University Press, pp. 19–66.

Smith, Murray (1995). *Engaging Characters: Fiction, Emotion, and the Cinema*. New York: Oxford University Press.

Solomon, Charles (1995). *The Disney that Never Was*. New York: Hyperion.

Sotiaux, Daniel (Ed.) (1982). *Le Cinéma d'animation en Belgique*. Brussels: CNGPEO.

Stephenson, Ralph (1973). *The Animated Film*. London: Tantivy.

Strauven, Wanda (Ed.) (2006). *The Cinema of Attractions Reloaded*. Amsterdam: Amsterdam University Press.

Tchernia, Pierre (1998). "Préface." In Dominique Auzel, *Emile Reynaud et l'image s'anima*. Paris: Editions du May, p. 5.

Tharrats, Juan-Gabriel (2009). *Segundo de Chomon: un pionnier méconnu du cinéma européen*. Paris: L'Harmattan.

Timby, Kim (2007). "Portraits animés." *1895* 53: 109.

Vignaux, Valérie (2007). "Archives et histoire du cinéma: Emile Cohl, un cinéaste hors cadre ou de l'indépendance élevée au rang des beaux-arts." *1895* 53: 13–18.

Vignaux, Valérie (2009a). "Ecrire l'histoire française du cinéma d'animation: généologie et séries culturelles?" *Marius O'Galop et Robert Lortac, deux pionniers du cinéma d'animation*. Ed. Valérie Vignaux. 1895 59 (December): 9–21.

Vignaux, Valérie (Ed.) (2009b). *Marius O'Galop et Robert Lortac, deux pionniers du cinéma d'animation*. Special issue, *1895* 59 (December): 30–37.

Vimenet, Pascal (2007). "Sculpteur moderne." In *Du praxinoscope au cellulo: un demi-siècle de cinéma d'animation en France*. Ed. Jacques Kermabon. Paris: Centre National de la Cinématographie, pp. 30–37.

Wells, Paul (1998). *Understanding Animation*. London: Routledge.

Wells, Paul (2007). "Animation." In *Schirmer Encyclopedia of Film* Vol. 1. Ed. Barry Keith Grant. Detroit: Thomson-Gale, pp. 85–96.

Whissel, Kristen (2007). "Pre-Cinema." In *Schirmer Encyclopedia of Film* Vol. 3. Ed. Barry Keith Grant. Detroit: Thomson-Gale, pp. 297–305.

Zahed, Ramin (2009). "Michel Ocelot, Director, Azur and Asmar." *Animation Magazine* (March 3); accessed March 23, 2009 at www.animationmagazine.net/article/9670.

Further Reading

Aumont, Jacques (1996). *A quoi pensent les films*. Paris: Séguier.

Auzel, Dominique (1992). *Emile Reynaud et l'image s'anima*. Paris: Editions du May.

Boland, Bernard (1980). "Le Roi et l'oiseau." *Cahiers du Cinéma* 310 (April): 52.

Bordwell, David (1985). *Narration in the Fiction Film*. Madison: University of Wisconsin Press.

Carrier, David (2000). *The Aesthetics of Comics*. University Park: Pennsylvania State University Press.

Casetti, Francesco (2008). *Eye of the Century: Film, Experience, Modernity*. Trans. Erin Larkin and Jennifer Pranolo. New York: Columbia University Press.

Cholodenko, Alan (2008). "The Animation of Cinema." *Semiotic Review of Books* 18 2: 1–10; online at www.chass.utoronto.ca/epc/srb.

Crafton, Donald (1996). "The Silent Film: Tricks and Animation." In *The Oxford History of World Cinema*. Ed. Geoffrey Nowell-Smith. New York: Oxford University Press, pp. 71–78.

Creton, Laurent (2004). *Histoire économique du cinéma français: production et financement 1940–1959*. Paris: CNRS Editions.

Dagognet, François (1922). *Etienne-Jules Marey: A Passion for the Trace*. Trans. Robert Galeta and Jeanine Herman. New York: Zone Books.

Ezra, Elizabeth (2000). *Georges Méliès*. Manchester: Manchester University Press.

Faber, Liz, and Helen Walters (2003). *Animation Unlimited*. London: Laurence Kine.

Frazer, John (1980). *Artificially Arranged Scenes: The Films of George Méliès*. Boston: G. K. Hall.

Frizot, Michel (1984). *La Chronophotographie*. Beaune: Association des Amis de Marey.

Ghali, Noureddine (1995). *L'Avant-garde cinématographique en France dans les années vingt*. Paris: Editions Paris Expérimental.

Hammond, Paul (1974). *Marvellous Méliès*. London: Gordon Fraser.

Hendricks, Gordon (1975). *Eadweard Muybridge: The Father of the Motion Picture*. New York: Grossman.

Jean, Marcel (2006). *Le Langage des lignes et autres essays sur le cinema d'animation*. Montreal: Les 400 Coups.

Jenkins, Charles Francis (1970) [1898]. *Animated Pictures*. New York: Arno Press.

Joubert-Laurencin, Hervé (1997). *La Lettre volante: quatre essais sur le cinéma d'animation*. Paris: Presses de la Sorbonne Nouvelle.

Leskosky, Richard J. (1993). "Phenakistoscoep: 19th Century Science Turned to Animation." *Film History* 5, 2: 176–189.

Leuba, Marion (1995). *Marey: pionnier de la synthèse du mouvement*. Beaune: Musée Marey.

Mannoni, Laurent (2005). *The Great Art of Light and Shadow: Archaeology of Cinema*. Trans. Richard Crangle. Edinburgh: Edinburgh University Press.

Marey, Etienne-Jules (1874). *Animal Mechanism: A Treatise on Terrestrial and Aerial Locomotion*. New York: D. Appleton.

Moritz, William (2004). *Optical Poetry: The Life and Work of Oskar Fischinger*. Eastleigh, UK: John Libbey.

Musser, Charles (1993). *The Emergence of Cinema: The American Screen to 1907*. Berkeley: University of California Press.

Neupert, Richard (2007). "L'Espace narratif et le dessin animé français." In *La Fiction éclatée* Vol. 2 Paris: L'Harmattan, pp. 179–188.

O'Pray, Michael (1998). "The Animated Film." In *The Oxford Guide to Film Studies*. Ed. John Hill and Pamela Church Gibson. New York: Oxford University Press, pp. 434–439.

Pagliano, Jean-Pierre (1986). *Paul Grimault*. Paris: Editions Pierre Lherminer.

Pagliano, Jean-Pierre (1995). "Of Rats and Men." *Sight and Sound* (May): 61.

Pagliano, Jean-Pierre (1996). "Ladislaw Starewicz: Cut Off their Tails with a Carving Knife." In *Projections*, 5. Ed. John Boorman and Walter Donohoe. London: Faber and Faber, pp. 118–125.

Pilling, Jayne (Ed.) (1997). *A Reader in Animation*. London: John Libbey.

Rancière, Jacques (2009). *The Future of the Image*. Trans. Gregory Elliott. London: Verso.

Rossell, Deac (1998). *Living Pictures: The Origins of Movies*. Albany: State University of New York Press.

Schwartz, Vanessa, and Jeannene M. Przyblyski (2004). *The Nineteenth-Century Visual Culture Reader*. New York: Routledge.

Taylor, Richard (1996). *Encyclopedia of Animation Techniques*. Philadelphia: Running Press.

Telotte J. P. (2010). *Animating Space: From Mickey to WallE*. Lexington: University of Kentucky Press.

Vignaux, Valérie (Ed.) (2007). "Emile Cohl." *1895* 53 (December).

Vignaux, Valérie (2009). "Ecrire l'histoire française du cinéma d'animation: généologie et séries culturelles?" *Marius O'Galop et Robert Lortac, deux pionniers du cinéma d'animation.* Ed. Valérie Vignaux. *1895* 59 (December): 9–21.

Vigo, L. (1980). "La Longue marche de Paul Grimault." *Jeune Cinéma* 128 (July-August): 3–10.

Vimenet, Pascal (2008). *Emile Cohl.* Montreuil: Editions de l'Oeil.

White, John (1987). *The Birth and Rebirth of Pictorial Space.* Cambridge, MA: Belknap, Harvard University Press.

Wiesmann, Donald L. (1970). *The Visual Arts as Human Experience.* Englewood Cliffs, NJ: Prentice-Hall.

Willoughby, Dominique (2009). *Le Cinéma graphique: Une histoire des dessins animés des jouets doptique au cinéma numérique.* Paris: Editions Textuel.

Index

French Animation History
© Richard Neupert. Published by John Wiley & Sons

Craig, Daniel, 153

Crary, Jonathan, 15

Crazy Ray, 55

Crécy, Hervé de, 163

Crisp, Colin, 60

cultural identity, 124–126

cut-out animation techniques, 26, 31, 35, 37, 38, 41–46, 48, 51, 53, 55, 58, 74, 76–77, 93, 95, 97, 109, 113, 115–118, 120, 122, 127–128, 132–133, 138, 140, 157, 163, 167

Dada, 55–56

Dagrada, Elena, 33

Dauman, Anatole, 122

Dauney, Robert, 153

Dauphin, Claude, 65

Day in the Country, A, 110

Déboires d'un piéton, Les, see Challenges for a Pedestrian

Delabarre, Olivier, 164

Delmeule, Camille, 166

Delpy, Hippolyte Camille, 24

Demeny, Georges, 16

Demoiselle et le violoncelliste, La, see Young Lady and the Cellist, The

Demy, Jacques, 106

Denis, Claire, 128

Denis, Sebastien, 30, 53, 92–93, 103, 112, 117, 121, 147, 161

Denslow, Philip Kelly, 4

Dents du singe, Les, see Monkey's Teeth

dialogue balloons, 41, 48, 49

Diaphana, 136

Disney, Walt (and Studios), 2, 3, 23, 61, 66, 68, 80, 88, 91, 99, 101, 104, 106, 107, 112, 114, 121–124, 134, 141, 143, 150, 161, 169

distribution, 2–3, 46, 72, 88, 90, 100, 124–125, 128, 131

Do Like the Darkie, 48

Drame chez les fantoches, Un, see Puppet's Dream

Dreams of a Rarebit Fiend, 42

DreamWorks, 163

Dubois-Herry, Cécile, 165

Dubout, Albert, 110–111

Duchamp, Marcel, 1, 15, 44, 56

Dudok de Vit, Michael, 148

Dulac, Germaine, 54

Dulac, Nicolas, 5–6, 9, 21, 33

Eclair Studios, 39–44, 45, 46

Eclipse Studios, 37–39

Ecole Georges Méliès, 165

Ecole Supérieure des Métiers Artistiques (ESMA), 165–166

ecological themes, 122, 148, 149

Edera, Bruno, 105

Edison, Thomas, 5, 11, 12, 13–16, 17, 18, 21

Editing Table, The, 106

Eggeling, Viking, 54

Eisenstein, Sergei, 21, 79, 81

Eizykman, Claudine, 83

Electric Hotel, 20

Elissade, Serge, 149–150

Emak Bakia, 56

Emile Cohl Prize, 102, 107, 120

Enchanted Fortune, 93–97

Enfants de la pluie, Les, see Children of the Rain

En passant, 90

Entr'acte, 55

Epouvantail, L', see Scarecrow

Epstein, Jean, 57–58

Escargots, Les, see Snails, The

ethnic imagery, 47–48

Etoiles nouvelles, 90

European animation (context), 124–126, 129, 131, 136, 140, 142, 161

European Union, 125–126, 161, 167

Even Pigeons Go to Heaven, 168